CULTURE, PLACE, AND NATURE
Studies in Anthropology and Environment
K. Sivaramakrishnan, Series Editor

Centered in anthropology, the Culture, Place, and Nature series encompasses new interdisciplinary social science research on environmental issues, focusing on the intersection of culture, ecology, and politics in global, national, and local contexts. Contributors to the series view environmental knowledge and issues from the multiple and often conflicting perspectives of various cultural systems.

Shifting Livelihoods

GOLD MINING AND SUBSISTENCE
IN THE CHOCÓ, COLOMBIA

Daniel Tubb

UNIVERSITY OF WASHINGTON PRESS

Seattle

Shifting Livelihoods was made possible in part by a grant from the Busteed Publication Fund of the Faculty of Arts of the University of New Brunswick, Fredericton, and a Harrison McCain Foundation grant in aid of scholarly book publishing.

Copyright © 2020 by the University of Washington Press

Composed in Warnock Pro, typeface designed by Robert Slimbach
Cover design by Katrina Noble
Cover photograph: Flecks of gold appear at the bottom of an artisanal miner's shallow wooden pan. Photograph by the author.

24 23 22 21 20   5 4 3 2 1

Printed and bound in the United States of America

All rights reserved. No part of this publication may be reproduced or transmitted in any form or by any means, electronic or mechanical, including photocopy, recording, or any information storage or retrieval system, without permission in writing from the publisher.

UNIVERSITY OF WASHINGTON PRESS
uwapress.uw.edu

LIBRARY OF CONGRESS CATALOGING-IN-PUBLICATION DATA
LC record available at https://lccn.loc.gov/2019047809
LC ebook record available at https://lccn.loc.gov/2019047810

All interior photographs, charts, and maps are by the author.
The book epigraph is from David Sánchez Juliao, "El flecha," in *Una década: 1973–1983* (Bogotá: Plaza y Janes, 1983). Translated in Ann Farnsworth-Alvear, Marco Palacios, and Ana María Gómez López, eds., *The Columbia Reader* (Chapel Hill, NC: Duke University Press). Used by permission of Paloma Sánchez.

To the gold miners of the Chocó

Well ever since I was livin' here, in this place where a black man has got no alternative aside from the ring and lookin' for fame—shit, man—yeah, because all the other jobs *viejo* Deibinson [Davidson], you know it man, are jobs for white people. *La madre.* That's right, not unless no shit man you're black and you get yourself in one of those jobs where you better be hustling man and wearing your little Holy Trinity charm (one-true-god-and-three-holy-persons). Yeah, because I don't have a damn clue how in this country a carpenter, a bodyshop welder, a bricklayer, water carrier, shoe shiner, Marlboro hawker, Kent cigarettes bit-seller, wheelbarrow pusher, sack hauler, brothel bouncer, busboy, old-whore's pimp, bus assistant, birdcage maker, snowcone seller, lottery ticket seller, writer (do not get mad at me, *viejo* Deibi, do not get mad, *please*), manager of a sidewalk stand, errand boy, peanut seller, accordion player, serenade singer, baptism photographer, gigolo for faded beauties, church sexton, newspaper hawker, coffee seller, tire repairman, car mechanic, or cable splicer, can survive. You barely make anything in those jobs, *viejo* Deibi, you know that, you cannot even make enough money to fool your hungry stomach, no shit.

—DAVID SÁNCHEZ JULIAO, "THE ARROW"

CONTENTS

Foreword by K. Sivaramakrishnan   xi

Preface   xv

Acknowledgments   xxv

Maps of Colombia and the Chocó   xxix

Introduction: Life during a Gold Rush   3

PART I
PRODUCTION: SUBSISTENCE AND THE DUAL HOUSEHOLD ECONOMY

CHAPTER ONE
Gold and the Household Economy   39

CHAPTER TWO
Gold and the Cash Economy   64

PART II
ACCUMULATION: *REBUSQUE* AND THE CASH ECONOMY

CHAPTER THREE
Family Mines and Small-Scale Mining   85

CHAPTER FOUR
Rebusque on the Precarious Periphery   104

PART III

TRANSFORMATION: MONEY LAUNDERING AND SPECULATION

CHAPTER FIVE
Simulated Extraction and Gold-Based Money Laundering   133

CHAPTER SIX
Speculative Projects and Multinational Mines   149

Conclusion: Life after a Gold Rush   172

Notes   183

Bibliography   195

Index   209

FOREWORD

The Chocó, in northwestern Colombia, is drained by three rivers that, with their many tributaries, form a network whose waters wash gold-flecked gravel downstream. In an ethnography that rises from the muddy shallows of the rivers that course through valleys and rain forests, Daniel Tubb narrates the lives of artisanal gold miners and forest farmers. *Shifting Livelihoods* begins with accounts of usually invisible people in this difficult terrain and ranges across issues of regional history and political economy. The story travels from extractive economy to political violence, across speculation and illicit trade, and details the extraordinary courage and generosity of people making an arduous, precarious living in the poorest parts of Colombia. As he carried out the work that informs this study, Tubb lived for eighteen months with, and visited off and on over nearly a decade, Afro-Colombians who compose the majority of the sparse population of the area.

Research on extractive mining cultures and industries in Latin America is a well-cultivated field. Much of the earlier work examined the effects of global capitalism on local societies overtaken by mining. Often these studies focused on the inequality, labor relations, and hazards produced by the spread of intensive extractive industries, within an overall and determining perspective of capitalist incorporation of precapitalist societies.[1] More recent work takes the discussion in several interesting directions. One strand attends to the persistence of speculative interest in subsoil resources in South America and how these imagined resource landscapes were formed and came to shape environmental and sociopolitical outcomes from mountain to lowland across the Andes and Amazonia, as well as in coastal wetlands and rain forests.[2]

Another key strand, and a refreshing perspective, is Tubb's situation of mining in a wider economy of livelihood production, where poor outsiders—settlers and drifters alike—incorporate panning for gold into a spectrum of activity that is necessary to eke out an existence in this dangerous terrain. He seeks out and describes the living lands and rivers of the department of the Chocó in the language of the people who wrest sustenance from this capricious terrain. Thus, he fashions the locally used term *rebusque* into a theoretical tool that helps him understand how people remain in quest for what is always temporary, shifting, and unpredictable. In this account, artisanal gold mining—combined with farming, hunting, petty trading, and forays into illicit economies—contributes to a portfolio for survival that requires innovation and resignation, riding luck, and suffering through adversity. The fluidity of lives and riverine landscapes intermingle in his narrative; sophisticated but unstable accounts of value, accumulation, and getting by are heard and reported.

Tubb demonstrates the importance of studying the subtle transformations of value and social relations that link gold in the river eddies of the Chocó to transnational banks and national treasuries. From a vantage point in the muddied lives of poor artisanal miners, he discusses interlocking spheres of exchange, rather than providing another linear, simplified account of how precious metal buried in natural environments becomes a vehicle for speculation and profiteering in global markets. This work is done through ethnographic veracity and engagement with literature in economic anthropology, environmental studies, agrarian transitions, and the anthropology of local knowledge and forest societies in Latin America.

In 2016 the Constitutional Court of Colombia seemed to come to the aid of the Indigenous and Afro-Colombian residents of the Atrato River basin by declaring the river a person capable of holding rights and recognizing it as the life force in the aquatic landscapes and aquatic cultures that have shaped the region over centuries. Tubb examines the intertwining of biological and cultural diversity—both under severe threat—in the lives and villages of those most intimately connected to these processes of natural and cultural regeneration and adaptation. This work is both timely and important, as the idea of conferring personhood to rivers and lakes is spreading across the Americas and Asia. Tubb brings those issues into a sophisticated discussion of local livelihoods in poor, minority, and Black and Indigenous community settings. The book thus moves across abiding issues to current developments, noting that, as the river and the lives and livelihoods it sustains gasp for air, no magic wand of policy or analytical flourish will bring easy relief. A long, enduring set of struggles and contests enters new phases and is seen through new lenses.

With all that is offered by this book by way of scholarly insight—and there is plenty of that for the attentive reader—it remains at its heart a compelling story.

K. SIVARAMAKRISHNAN
Yale University

PREFACE

Leidy[1] cleared gravel and stones from a wooden sluice wedged in a gully between two slopes. Caked mud-streaked her legs, and dirty water coursed around her feet and along the sluice. The sluice was a plank of wood with roughly cut boards nailed on both sides over a metal grill and a red sack. At the far end of the sluice, Leidy's mother worked. Her gray skirt hung over black rubber boots. Leidy's younger sister was there too, dressed in denim short-shorts, a purple T-shirt, a bandana, and a rakish smile looking back at my camera. The younger women were too elegant for the work at the mine.

An hour before, the four of us had hiked the twenty minutes from the river to their mine. We had trailed half a dozen men and boys from a small community in the Chocó, Colombia's northwest Pacific region of rain forests and rivers. I carried my camera, Leidy a digital music player, and one of the boys a blackened pot with a bag of rice inside; another young man balanced a gasoline-powered water pump on his upper back. The others carried shovels, wooden pans, and metal spikes—the tools of their trade as artisanal gold miners. We had begun at a cobble beach, passed through the jungle, and then come to a wide-open space of sand and mud and gravel that had been dug up by a pair of excavators made in Japan. Below an embankment and beside a large pool, a family used streams of water from a pump to cut through gouges left by the excavators, owned by illegal and informal small-scale miners who had packed up and gone upriver to mine away a hillside above a productive tunnel and start a new excavator mine. Where gravel met forest, trees peered over a kaleidoscope of purple-grays, red-browns, and silver-blues. On that hike, we followed a capricious path that meandered through a blasted landscape that once had been jungle.

Back in the sluice, with Leidy standing on that wooden plank with the metal grill and the red sack between the two slopes held up by the tangled roots of trees long gone, the three women worked with their hands. They chatted and laughed in contagious hope. It was 2010, my third visit to such a mine, and all of us—Leidy, her mother and sister clearing the sluice, the young man hauling the pump, the family carving into the earth with their jets of water, the workers gouging away the tree cover with excavators, and I, asking too many questions and taking too many photographs—were after gold.

How does a gold rush shape the lives of those who live alongside it? There is no single answer. Dwelling on the hopes and the dreams, the successes and the failures, the strategies and the tactics of those after *el oro* in the most impoverished region of Latin America's second-most inequitable country tells unexpected stories of the production, accumulation, and transformation of value. I offer contradictory stories in three parts. In the first, gold is a high-value export commodity, which makes panning the core of a rural livelihood strategy and a complement to subsistence household production. In the second, the metal is embedded in a cash economy, which offers a way for miners from the Chocó and elsewhere to attempt to accumulate a little cash. In the third, gold is part of global legal and extralegal flows of capital, in which value undergoes processes of transformation, rather than creation. Together these three parts, which each consist of two chapters, create a study of gold embedded in informal and precarious shifting livelihood strategies.

While there is a large literature on the informal economy, and "precariousness" has entered the lexicon of social scientists, the colloquial Colombian term for it all is *rebusque*, translated here as "shifting." This word aims to capture the temporary, contingent, creative, and mobile world of informal work represented by *rebusque*. My use of it draws on an older English etymology, rather than the quotidian contemporary meaning. "Shifting," as I use it, does not mean working for a set period at a factory but instead references the odd jobs and short-term hustles of the many *rebusques* described in the epigraph taken from Colombian writer David Sánchez Juliao's short story "The Arrow," which itself is about the various forms of informal work that a failed boxer employs.[2] *Rebusque* refers to the many forms of unstable work available to the most marginalized populations in Colombia. Shifting encompasses various features of *rebusque*. One shifts by one's own devices to succeed and get on, one shifts to live with difficulty by managing and makeshifting and employing evasions and practicing indirect methods through frauds and temporary expedients, and one shifts for oneself to provide for one's own safety, interests, and livelihoods when there is no outside aid.[3] Shifting captures the ontology of informal work, and a way of thinking about and living through various forms of *rebusque*.

The stories in the following pages come from the work of Leidy and the others like her whom I spent time with learning how to mine. My geology is theirs. My knowledge comes from the labor of moving gravel, digging holes, and panning. I learned mostly from people like Leidy who were the descendants of enslaved men and women brought from Africa who had panned for gold hundreds of years before. This book emerges from the bottom of a mine pit, and it relies as much on the insight that can be gained from this work as it does on rumors and half-truths heard in late-night conversations, read in media accounts, and gathered from other sources. Stories from the mud are not the only stories that could be told of gold.

Downtown Bogotá, the cold, gray, concrete capital of over ten million in the Andes Mountains, houses the elegant Gold Museum. Carefully lit and exquisitely curated artifacts stand in testament to the skills, metallurgies, and cosmologies of pre-Columbian Indigenous peoples who lived in what is today Colombia. Their descendants still do. The exhibits draw tourists from around the world to gaze at the carefully wrought statues and figurines, masks, cups, and other objects made of metals mined in the alluvial gravel of the hot lowlands of Colombia. The exhibits make little mention of contemporary miners, however. In 2010, just a few panels in the last room on the top floor dwelt on the lives of those who, like Leidy, were still digging for gold. While many Black miners in the Chocó still used hand tools, other miners were migrants from different regions who used heavy machinery.

That morning with Leidy, she kept the sluice clear. Water from a rain-filled reservoir rushed along the gulley and pulled sediment, mud, gravel, stones, and pebbles down over the plank with the red sack nailed in place. Over the day, the heavier gold that had lain hidden under the earth would settle to the lowest part of the sluice to be collected later. While I spent much of the next eighteen months clearing sluices, on that particular day with Leidy, I took photographs. That morning at five o'clock I had gone to the village where Leidy had grown up so that I could explain to her neighbors how I had come with the hope of writing a book. Drawing on work from economic anthropology about Andean peasants,[4] I was interested in the way gold was embedded in how people think and talk about their economies. In what I now think of as an awkward and improvised presentation in a one-room school with a dozen men and women squeezed into wooden seats designed for children in the heart of a village of twenty or so houses on a muddy slope above a fast-flowing river, I explained that I wanted to learn to mine in order to write what has become this book. Months later, I realized that my accent was strange and my request bizarre. Still, over time, people warmed to the idea as they realized I was sincere. *Free labor!* Soon, they were showing me things, asking me to take photographs, and teaching me to mine. Soon, too, I asked for and received permission for the project from the larger Afro-Colombian peasant organizations in the area.

From September 2010 to April 2012, I spent most of my time in one village on a river learning the work. I labored alongside Leidy, Martina, her husband Pedro, their neighbors Don Alfonso and Esteban, and others who were all twenty-first-century artisanal miners. I was enthusiastic, if not terribly efficient. I rose before dawn, hauled fuel, dug trenches, and threw stones. I spent a little time underground. I often visited a small-scale operation after the two excavators arrived from the mine downriver near Leidy's community to work the lands above Martina and Pedro's village.

I found ways to help. I became proficient in some techniques. Difficult tasks became mundane, even though most of the time I stayed a neophyte. With Martina, I cleared stones from the sluice. The sluice was half a dugout canoe, which fed into a plank of wood with the sides nailed over a sack. As Martina and Pedro dumped stones and sand and gravel dug from the pit, I kept the sluice clear. Their *bateas* were the primary tools. Pedro sent wooden pans full of mud sailing up from the bottom of the pit to pass the empty pans sent sailing down by Martina. I cleared away the stones and gravel left in the sluice by the steady pull of a trickle of water. If I worked slowly, the stones would pile up and Martina would come over and clear everything in one motion, which left me embarrassed. Over time, I learned some of her tricks. Do not pick the stones one at a time, scoop them *en masse*. The work was physical and skillful.

This book, in part, is a study of that skilled work, and the freedom that it can give. The pages that follow draw on the time I spent working with miners. From those labors, I address the diverse economies of Martina and Pedro and others who earn their livelihood using wooden pans and hand tools alongside hunting, fishing, urban migration and trade, and other shifting livelihood strategies of *rebusque*. My focus is on the labor and livelihoods of miners embedded within the broader connections of gold.

My arguments emerge from an apprenticeship in the skilled techniques of mining.[5] I labored to become conversant in mine work. Throwing stones, digging, shoveling, and picking gave me insight on what the yellow metal meant, how to find it, and what to do with it. These activities opened a window onto the practicalities and ambiguities of mining. Some tasks became familiar. If familiarity is a necessary step to understanding, learning to mine helped me develop an intimate, practical, and embodied understanding of the work. It also created a space for a mutual trust and friendship that facilitated my ethnographic endeavor. Quotidian interactions, informal conversations, and deepening relationships created friendships. Learning to mine helped build confidences, which are the truck and trade of ethnography. It helped me learn both what is important and what to ask (and not ask). It gave me an opportunity to meet miners, and was a ready, intelligible explanation for my presence. It helped me build human connections and develop social competencies.

The fact that I became an enthusiastic, if ultimately incompetent and inexpert, miner, helped me become aware of what was important to miners, while also giving me some of the habits required to navigate everyday tasks. In addition, if the men and women who worked at their mines all day assumed the role of skilled experts, I assumed the role of their novice, someone to be taught and protected. This temporary inversion of knowledge and power was notable because, too often, outsiders and visiting researchers would arrive unexpectedly in the late afternoons, just as miners were returning from the bush the most tired and dirty. By working alongside them, by being as tired and as dirty, my research became more legible. Everyone knew what my method was because they saw me doing it.

My ethnographic participant observation was not enough, however. I also read. I read newspapers, magazines, archival documents, websites, and a burgeoning literature on mining in Latin America and beyond. Once I had finished my fieldwork in 2012, I spent a year reading corporate reports, financial statements, and websites of companies based in Canada with projects in the Chocó, as well as activists' reports and newspaper articles. I studied and mapped gold mining statistics. I followed my intuition to reach a new understanding of a gold rush.

I first met Leidy in November 2010 in the town of Paimadó at a workshop organized by a nongovernmental organization funded by a European development agency. We had taken a long motor launch with a dozen others to Paimadó, which was being washed away by illegal dredging operations owned by Brazilian small-scale miners. A national news magazine had covered the story many times, demonizing the dredges and their owners. A decade later, things in Paimadó are far worse: more dredging, more damage, and more stories, which make the situation out to be, by all accounts, an unfolding environmental disaster. Many recent accounts of mining focus on the largest mines owned by multinational corporations; issues of corporate social responsibility, social license, social movement opposition, and the damage to the environment are center stage. This is also the case in the research on "neo-extractivism" in Latin America. What this literature misses, though, is that much of the gold mined each year comes from what are called artisanal and small-scale mining operations, the former being the kind of miners who were washing away Paimadó as they dredged for gold. This is a global phenomenon.[6]

That shiny, glittering metallic element has shaped the world for a long time. Gold is a financial instrument, a commodity, and a holder of wealth. Some estimates are that there are about 171,300 metric tons of gold in the world worth about $8 trillion, with 52,000 metric tons still to be mined.[7] Gold has a role in international finance, with a relationship between investments in gold and stock market collapses. Gold is imagined as a safe investment and a place to put money when all else fails. Gold plays a role as a hedge at the center of the international economy. Gold is the commodity currency of choice for "metal-heads" (speculators), libertarians, drug traffickers, and the rest. Prices are set by a handful of banks overlooking the foggy River Thames in the City of London.[8]

This book is not about any of that. Instead, it is about what happened when prices reached $1,900 a troy ounce in 2011, which smashed records set in the early 1980s, and reshaped a way of life on a river in western Colombia, as thousands of men and machines began to set up jungle camps and as multinational corporations sought out new projects.

Focusing either just on large-scale operations or on the ways that gold is used suffers from three distinct problems. First, it ends up considering not the here and now of mining but instead a subjunctive tense—the potential or the future disasters that large-scale projects portend, rather than what is already happening. Considering what a large-scale mine *might* do is a different task than documenting what artisanal and small-scale mines *have* done. Yet, in 2012, fears were of future mines, not already existing mines. Second, it ends up taking for granted where the value itself is produced and accumulated in the mining industry, rather than considering how gold is embedded in wider relations of trade and finance. Third, it ends up emphasizing the boom-then-bust of resource projects, rather than all of the impacts of a project before they actually come online. Small-scale and artisanal miners reshape landscapes, riverscapes, and lives, even as the value in the process can come from under the ground and from the more immaterial global machinations of contemporary capitalism, both legal and illegal. After all, in the Chocó, physical gold is used to launder drug money, while the idea of gold supports speculative mining projects.

The gulley where Leidy stood in the mud had been worked by the three women because it was a family endeavor. Leidy's father had died the year before, electrocuted in an accident while he was fixing a high-voltage transmission line that connected his village through many kilometers of rain forests. In her front room, Leidy kept a photograph of her father lying in an open casket. That morning, where we worked, the excavators had moved on, and the three women were after the little metal that was left behind. While their work had the potential of a lucky strike, mostly it gave them a little extra cash, which helped Leidy support her family. She relied on this money, along with cash transfer payments for single mothers brought in by the Colombian government by helicopter from a military base and her *rebusque* consisting of different short-term hustles. The three women in the gully were a tiny example of the much larger phenomenon that was sweeping their river and the region.

During the heady days of the rising prices in the late 2000s and early 2010s, illegal and informal small-scale operations expanded throughout the Chocó and other regions, including the Lower Cauca, the South of Bolívar, and Nariño. But this mining was often of an altogether different degree than the manual labors of Leidy and her family. The evidence was all around. Talk turned to stories of lucky strikes, easy money, and fortunes made and lost. A parish priest had saved a church from one village before the village itself was erased from the landscape by earthmovers owned by outsiders who may have been invited in by the villagers themselves. Plazas in front of country schools were metamorphosed into holes that became ponds to farm fish. Trucks crawled over the Andes hauling excavators collapsed like sleeping dinosaurs for easy transport with yellow signs that read "Wide Load."

Leidy, her sister, her mother, and much of the rest of the population of the Chocó were the descendants of the escaped or manumitted enslaved men and women brought from Africa to mine in those jungles. The other 10 percent or so were Indigenous Embera communities or the mestizo population. If tales of El Dorado had brought the Spanish to open the veins of Latin America looking for minerals, it was gold from Colombia and silver from Mexico and Potosí that were the basis of Spanish colonial wealth.[9] In the same way, mining shaped the settlement patterns of colonial Colombia, because hundreds of years ago contemporary urban areas were agricultural zones growing food to feed slave gangs in mining regions.[10] More recently, the story is similar. In the 2000s, the promise of fast cash lured outsiders to the Chocó from the neighboring province of Antioquia to escape violence and find gold. *Garimpeiro* miners from Brazil who had run out of easy metal in the Amazon came as well. I heard rumors of Koreans, Chinese, and Americans who had lost money in the business of supplying heavy machinery and had turned to digging with excavators.

The scale (and apparent acceptance) of the mining I witnessed used to be the exception. Mechanized operations arrived with the Chocó Pacífico

Mining Company in the early part of the twentieth century. In the 1960s, in one town, dozens of members of a community came out with machetes to protest the New York–based company because it wanted to dredge their cemetery.[11] By 2010, many of the machines I saw were owned by outsiders and yet had been invited in by local families. What had changed? Why did some families support such endeavors? Why did others not?

When talking about mining, it is easy to resort to stereotypes: illegal miners are the biggest source of profits for armed groups; miners are involved in trafficking cocaine; miners are the cause of an unfolding environmental disaster. The story is more complex, however. By 2013, the miners who used heavy machinery and excavators were occupying an airport and organizing marches against state repression. While their mines were being made illegal, the projects of foreign multinational corporations were being supported by the Colombian state. Still, the Chocó was in fact experiencing a disaster, as mercury contamination damaged rivers, fish stocks, and human health, and as poor families opened up their lands to bring in the heavy machines to extract whatever they could.

There may be little that is unique about the ways the boom reshaped the Chocó, however. Similar rushes have occurred around the world.[12] Accounts of the Amazon in the 1980s, where thousands descended on remote jungle camps, read eerily similarly. Stories from Venezuela in the 1980s and late 2010s tell of illegal miners destroying rivers and Indigenous communities. Peru's Madre de Dios region is another example, as is the way coltan is mined from the fields of the Democratic Republic of the Congo. Artisanal and small-scale miners work in northern Myanmar and West Africa, while rivers in Indonesia are featured in Hollywood movies.[13] The Discovery Channel has a reality show about miners in the Canadian Yukon and Alaska. There is a global gold rush, which in many places is being demonized. Globally, it is easy to paint all miners with the same brush, making this illegal and informal industry the biggest threat to rivers around the world. But this misses the quotidian lived experience of such mining.

By 2018, millions around the world made a living mixing digging for gold with farming, hunting, slash-and-burn agriculture, temporary work, out-migration, and other activities. Some of the poorest and most marginalized around the world have traded their machetes for shovels to become what specialist on gender and community livelihoods Kuntala Lahiri-Dutt calls extractive peasants.[14] While the Chocó's is far from an isolated gold rush, it is one in which the particular matters. While what was unfolding can be seen as a catastrophic form of uncontrolled illegal and informal extractive activities, the industry also provided a livelihood for Leidy, her mother, and her sister that afternoon. It is this contradiction that makes it so urgent to understand the perspectives of the miners themselves.

I take such a perspective in the following pages, but mining is just one part of the story. There are other parts. Rural families have watched their ways of life come under attack from cocaine trafficking, from government corruption, and from illegal logging. The Chocó is a key route for coca production and cocaine shipments from the interior to the Pacific Ocean and north to Central America on their way to the United States. In this, the most impoverished region in Colombia, many live on as little as a dollar a day. Access to food is insecure, work is scarce, and flooding, war, natural disaster, and the ongoing search for a livelihood displace people from their territories in riverine valleys to the cities and other areas of highland Colombia. The population of 350,000 Black descendants of enslaved women and men brought from Africa and of dozens of Indigenous communities and mestizo settlers has experienced the boom times in diverse ways. This book is about how the miners (whom I knew best) experienced the gold rush.

This book follows six or so mines over six chapters, divided into three parts. Some mines were worked by Black families who mixed gold production using hand tools and manual techniques with various livelihood strategies. Other mines were worked by men and women from other regions of Colombia, who deployed heavy machinery and mercury as a way to accumulate cash. Still other mines may or may not have been worked at all, as they were instead used to support money laundering or speculative investments. Part 1 dwells on the artisanal production of two mines worked using hand tools and manual techniques embedded in what I call a dual household economy.[15] Part 2 considers small-scale accumulation, focusing on a mine owned by a Black family who decided to invite in outsiders in an attempt to get rich quick. Part 3 turns to the global connections of gold, with forms of value transformation through cocaine money laundering and stock market speculation. These three parts follow connections out from a rural way of life in the Colombian Pacific to places far beyond the Chocó, through the networks of the drug trade and speculative capitalism. Throughout it all, each chapter always returns to a place and the lived experience of men and women like Leidy and her neighbors who find their shifting livelihoods through *rebusque*.

Taken together, the stories tell of unexpected resilience—of muddling along and finding creative ways to confront a lack of opportunity through various forms of *rebusque*. Gold becomes one strategy, among others. It is an integral part of place-based livelihood and a way of life that is both supported by and threatened by the arrival of outsider-owned excavators and dredges. The metal offers a path toward a livelihood, a certain freedom, and the good life, even as it is contingent, contradictory, and precarious. The path has dramatic economic and environmental consequences, which may be why, for decades, the response of Colombian governments has been to criminalize certain types of small-scale and artisanal mines. Without downplaying environmental and social costs, in particular its gendered and racialized impacts wherein Black women like Leidy, her mother, and her sister were especially marginalized, this book explores complex forms of livelihood to offer different narratives of a gold rush. The first part of the book focuses on artisanal mines, the second on small-scale mines, and the third on a different scale than production and accumulation, where the yellow metal facilitates the transformation of value either through gold-based money laundering by narcotraffickers or through speculation by Canadian mining companies.

This book is an account of learning how to mine. It is an ethnography of a gold rush, and it is awash with description and analysis. It draws on real people, actual places, and true happenings, although I have afforded some anonymity to the living and dead. Fictitious names protect the identities of miners, their families, and other nonpublic figures. Full names, however, are real. While I write about real places—mines, villages, and towns—and while the rivers have their own bends and curves and particularities, they all shall remain nameless in a nod toward protecting those who still live there. I have adopted generic terms for villages and rivers and other real places for the same reasons. Events I observed occurred on the river I know best in September 2010, between November 2010 and April 2012, in September 2013, in October 2014, and in May 2017. The dialogues in quotations are translations reconstructed later from jottings or, in a few cases, from transcriptions of digital recordings of interviews. I took notes immediately after conversations or in the days and weeks that followed them. While I recorded some interviews and conversations with an audio recorder, most of the dialogue is my imperfect rendition made from notes written after the fact.

Photographs open and close each chapter. The photographs are my own, and I did not collaborate with anyone. During my fieldwork, I often had a camera with me, and photography and video was something I spent energy on. However, as I began to draft these pages, I realized I had time to learn to write well, but not also to master photography. Of the photographs I have not used, some served as memory aids for the writing. Of the photographs I have used, each expresses not just an illustration of the text but an additional layer of meaning. Some invite their own stories, and all serve to enrich interpretations of shifting livelihoods and gold mining in the Chocó.

ACKNOWLEDGMENTS

Why a gold rush? The farm where my parents live is a twenty-minute drive from Eldorado—not the mythical Latin American city, but a real one. Eldorado is a long-abandoned mine in Eastern Ontario, Canada, which was home to a short-lived gold rush in the 1860s. Little remains today but a crumbling rural hamlet with an exotic namesake. Nearby is a village named Deloro, former home to a smelter that closed in 1961. Both names must be the first Spanish words I ever learned, and yet I never even realized that in the late 1990s when my mother, Louise Livingstone, worked as a journalist at a local paper. Between stories of council meetings, soccer tournaments, and school plays, she wrote of the contamination and need for a cleanup at the old mine and the old smelter. It was when the metal was exhausted from Deloro before the First World War that the smelter opened. Over the next few decades, Deloro smelted first silver, then cobalt for airplanes, and then, my mother thought, uranium for the Manhattan Project. When the smelter closed, a mishmash of slag, tailings, contaminated water, heavy metals, arsenic, mercury, and low-level radioactive material was left. My mother wrote of the need for a cleanup, of the men who worked and died at the smelter, and of the village where a handful of retired workers lived. This book is about a different gold rush and different mines in a different country, but in writing it, I have followed my mother's footsteps. This book is for her. She has read the first, second, and final drafts of everything I have ever written.

If I sometimes imagine writing as a solitary task undertaken in the predawn hours before the bustle of fieldwork, family, and teaching, my memory is both true and false. True because the predawn hours were when I did much of my writing, false because this book emerged alone but also in conversation. My interlocutors were many, in Colombia and beyond.

My most profound gratitude goes to the women and men who welcomed, with amused smiles, my attempts to learn their craft. I have woven together stories about the people I call Leidy, Laura, Martina, Pedro, Antonio, Héctor, Elisabet, Fernando, Mauricio, Miguel, Don Alfonso, Diego, Esteban, Marco, Ernesto, Sofía, the Chief, Rodrigo, Julio, Luis, Geraldo, José, Carlos, Juan David, Andrés, Meta, Felipe, and Ximena. Others who taught me to mine and who made this work possible are not represented in these pages. To everyone, my thanks.

My gratitude as well to the Black community council, which gave me an identity card, a letter, invitations to countless meetings, and permission to learn to pan on their collective territory. In Quibdó and beyond, my thanks to too many unnamed people for their conversation, insight, and assistance. In Bogotá, conversations with Claudia Mosquera Rosero-Labbé at the Universidad National de Colombia shaped my work on Afro-Colombia. Eduardo Restrepo at the Pontificia Universidad Javeriana discussed fieldwork with me over small cups of black coffee. His conversations and bibliography were *imprescindible*. Ximena Gonzáles, Elisabet Pèriz, Johana Rocha, and Andrea Torres at the Centro de Estudios para la Justicia Social (Tierra Digna) let me accompany them on their early visits. The women from Tierra Digna are impressive *guerreras* fighting (and winning) legal battles for land, water, and justice.

I am grateful for the intellectual nourishment provided by a scholarly community at Carleton University in Ottawa, Canada. Peter Gose turned me into an ethnographer and encouraged me to engage with mining as a practice. Cristina Rojas gave advice, introduced me to her *colombianista* colleagues, and did so much more. Blair Rutherford dispensed impeccable questions. Louise de la Gorgendière pushed me to begin before I felt ready. Jen Pylypa hosted a writing group where Leanne Davis, Matthew Hawkins, Cheryl Matthew, Marieka Sax, and I turned our fieldwork into ethnography. Comments by Graeme Auld at Carleton University and John-Andrew McNeish at the Norwegian University of Life Sciences improved my thinking. Wangui Kimari introduced me to ChocQuibTown, and by extension the Colombian Pacific. The Institute of Political Economy provided me with an interdisciplinary home, fostered in no small part by Donna Coghill.

The book was nurtured while I was a visiting fellow at Yale University's Agrarian Studies Program in New Haven, with help from James C. Scott and K. "Shivi" Sivaramakrishnan and a community of graduate students, postdoctoral fellows, and scholars. Marcela Echeverri welcomed me to Yale with a workshop series on Colombia. Most of all, I learned from the other visiting fellows and graduate students. Guntra Aistara, Aharon de Grassi, Jonathan DeVore, Alba Díaz Geada, Julie Gibbings, Chris Gratien, Jennifer Lee Johnson, and José E. Martínez-Reyes and the participants in the Program in Agrarian Studies all commented on various chapters. Aniket Aga, Chandana Anusha, Deepti Chatti, Luisa Cortesi, Karine Gagné, Sahana Ghosh, Amy Johnson, Alyssa Paredes, Elliott Prasse-Freeman, Amy Zhang, and other members of the Environment Anthropology Collective commented on early drafts of as well.

I completed revisions at the University of New Brunswick, Fredericton. Susan Blair, Gabriel Hrynick, Koumari Mitra, Amy Scott, and Melanie Wiber welcomed me to our small but vibrant department. In Fredericton, I participated in writing groups. Critiques by Liz Clarke, Stefanie Kennedy, and Carolyn MacDonald helped improve chapter 3. Group writing with Andrea Bombak, Tia Dafnos, Tracy Glynn, and Suzanne Hindmarch helped carve time for revisions. Online Andrea Carrion, Alder Keleman, Chris Shaw, Kate Turner, and others helped me begin and end. Claudia Rocha read my first draft and provided her encouragement. Undergraduate students at the University of New Brunswick, the University of Victoria, Purdue University, and St. Thomas University read or listened to many chapters. My thanks to my students for their many insights on the literature we read together, which shaped this text.

The ideas in this book have been tested at various conferences, including the annual meetings of the American Anthropology Association, the Latin American Studies Association, the Canadian Association of Latin American and Caribbean Studies, and the Canadian Anthropology Society, as well as presentations at Yale University; Brown University; the University of Toronto; the University of California, Irvine; Carleton University; the University of New Brunswick; and Dalhousie University. Conversations with various scholars shaped these pages, including Yesenia Barragan, Tom Beckley, Ingrid Johanna Bolívar Ramirez, Brian Brazeal, Filipe Calvão, Angela Milena Castillo Ardila, Marjo de Theije, Ann Farnsworth-Alvear, Elizabeth Ferry, Kirsten Francescone, Tracy Glynn, Ricardo Grinspun, Pablo Heidrich, Eric Hirsch, David Kneas, Melis Laebens, Catherine C. LeGrand, Liisa North, Susan O'Donnell, Pilar Riaño-Alcalá, Aída Sofía Rivera Sotelo, Mary Roldán, Caroline Shenaz Hossein, James H. Smith, Luis van Isschot, and Daniel Varela Corredor.

An earlier version of chapter 3 appeared in the journal *Extractive Industries and Society*, and further reflections on the Chocó appear in other places.[1]

Fieldwork support came from Canadian Social Sciences and Humanities Research Council fellowships, an Ontario Graduate Scholarship, the Department of Sociology and Anthropology at Carleton University, and a Michael Smith Foreign Study Supplement. The University of New Brunswick gave me a teaching release in my first semester, while support from the Office of Research Services enabled me to bring a draft of this book back to Colombia in May 2017. Additional support for publishing this book was provided by the Busteed Publication Fund of the Faculty of Arts and a Harrison McCain Foundation grant in aid of scholarly book publishing, both from of the University of New Brunswick, Fredericton.

Along the way, over a decade, Marieka Sax offered conversations and comments and critiques that have shaped and deepened my thinking. From camaraderie during the first days planning to go to the field, to the research itself, to starting then finishing this book, to revising the first draft, and all the rest, my thanks go to Marieka.

Deft editing by Erin Seatter, my brilliant brother Ed Tubb, Karen Caruana, and Colin Waters improved the prose immeasurably. Isaac Barclay provided impeccable assistance in the final rounds of revision. My freelance development editor Fazeela Jiwa guided me down the final, hardest stretch of revision with her careful critique. University of Washington Press executive editor Lorri Hagman and Culture, Place, and Nature series editor K. "Shivi" Sivaramakrishnan provided guidance with patience. Hanni Jalil-Paier, Julie Van Pelt, and the rest of team at the University of Washington Press shepherded this book into print. Richard Isaac saved me many embarrassments with a detailed final copy edit. Three anonymous reviewers read the manuscript in its entirety, while others commented on the article drafts that have become chapters 3 and 5. Their commentary prompted much rethinking and restructuring. Errors in fact or analysis remain my own.

Mostly, my memory of solitary writing is false because I have been lucky enough to share my life with my greatest loves, Mercedes, Camilo, and Lila. Camilo would rather have eaten more pancakes on Sunday mornings than let me write. Lila was born as I revised these words. Mercedes listened to large sections of the book read aloud and accompanied me to the field, then to write in Ottawa, then to draft in New Haven, then to revise in Fredericton. She knows most everyone in what follows, and it was she who sat me down so long ago with her legal mind and a stack of sticky notes to map out the structure of this book.

To Mercedes and Camilo and Lila, my gratitude and love, always.

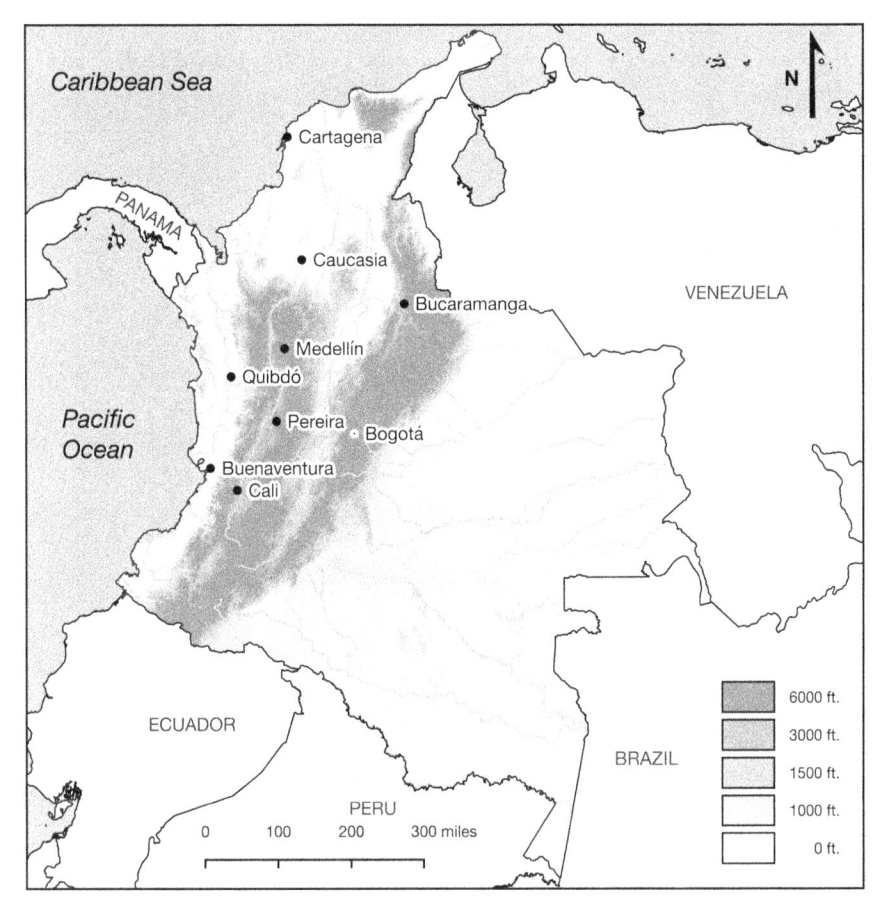

Colombia

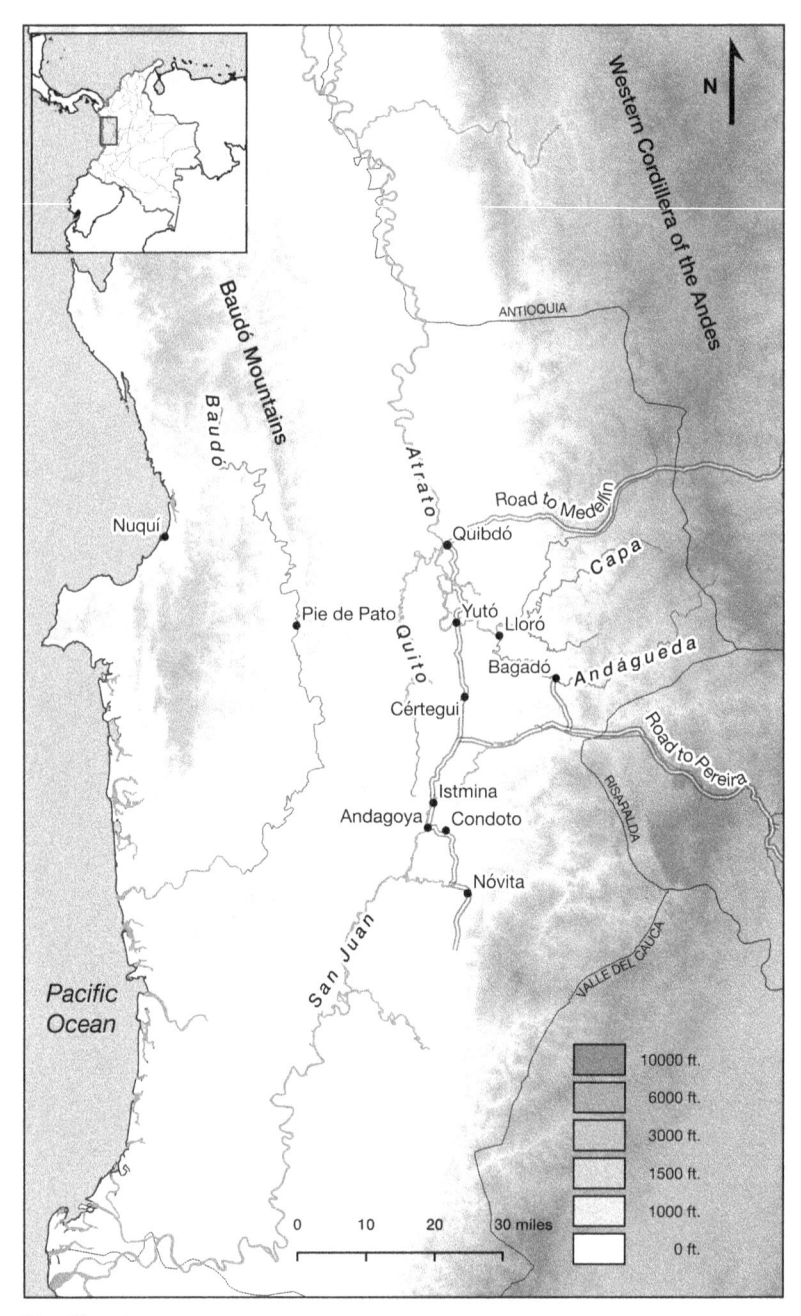

The Chocó

SHIFTING LIVELIHOODS

Introduction
Life during a Gold Rush

CRESTING a rise, Antonio and I stopped and surveyed the mine. Two distant excavator machines were dwarfed by what they had dug up. With the jungle and topsoil gone, a moonscape of gravel was left. The machines trapped gold with mercury, and their tailings gushed into a sluice and down to a stream and through the forest to paint the river the color of coffee with milk.

"It's beautiful," I swear I heard Antonio say.

My warmest memory of Antonio is from months earlier as he looked down from his perch above his father Pedro's mine. Antonio had his rubber boots kicked forward, and his index fingers pointed both directions. He was all smiles. We were joking on a break from digging at the family mine. We used wooden pans and a network of channels cut into the hillside. Over months, we worked so slowly that the vegetation seemed to advance over our leftover gravel faster than we made it.

When I looked out beyond the rise at those two excavators, I saw the trees wrenched and the landscape flattened. I thought of Antonio and Pedro's mine compared to the mines of his neighbors, which had been swamped by the two excavators owned by strangers. I saw something ghastly over that rise. Antonio did not.

Antonio saw an efficiency over his hand tools. He felt satisfaction at what had taken the machines a matter of months, which would have taken him and his father a lifetime. I imagined the jungle gone and the river polluted. We had different ways of thinking about, understanding, feeling, and experiencing the same excavator operation. His vision was not what one would assume reading newspapers, magazines, nongovernmental organization reports, or some of the scholarly literature. In these accounts, the

Excavators dig deep and wash the earth over a classifier (the machinery at far right) to leave behind a mined-out landscape.

impression given was that the small-scale miners of the northwest Colombian department[1] of the Chocó—the men with those excavators—were frontier gangsters clearing the land in a quest for wealth. Spend enough time, and such accounts are unsatisfying. Antonio's vision was at odds with what I saw, expressing a different way of thinking. His was the ontology of a miner.

This book considers the ways Antonio and others experienced the boom times of a gold rush and the ways that this gold rush was embedded in wider legal and extralegal economies. It would be easy to fall into a narrative found in much writing about the commodification of nature and natural resource extraction, but I strive for a different complexity by weaving together stories about the lives of artisanal and small-scale miners and those who live in the communities where these miners work. Gold enables some forms of autonomous livelihood, even as it disables others. Mines create freedom and unfreedom; they are at once destructive and constructive. The conditions of extraction and the environments affected and the miners themselves matter at least as much as the mere presence of mining. This book offers insight on the contradictory ways that gold both liberates and subjugates as mines become sites of exploitation and emancipation. What results is a twofold investigation: First, stories of lived experience drawing on the lives of a handful of miners on artisanal and small-scale gold mines. Second, stories of money laundering through gold by cocaine traffickers and speculation on mining projects by multinational corporations wherein gold facilitates other economic processes. These accounts, nevertheless, remain stories from the margins, because their setting is the poorest and most discriminated department in Colombia and because the stories focus on those who make a living through "precarious" and "informal" shifting livelihood strategies—strategies which themselves offer a certain freedom, especially when compared to the nonexistent alternatives.

FORESTS, RAIN, CULTURE, AND THE RIGHTS OF A RIVER

The department of the Chocó appears in satellite images as a cloud-dappled emerald strip between the Pacific Ocean to the west and the Caribbean Sea to the north, at the frontier of South and Central America in northwest Colombia. The Pacific forests are occasionally broken by rivers, invisible mines, roads, villages, towns, and cities. The coastline from southern Panama to northern Ecuador is about five hundred miles long; the forests are less than eighty miles wide. To the north is the impenetrable—except to those who know the routes—Darien Gap that separates Colombia from Panama. It is impenetrable because there are no roads between South and Central America. The forests and then the ocean itself are the western limits of the Colombian departments of Nariño, Cauca, Valle del Cauca, and the Chocó. Along the eastern edge of the forests, the Andes rise higher than 13,250 feet before falling again to the valley of the Cauca River. On the Pacific side, trees scrabble for purchase on barren soils, and rotting vegetation perfumes the air. Environmentalists call the forests of the Colombian Pacific the "lungs of the world," the "Chocó biogeographic region," and a "biodiversity hot spot."[2] Venture into the undergrowth, and the shadows deepen and the leaves close in and the dark mutes the green, as short sight lines give the forest a false sense of permanence and the tropical jungles become fraught with real and imagined dangers as the foliage makes it impossible to see more than few feet into the darkness. On the river that flows by Antonio's village, on a cloudless evening, the Andes are visible from the middle of the water. On chilly mornings, tendrils of fog drift across the water to the edge of the river and what are the wettest forests on the planet.

Between the Pacific Ocean and the Andes Mountains, it rains a lot. Some days are hot and bright and sunny, despite following nights of torrential rains. Some days are heavy rain interspersed with sunshine. Some days it rains in the morning and clears in the afternoon. Some dry days turn into weeks of drought. Some wet days become weeks of rain. Sometimes, El Niño, that tropical depression off the western coasts of Colombia and Ecuador, sends clouds into the Chocó fueled by the warm waters of the Pacific so that an ocean's worth of evaporation crashes into the Andes as the heavens open with biblical proportions. Their description as the wettest forests in the world is no hyperbole, at least according to statistics on average global rainfall.[3] Some municipalities record the world's highest annual rainfall: forty-three feet and seven inches in one year. If the rain supports the forests and fills the rivers, those who live on the edges of both have a special relationship with water.

The culture is an aquatic one.[4] The flow of the river is the topic of daily conversation. Antonio, his father Pedro, and his neighbors Esteban and Don Alfonso read their rivers. They speak about its depth, and the quality of the water. "Will it flood?" "Did it flood last night?" "Is the river clear?" "Did it rain in the mountains?" The rain on a metal roof makes sleep elusive and travel impossible. When I first visited the village where Antonio lived, I anxiously packed my cameras and digital audio recorder and computer into plastic bags with tins of silica gel to protect everything from the humidity. A year later, on the back of a dirt-bike-taxi rushing through darkened streets in the departmental capital Quibdó, I realized the less one wears in the rain, the better: shorts, a T-shirt, and plastic flip-flops are plenty. Walking in the rain is like taking a shower, and still people bathe twice a day. Spend enough time, and rain becomes a nonevent, remarkable through its absence.

When the rains do not come, the sky widens with towering clouds floating in masses of blue. The days of a burning yellow sun leave the rivers dwindled, the rain barrels emptied, the trees parched, and the landscape dried. Talk turns from the river to *el verano*, or the dry months, and the lack of rain. After all, as the saying goes, water is life. When the runaway former enslaved peoples, descendants of the men and women brought from West Africa to mine gold for the Spanish, founded their communities in the Colombian Pacific, they built close to the edges of the rivers to have easy access to water. People drink river water. Fishers catch fish with lines or nets or traps fashioned from wood. Children spend afternoons cartwheeling into the water. Young boys teach themselves to navigate with poles in dugout canoes. Families travel in flat-bottomed wooden launches with nine-horsepower outboard motors. Women and girls carry clothes in red plastic bowls to the river's edge to scrub on wooden washboards and then let dry on the sun-warmed river stones. And wheelbarrows dump black garbage bags—with diapers, T-shirts, plastic, soft drink bottles, and the other collected human refuse—into the rivers. The bags float downstream until they wedge in submerged roots of trees, so that when the waters fall the garbage is left high and dangling meters above the now-low river.

This deluge of rain moves much more than human refuse. When the rains come, the rivers flood and wash into towns and villages. When a flood swept away his village two decades ago, Antonio's father Pedro carried Antonio and his two siblings to safety in the middle of the night on his shoulders. Pedro and his neighbors rebuilt their village. The new village is a triangle of twenty or so cinderblock houses built on high ground a short walk from the river. When it rains, the river rises as much as ten feet to overflow its banks, pull at bridges, and tear complex entanglements of trees and branches and roots and earth into the water. Although the flooding river never quite reaches the new village, the heavy rains mark the arrival of *el invierno*, or the wet months. The rains can last a week or a month. These rains have washed down the western slopes of the westernmost range of the Colombian Andes for millennia. The rainwater has shifted trillions of particles of gravel and cut knifelike into the banks of the rivers to create what appears to be sheared embankments that become visible when the river levels fall. The sediments reshape the currents and create sandbars that damage delicate propellers.

The rain works and reworks the landscape as well, so much so that over geological millennia, tiny yellow flecks of gold have concentrated in the muds and gravel of the bottom of the river. These rains have left gold-rich gravel in old riverbeds spread across the landscape. Pedro and Martina and Antonio and thousands of others wake up just before dawn, bathe in nearby rivers, and travel by foot or canoe or perched on motorcycles, buses, and trucks to mine the alluvial gravel. These men and women know where to find the metal because they follow the old watercourses left by the rain. They read the landscape and they know where the water used to run. In the interoceanic forests of the Chocó, the Great Biblical Flood is ongoing as the sand, gravel, trees, and metals continue to be rain-shifted.

All of this water ends up in one of the Chocó's three aquatic arteries. The Atrato River drains north to the Caribbean Sea. The San Juan empties southwest to the Pacific Ocean. The Baudó descends from a low coastal mountain range called the Serranía del Baudó on its way to the Pacific. The Atrato and the San Juan each have dozens of tributaries—streams and rivers that cut down from the Andes. It is this aquatic network that has, over geological time, washed sediment and gravel down from the mountains into the lowland plains, scattering specks of gold in alluvial gravel. Those specks have been sought for at least half a millennium by men and women using wooden pans and sluices. By the 2000s, hundreds of multistory excavator machines on caterpillar treads were doing the same search.

As a consequence of this uncontrolled boom in mining by excavators, the Atrato River became a legal person in November 2016 through a landmark decision of the Constitutional Court of Colombia.[5] The court, the country's highest, which renders judgments on matters regarding the 1991 constitution, declared the river a holder of rights. It was a legal response to a mining boom that has devastated the environment and the lives of those in the Atrato basin over the last thirty years. The basin, described in the court decision, encompasses 40,000 square kilometers (60 percent of the whole department), starts in the Andes, has 150 tributaries, has eight ports navigable by vessels of up to 200 metric tons (200,000 kg), and is home to Black and Indigenous communities, which make up 97% of the population.

Antonio and Pedro and many of the others in this book are connected through residence or kin to one such Black community. For them and for the hundreds of thousands of descendants of enslaved men and women brought from Africa, the rivers of the Chocó are the center of their place-based regional identity. The Atrato, the San Juan, the Baudó, and the dozens of other rivers are cultural spaces, places of quotidian livelihood, and important providers of transport, food, laundry, drinking water, and playgrounds. In both the Chocó and the wider Colombian Pacific, rivers represent rich symbolic and cultural values for those who mix gardening and fishing and hunting with artisanal mining and shifting livelihoods. The decision to grant judicial personhood to the Atrato River was an attempt by the court to protect this aquatic way of life against the predations of uncontrolled resource extraction.

In Colombia, the Constitutional Court wrote, gold represents $2.5 billion, or 2.3 percent of the gross domestic product, which is a fifth of all exports and which makes Colombia the sixth largest gold exporter in Latin America and twentieth worldwide. Mining provides work to 350,000, while excavators and bulldozers and dredgers devastate fragile ecosystems. These miners move tens of thousands of tons of material each year, releasing mine runoff that renders rivers unnavigable, that makes water move slowly and carry less oxygen and be undrinkable. Mercury, which miners release hundreds of tons of a year, makes its way into the food system to impact human nervous, renal, cardiovascular, and respiratory systems. Mines breed mosquitos, which bring malaria.[6] Armed groups on the left and right fund their wars by taxing miners and laundering their drug profits through gold. If the court paints Black and Indigenous communities as the victims of mining, it puts the legal rights of nature and the environment at the core of the state's response to the crisis. The idea is a form of posthuman, biocultural rights tied to the rights of ethnic communities to administer and control their own lands. In declaring the Atrato basin a subject of rights, the court required the protection, conservation, maintenance, and restoration of "diverse cultural practices, languages, and relationships with plants, animals, microorganisms and the environment that contribute to biodiversity, as well as the spiritual and cultural practices of local communities."[7] To achieve this end, the court created an independent expert panel and a Commission of Guardians of the Atrato. It ordered plans to decontaminate the river, to protect ways of life, to undertake further study, and to end the gold rush.

The challenges for the Atrato River to exercise its right are twofold. First is the challenge of actually implementing the various declarations of the court. Others may help tell the story of this process. Second is the challenge that perhaps the court got something wrong. The court's decision foregrounds the negative aspects of mining, and yet the decision remains silent on the ambiguities, tensions, and complexities connected with the experience of a gold rush. The court had little good to say of miners from other regions of Colombia, little of the metal as a source of cash that brought, temporarily, work and higher incomes to rural communities, little of migrants moving to the Chocó to find some money, little of who those migrants were and why and how they came to the region, little about the motors and the appliances and the cellphones and the expensive liquors and the beautiful clothes that flew from store shelves, little of the men who filled the bars and the music they played that was the soundtrack to the gold rush, and little of the Black and Indigenous communities and their diversity of perspectives, which moved from outright hostility to embracing mining through the development of internal regulations in a form of legal pluralism. In short, the court saw little of the beauty Antonio saw from that rise in the jungle, and only the horror I saw.

Certainly, the problems left by decades of mining—mercury contamination, water quality degradation, loss of fish, acid runoff, gender-based violence, and displacement—are profound. Yet, the court's tools of prohibition may not work. Over forty years, criminalization has been used against Colombia's other most famous illegal export—cocaine. The drug war has prohibited cocaine production, criminalized its export, and enforced these policies with soldiers. The drug war has failed to prevent production; in 2017 Colombia exported more cocaine than ever before, and the industry has fueled decades of internal conflict. Colombia's civil wars have killed 200,000, displaced six million, and disappeared tens of thousands.[8] Despite a peace process in 2016 with the main guerrilla army, the Chocó in 2019 was anything but postconflict.

The story of a gold rush is not unique to Colombia. Around the world, what is called artisanal mining (e.g., using hand tools and manual techniques) and small-scale mining (e.g., using excavators and dredges) has been practiced for decades.[9] These practices have increasingly been criminalized globally, and many states have engaged in practices pioneered in Colombia: blowing up mines, burning machinery, and imprisoning miners. The Atrato River will have difficulty in exercising its rights if mining for gold continues to be understood as a simple story. This book offers a more complex narrative by considering the period from 2010 to 2012, when the price of gold was at its highest, when the boom times looked like they would never end, and when foreign multinationals were prospecting for gold. It builds this narrative from fieldwork in the mud digging at various mines near Antonio's village and from a reading of media accounts and other sources.

PRIMITIVE ACCUMULATION AND ARTISANAL AND SMALL-SCALE MINING

That afternoon with Antonio, our boat had been low in the water. We were five: Antonio, Elisabet, Héctor, Fernando, and myself. A small troupe on a Saturday afternoon day trip. Picnic-like. Festive. As we made our way first by boat and then on a trail that led to the rise, it was on Héctor's insistence that I took photographs.

What can photographs of mines carved out of the jungle *not* conjure? I remember the wooden pans that Pedro and Antonio used while working for themselves, the rusting excavators with their football fields of blighted land, the fears of multinational corporations and their projects for open-pit megamines carved into the hills high in the Andes, the Black community organizations holding workshops in response, the possibilities of wealth that lured men to jungle camps far from home, and the Black men and women displaced from their homes by these outsiders.

On a global scale, my memories of lands and forests owned by Black families washed into the rivers by the work of the excavators and of the fears of the multinational corporations that would do the same, at first, resonate with the story of the expropriation of the farms, forests, and livelihoods of independent peasants who were displaced by sheep in the Highland Clearances of nineteenth-century Scotland, which German philosopher, political theorist, and economist Karl Marx described as primitive accumulation.[10]

Sheep are not gold, and the nineteenth is no twenty-first century, but an analysis of primitive accumulation in which people are displaced by production for foreign markets resonates in Colombia. The expansion of banana, oil palm, and sugar plantations in the zones of tropical agriculture, the coal mines in the Caribbean coast, the oil refineries in the hot lowlands, and the drug camps and the cattle ranches in so many regions are all forms of commodity production, often for foreign markets. Over decades, hundreds of thousands have been displaced from their homes by corporations, landowners, businessmen, and their paramilitaries and soldiers to make way for the production of commodities for foreign markets. Marx could have written of the Colombian peasantry in the twentieth and twenty-first centuries that their "history, the history of their expropriation, is written in the annals of mankind in letters of blood and fire."[11]

With primitive accumulation, Marx sought to describe human displacement and the earliest stage of capital accumulation. The clearances provided wool from sheep grazing on lands once lived on by Highlanders, and the capital that pushed the industrialization of cities in Northern England. In no small part, Highland wool built English factories. More broadly, colonialism—the Spanish in Latin America after gold, the Dutch in Indonesia after spices, the English in East India after tea, and so on—did (and continues to do) the same. Processes of primitive accumulation have dispossessed innumerable peoples in a search for raw materials, which in turn helped fuel the expansion of capitalism. "The treasures captured outside Europe by undisguised looting, enslavement and murder flowed back to the mother country and were turned into capital there," wrote Marx.[12] While its trenchant critique resonates in Colombia today, primitive accumulation remains a totalizing narrative, which risks simplifying away complexities of life on the frontier. Drawing on Marx, one is tempted to dismiss Antonio's comment looking out over that rise as a false consciousness. However, to do this would miss important questions. A story of primitive accumulation in which gold merely "comes dripping from head to toe, from every pore, with blood and dirt"[13] is unsatisfying. Blood and dirt abound aplenty, but so does much more besides. Why, for example, were some excavators welcomed in by Black landowners? Were artisanal miners like Antonio and Pedro really involved in primitive accumulation? How can metal for foreign markets benefit locals? Was the equivalent of the Lowland laird dispossessing his Highland crofter one of those men driving a red excavator wearing a Hawaiian shirt?

This man, who had carved out the landscape over the rise in front of our small troupe, was what everyone called a *retrero*, a term derived from the Spanish word for excavator (*retro*, short for *retroexcavadora*) and referring to an owner and worker of an excavator mine. He was one of thousands working on similar operations throughout the Chocó. The term *retrero* was common, but the *retreros* themselves sometimes used the phrase "small-scale mining." Activists and other observers used the terms "medium-scale" or "mechanized mining." While in the Chocó, the terms used were "artisanal" and "small-scale" in ways that reflected Colombia's mining legislation before 2001, scholars often deploy a more technical approach, noting differences based on scale, technique, and legal status.[14]

In one such category, "microscale" refers to shifting under 5 metric tons of ore a day, "small-scale" 5 to 300 metric tons, "medium-scale" 301 to 1,000 metric tons, and "large-scale" more than a 1,000 metric tons. Other relevant categories were legal or illegal, formal or informal, and manual or semimechanized. Artisanal mining, following this nomenclature, refers to Afro-descendant, microscale, legal, informal, manual miners relying on hand tools and water pumps. This was what Pedro, Antonio, Elisabet, Héctor, Fernando, and even I did. Indeed, later that year, Héctor and one of his brothers would open their own mine in the jungle, just as many young men did along the length of the river. The small-scale miners, like that *retrero* dressed in a Hawaiian shirt, were whom Antonio and I observed ripping up the jungles. The man worked on an outsider-owned, medium-scale, illegal, informal, mechanized mining operation that relied on heavy machinery, primarily excavators on land and two-story dredging machines on water. Despite the differences in scale, the excavators used the same principles as the artisanal miner: dig to the bedrock and wash. While Antonio's family relied on water and gravity to sort metal from the earth, small-scale miners used their machines and the toxic heavy metal mercury to get the gold from gravel where once had been the complex entanglements of a vibrant jungle landscape.

NATURE COMMODIFIED: STAPLES AND RESOURCE EXPORTS

Both the Highland Clearances and the European colonial expansions relied on processes that commodified nature. Today, digging for minerals, pumping gas, logging trees, netting fish, harvesting soya, and mining bitumen are each their own transformations of natural phenomena into substances for sale on global markets. Minerals, plants, and animals have long been ripped from one place to be sold for the enrichment of another. There are many ways to understand such resource economies. In the middle part of last century, a group of economic historians in Canada began to think about how producing particular commodities shaped the places doing that production. Developing Marx's focus on production, but not his broader critique, these historians were interested in how the ebbs and flows of the trade of natural resources such as fur, gold, timber, cod, and other staples had shaped the structures of the economic history of Canada, for better and worse.[15] This staples approach, applied to the Chocó, would begin with an economic history of the department told through mining.

Gold has been a central defining export of the Chocó ever since the Spanish conquistador Pascual de Andagoya arrived in the sixteenth century.[16] Indigenous peoples; enslaved men and women brought from Africa by the Spanish;[17] their escaped and manumitted descendants in the nineteenth, twentieth, and twenty-first centuries; the British and US companies in the twentieth century; the excavators and dredging operations owned by Colombians and Brazilians; and the prospecting firms listed on Canadian stock exchanges in the late twentieth and early twenty-first centuries have all been after the metal. By the early twentieth century, British and American mining companies were dredging rivers and building a company town in Andagoya—named after that conquistador—replete with screened-in porches and tennis courts for the white management. After the Chocó Pacífico Mining Company was nationalized in the 1970s and after the nationalized company went bankrupt in the 1980s, the town of Andagoya fell on hard times.[18] During this time, global gold prices hit records in the 1980s, and scattered informal mine camps were built by transient miners, mechanics, assistants, diggers, washers, cooks, cleaners, and other men and women after gold. Shacks and canteens were built from wet lumber over a few days and roofed with ubiquitous heavy black plastic and walled with bright green tarpaulins.

The communities around these makeshift small-scale mine camps could be studied with a tight-angled perspective focusing on the men and women whose lives were shaped by living on such mining frontier, or one could put these particular mines into the wider patterns of how a gold rush has impacted the Chocó more broadly. On the river I know best, there had been at least six dozen excavators operating in the year before I arrived in 2010. Almost all of these mines were illegal. Indeed, in news accounts, these miners were typecast.[19] The small-scale miners—these illegals who moved to the Chocó—came from other mining regions of Colombia. Miners arrived in the 1980s, became less prevalent in the 1990s, and then came back in the 2000s and 2010s as the world gold price rose and the Colombian peso fell.

By 2009, the production figures for the Chocó were increasing rapidly.[20] Municipalities in the Upper Atrato and Upper San Juan watersheds were the largest producers of gold in all of Colombia, on paper.

What were the impacts of this mining boom? Excavator mines have transformed the forest landscape of lowland Colombia to feed global markets for decades. The metal, once mined, concentrated, and refined, is used as a store of wealth, as an investment vehicle, as a part of the electronics industry, and as a status symbol. From bank vaults to dowry jewelry, from cellphones to earrings, from envelopes of dust to ingots hidden in suitcases, gold is a quintessential global commodity produced in thousands of artisanal and small-scale and large-scale mines and then processed by smelters and refineries. All of this has had profound impacts on the Chocó.

DEPENDENCY AND OPEN VEINS

By the 1960s and 1970s, as Canadian political economists[21] began to consider the impacts of a structural reliance of resource exports as a defining characteristic of the national economy, Latin American political economists advanced a theory of declining terms of trade to show how export-oriented resource extraction had shaped the continental experience of economic development.[22] Both approaches critiqued the dependency of selling commodities to foreign markets, which was a defining characteristic of lopsided national economies reliant on resource exports. It was in this context that Uruguayan journalist and novelist Eduardo Galeano described Latin America as a land of open veins. He wrote: "Latin America is the region of open veins. Everything, from the discovery until our times, has always been transmuted into European—or later United States—capital, and as such has accumulated in distant centers of power. Everything: the soil, its fruits and its mineral-rich depths, the people and their capacity to work and to consume, natural resources and human resources. Production methods and class structure have been successively determined from outside for each area by meshing it into the universal gearbox of capitalism."[23]

If the Europeans were first after that city called El Dorado and a supply of spices from India, they found neither. Instead they found wealth in the form of other nature turned into commodities: gold in Ouro Preto, Brazil; nitrate in Chile; sugar in Brazil's northeast; and later, rubber in the Amazon and oil in Venezuela. At the beginning, the defining export was silver from what is today Mexico's Zacatecas and Bolivia's Potosí. The latter was the most important. The city of Potosí was built below a mountain of silver, and was, for a time in the sixteenth century, one of the largest cities in the

Western Hemisphere. The mines of Potosí consumed, in Galeano's account, eight million Indigenous men who dug into the bowels of the earth, by releasing toxic gases. Today miners still dig for minerals, even as the city remains impoverished.[24] While the silver flowed from Potosí, it had little long-term benefit for the city, the region, or the continent. Indeed, the silver hardly even benefited Spain, as it flowed into the coffers of Northern European moneylenders and via mercantilist traders to the Philippines and to China. Clearly, Latin America as a whole and Potosí in particular have been sites of primitive accumulation fueling the development of foreign capital for centuries, while remaining themselves deeply impoverished.

While Potosí was the largest supplier of silver to the Spanish crown, the Chocó was the largest supplier of gold.[25] The metal came from slave camps in peripheral, ungovernable mining outposts where enslaved men and women from West Africa were smuggled in and gold was smuggled out. Further south, in what is today northern Ecuador, Black maroon communities controlled entire regions.[26] By the nineteenth century, the descendants of the enslaved, runaways, and freed men and women called themselves *libres*, or free. These *libres* settled the lower and middle reaches of the tributaries of the Atrato and San Juan Rivers, pushing Indigenous peoples upriver. The forests of the Chocó became a refuge for men and women whose way of life—slash and mulch horticulture and mining in isolated communities—relied on strategies of a free people hoping to keep it that way.[27] Despite such liberatory possibility, despite (or because) of almost five hundred years of mining, first as enslaved men and women for the Spanish and later as independent miners for themselves, Galeano's critique resonates. Like Potosí then and now, the Chocó was and is impoverished. The Chocó has the worst indicators of poverty, malnutrition, and education of all of the thirty-two administrative departments of Colombia.[28]

LONG-DISTANCE HISTORIES OF COMMODITY TRADE

Galeano suggests that a seminal moment of capitalist development was 1492, but anthropologists have given long-distance commodity trade a much older role in their accounts of world history. The world of the 1400s was already deeply interconnected. The European mercantilist expansion in the sixteenth century, which was fueled by primitive accumulation and colonial genocides in the Americas, Africa, and Southeast Asia, was one more transformation of already-existing trade relationships across vast distances, rather than a novel phase of world economic development. The tenth-century spice trade from Asia foreshadowed the sixteenth and seventeenth centuries' trade in furs from North America and gold and silver from Latin America. This argument, advanced by anthropologist Eric Wolf, was part of a tradition of *longue durée* history of a global scale pioneered by French historians.[29] The long tentacles of commodity trade have impacted all parts of the planet, and this movement of commodified nature can help explain the histories of all places and their peoples. Export trade has shaped kin orders, systems of rank and belonging, and tribute to European colonial powers, which were central to economic and social organizing around the world. Processes of primitive accumulation for foreign markets did not, however, result in an expansion of a universal system of ideas, ideologies, and ways of life. Nevertheless, the world that anthropologists documented from the end of the nineteenth century was a world that was already deeply integrated with wider systems of power and the trade of nature, commodified.[30]

The Chocó has long been a source, destination, and route for the production and transport of mineral, forest, and human cargos. It is easy to imagine the Chocó as an isolated and peripheral region lost in time, the exotic, darkest Africa on the edges of a whiter Colombia reproduced by Colombian Nobel Prize–winning novelist, short story writer, and journalist Gabriel García Márquez in his account of a visit there in the 1950s to report on a strike in the town of Andagoya[31] and in the concerns of my white friends in Bogotá who worried about my visiting the department. But the Chocó is a place where people's very way of life, economy, and culture have been shaped by global connections. The Atrato River was shut to all trade by the Spanish crown in the seventeenth century in an attempt to obstruct the contraband flow of as much as a third of the gold from the Chocó to Dutch and English pirates waiting on the Caribbean coast in the Bay of Urabá.[32] The Chocó became home to enslaved men and women transported up the Atrato River to the San Juan River, some to work as miners, others on a contraband transit route south to bypass royal taxes and avoid the Isthmus of Panama on the way to slave markets in Lima.[33] The San Juan became the world's major supplier of platinum in the eighteenth century, after Spanish metallurgists learned how to refine the metal. A title the region held until the early twentieth century, when South African and Russian production took over.[34]

When mining entered a cyclical decline in the nineteenth century, Black men tapped rubber in the forests to sell to itinerant merchants. Hard seeds from the tagua plant, called vegetable ivory, were picked for the world market in buttons, until the Second World War and the invention of plastics disrupted the demand for this once globally important nontimber forest product.[35] When the Chocó Pacífico Mining Company opened that company town in Andagoya and dammed one river for hydroelectric power and dredged the region for gold, its profits flowed to the International Mining Consortium and helped fund, not Yankee Stadium as *chocoanos* told me but Lewisohn Stadium, which was built in 1915 and demolished in 1973. The stadium was named after financier and philanthropist Adolph Lewisohn, who had interests in the mines in the Chocó. As the mining company went bankrupt, the important commodity changed as well. By the 1980s, tropical hardwoods were exported, while white gold—cocaine—was transported through the rivers and jungles of the Chocó for export to foreign markets via jungle airstrips and narcosubmarines.

These stories of long-distance trade disrupt the too-simple opposition between the global and the local. Mining is embedded in a global trade, and dwelling on these connections affords a novel view of gold. These export commodities, be they legal or extralegal, coexist on a continuum. From the fine-grained account of daily life in a regional economy dominated by minerals and drugs developed in the following chapters, what emerges is a place-based analysis of the Chocó that helps explain the local and global connections of producing gold, even when these are merely that a gold rush provides some a way to make a living.

THE NEO-EXTRACTIVISM CRITIQUE AND ARTISANAL PRODUCTION

A few times a week, people from nearby villages would congregate at a mine front to pan for gold. They looked like ants beside the giant excavators. It was a scene repeated throughout the Chocó. Dozens, perhaps hundreds, descended into each pit to pan and try to get a little cash. It was precisely this same small-scale industry that had gained such a terrible reputation. At a workshop in the National University in Bogotá in 2010, a community liaison officer who worked for a South African mining giant with exploration operations throughout Colombia (including the Chocó) showed photographs of the devastation from this informal and illegal sector. The focus was on the negative consequences of the production of artisanal and small-scale mining, and not the widespread fears of large multinational corporations.

Interest in "neo-extractivism" and large-scale resource development has been taken up widely in recent years, especially in Latin America.[36] Recent approaches to such resource industries have spent a long time returning to the themes brought up by earlier scholars—primitive accumulation, staples, and dependency. The neo-extractivist approach considers national economies in the Americas as primarily based on extracting minerals, hydrocarbons, and monocropped plantation agriculture.[37] This neo-extractivist critique sees the continent as once again a space of resource extraction, as Latin American states in the 2000s turned to resource production for foreign markets. Uruguayan social scientist Eduardo Gudynas described how Latin American governments have again come to rely on export-oriented resource economies for foreign markets. The left-leaning governments in Bolivia, Brazil, Ecuador, Venezuela, and Uruguay of the 2000s linked resource development to ideas of national progress. Right-leaning governments in Colombia, Chile, and Peru did the same. Dreams of such exports allowed politicians, bankers, and others to present natural resources as an economic motor. In Colombia's case, mining was cast as a locomotive that would pull the economy forward. Extractive industries were seen as the key to combat poverty and promote development. Neo-extractivism became central to contemporary developmentalism on the continent. A myth of progress based on the export of primary materials become central to regional economies and development strategies. The neo-extractivist critique was that natural resource exports without any value added would once again have negative social results, create enclave economies, destroy the environment, raise issues of permission in remote areas, displace communities, cause violence, promote criminal activities, lead to corruption, engender influence trafficking in permits, and result in the persecution of labor unions, social movements, and environmentalists.

Like political economists in the 1970s, the neo-extractivists tended to dwell on big questions, big projects, and big states. When applied to the Chocó, this leads to a misunderstanding of scale. From the Highland Clearances to the silver from the mines of Potosí to Canadian corporations today, the tendency is to focus on processes at their most massive scale with world-changing consequences, like the colonial adventures of the Spanish and the multinational corporations that are destroying rivers and landscapes. This focuses attention on the largest mines, some of which only exist in a subjunctive tense. Such mines are always just around the corner. They are imagined with desire by some and fear by others. Such a tendency to focus on the largest scale and future mines is to ignore the everyday and quotidian changes that are already taking place for miners and their families in the Chocó.

To put it another way, in 2010 when I arrived in the Chocó, most of the activists I spoke to spent time worrying about Canadian corporations. Boosters and critics alike saw such projects promising inevitable and imminent harbingers of change to the national economy, the local community, corporate profits, and the environment. Eight years later, none of those corporate mines exist in the Chocó. What did (and does) exist is mining taking place at a much smaller scale. Focusing on this smaller scale contests the almost universalizing tendency of the neo-extractivist critique. There are websites where resource projects are catalogued and listed, which help conjure the existence of mines that, as of yet, may not exist. This casts multinational corporations and their megaprojects as all similar, which misses actually existing resource extraction. When I was doing fieldwork, the discussion of mining in Colombia focused on the largest-scale operations of Canadian corporations, while the actually existing small-scale mining appeared in newspaper accounts and magazine articles. Civil society organizations were concerned about the threat of large-scale, open-pit megamines owned by Canadian multinational corporations. These mining corporations have never produced an ounce of metal in the Chocó.

More broadly, the neo-extractivist account seems to cast entire continents as centers of extractive capitalism to take resources from people, often Afro-descendant and Indigenous communities, with dramatic reconfigurations caused by megaprojects, massive mines, and gargantuan dams. These accounts are of marginal places, places that are the centers of economies based on resource extraction. Yet, in the neo-extractivist critique, there is a tendency to see extractive economies as crushing Indigenous and Black peoples. This misses the ways that rural peoples are both already articulated with their own resource projects into global networks of trade and how they can sometimes find their own forms of agency. Life in such peripheries is not always reduced, constrained, and converted into mere commodities, as extractive economies can create possibilities that enable alternatives. Much of the neo-extractivist literature misses the ways that production that occurs at much smaller scales can offer autochthonous possibilities, which contradicts a facile reading of the resource curse.[38]

DUAL HOUSEHOLD ECONOMIES ON THE RESOURCE FRONTIER

While the literature on natural resource extraction often stresses the negative consequences for people and livelihoods that came from a reliance on extractive economies, some marginalized peoples around the world do find something fruitful in global connections by finding ways to turn commodities to their own ends. For example, hunting, fishing, and rice, plantain, and tropical slash-and-burn agriculture provided a reliable if marginal source of subsistence production for the domestic household economy of Dalik communities in the Borneo Highlands, Indonesia. It was the initially Chinese and then later Dutch markets for feathers, jade, amber, rubber, and other "nontraditional forest products" for which the Highland Indigenous peoples gathered and sold these products and which provided a source of cash that added to their household economy. The result was what anthropologist Michael Dove calls a dual economy of both inward-oriented subsistence production as a source of livelihood, and export-oriented commodity production as a source of cash.[39] The latter enabled the former. Far from a story of primitive accumulation, it was a global market for commodified nature that was a core part of the way of life of marginalized peoples. The *matsutake* mushrooms picked from the postindustrial forests of the Pacific Northwest coast offer another high-value, quasi-legal commodity, which supports the lives of formerly forest peoples who came to the United States as refugees from the US imperial wars in Southeast Asia.[40] For garbage pickers in urban Brazil, there is a similar liberatory aspect to their foraging on a large urban garbage dump.[41] For each, a source of cash supports a vibrant way of life on the margins of more mainstream economies.

The Chocó is a former slave society where rural families like Pedro's and others—descended from the enslaved—rely on a dual household economy similar to what Dove described. Nina S. de Friedemann, the grandmother of anthropology of the Colombian Pacific, wrote about how Black families rely on the household subsistence production of hunting and fishing and gardening as sources of food, as well as their kinship relations, labor regimes, and systems of descent, which find antecedents in the slave gangs of earlier times.[42] Artisanal miners have a dual household economy, where gardening and hunting and fishing provide subsistence and stability, while gold provides cash. Indeed, rural Black residents have long moved from one export-oriented, high-value staple tied to global circuits of capital to another. After all, gold and platinum and rubber and timber and tagua and cocaine have all been taken from the forests of western Colombia. Each bonanza brought with it a sudden increase in opportunities to make a little money. In the jungles of Latin America's most precarious periphery, this export-oriented commodity production, when undertaken by rural residents, supported household production strategies. This is what allowed some to find a modicum of agency and freedom.

The gold rush of the 2000s is just the latest chapter of a long history of exports that have impacted Black communities, in diverse ways. It is when these export-oriented activities are undertaken not by rural residents but by outside actors, like Canadian junior mining companies or money launderers or small-scale miners from other places, that whatever agency and freedom Black communities have is compromised. Historians of the region have begun to write about how the forests and these exports have created a freedom on the periphery.[43] Like other nontimber forest products, gold offers a form of liberation—forming part of a dual household economy that is central to the way of life of rural Black communities and a way to accumulate cash, even if this is just when miners provide a small market for sugar tea, cakes, and cookies to a Black woman with no other source of income.

REBUSQUE IN AN EXTRACTIVE ECONOMY

Elisabet, a Black woman, middle aged, with no partner, is not that different from her neighbors. Elisabet is from a country riven by an easy racism, which makes her position so precarious. Elisabet is from an area long abandoned (or never quite integrated) by the state. Elisabet lives on a river in the midst of an armed conflict. Elisabet has no job and few prospects of finding one. Elisabet—she gets by. Before that Saturday troupe with Antonio and me, Elisabet had taken a boat from her home to Antonio's village. She had left her house with its fine tiles and good walls built by her father's generation when he had worked for that American mining company. Her backyard had a half dozen pots filled with herbs to flavor the cooking with which she found a living through *rebusque*.

Rebusque is the Colombian Spanish word for insecure and informal work. The term applies to those who make a living on the precarious periphery through informal employment—over half the population. Elisabet is one example, as were the *retreros* described earlier, as are millions of other Colombians who live through *rebusque*. Examples of *rebusque* that I came across in the field were many: The teenagers, including Antonio, who moved to the southern jungle to pick the coca harvest for a season. A spry, older man named Don Alfonso, who returned decade after decade to pick coffee in the Andes or to trade in the city. The family who hustled cheap appliances on a street corner in a regional town. The healer who left the department of the Putumayo to sell traditional medicines in a market in downtown Quibdó. The young *paisa*[44] woman who came over the mountains from the city of Pereira to dance in the mine camps for a week, and even the young Black woman who organized the dancer's trip. The Black girls who go in the opposite direction, to Pereira, to spend their youth as live-in domestic servants. The logger who hauled out tropical hardwoods. The *paisa* family who moved from one small town on a river in Antioquia to another small town on another river in the Chocó to sell street food. All were looking for work by engaging in *rebusque*.

Anthropologist Tania Murray Li has written of the jobs that never materialized after the intensification of agriculture in Indonesia, as cacao plantations needed fewer workers than the peasant landscapes they replaced.[45] She describes rural peasants who left the lands that could no longer sustain them for the city, where they had trouble finding work. Manufacturing jobs, Li writes, were created mostly in China, and jobs in China are of no use to peasant farmers in either Indonesia or Colombia. This world without work applies in a way to my young and well-educated students in the developed world seeking stable jobs, but who find themselves joining the ranks of the underemployed "precariate."[46] Anthropologist James Ferguson, in his book on the poor in Southern Africa, makes a compelling case for a redistributive politics. Ferguson argues: "Africa's fast-growing cities are increasingly inhabited by people who lack both land and formal-sector jobs and who improvise complex and contingent livelihoods through a combination of petty trade, hustling, casual labor, smuggling, prostitution, begging, theft, seeking help from relatives or lovers, and so on."[47] Ferguson sees what people lack as not so much access to entrepreneurship but access to a livelihood. The problem is demand, not supply. Ferguson proposes a radical solution: Don't teach a man to fish, but instead give a man a fish through the redistributive politics of cash transfers. Without radical cash transfers, many Colombians survive through strategies similar to what Ferguson describes for Southern Africa. Sociologist Ulrich Beck coined the phrase "the Brazilianization of the West" to describe the expansion of this same world of informal work, which has led to the return of unstable, underpaid, nonunionized, and temporary employment in the West.[48] This insecure form of work is what Colombians call *rebusque*, which I translate as "shifting."

REBUSQUE, STRUCTURE, AND AGENCY

In this book, I mean "shifting" as a way to describe the temporary and mobile aspect of work so common in Colombia. Shifting, like *rebusque*, is a verb and a noun. As a verb, *rebusque* becomes *rebuscar*, and "shifting" becomes "to shift": to change between different strategies to make a living and find work; to move on the margins from one impermanent job to another; to reverse strategies; to make a little extra alongside a permanent job; to travel from one location to another to find work; to search for work in a world where there is—be it legal or illegal, formal or informal, permanent or precarious, poorly or well paid—not enough. As a noun, *el rebusque* becomes "the shift," be it the night shift or the day shift or the way mobile and precarious workers live through *el rebusque*. While there is much that is informal and precarious and insecure and illegal about the *rebusque* work available to Colombians, these words are not the same as *rebusque*. *Rebusque* on an illegal and informal mine applies to a customary right to a share of each wash in an excavator mine, as well as to the work of mining itself. Translating *rebusque* as "shifting" emphasizes the agency that Elisabet and others like her found in their livelihood of changing strategies, trying something new, moving after work, looking for an opportunity, and making a job for oneself.

For centuries, philosophers have pondered questions of structure and agency. How much choice does someone have within a given set of circumstances? What is most determinant? The opportunities provided by individual creativity, choice, and agency, or the limits imposed by one's race, class, and gender, or by place, social institutions, environment, and history? "Men make their own history, but they do not make it as they please; they do not make it under self-selected circumstances, but under circumstances existing already, given and transmitted from the past," Marx observed so long ago.[49] His case was for human structure limiting individual agency.

Elisabet's *rebusque* was what she did when things were stacked against her. She shifted between various moneymaking schemes. From her front room, she sold breakfast to visiting miners. From her back room, she fried doughnuts made with cheese and corn flour in a large pot over a wood fire. She had a dozen other odd jobs: as a breakfast canteen cook, a baker, a fast food saleswoman, a drinks maker, a seller of mail-order perfumes and colognes from catalogues, and sometimes a panner of gold. The combination gave her a certain agency. It was the very informality of it all that allowed her to make a little cash. What can be learned from this way of making a living in a world where there are few good jobs and few options? Mining and all the rest are what allowed Elisabet to find a little liberty. It is stories like Elisabet's *rebusque* that result in the unexpected optimism in the following pages, and in a call to protect the informal spaces that remain for this self-directed freedom, which is often absent in more regulated economies. Elisabet deploys the stratagems of the poor with her cleverly contrived tricks and schemes to get by or to get ahead by selling cakes and tea and breakfast to miners.

Elisabet found opportunities that enabled her own agency in her everyday *rebusque* of finding a livelihood in a mined-out environment amidst the structures of disempowerment that uncontrolled mining brings to a postslave society. Yet, to focus on structural forces risks dehumanizing individuals like her as they find their own forms of agency. The tension between structure and agency cannot be resolved, of course, but telling nuanced and complex stories offers a partial solution. Spend enough time and one begins to think the creative strategies of *rebusque* give some hope, especially as entire landscapes are transformed by rapacious processes of resource extraction. Not to overstate Elisabet's agency, of course. How much "choice" does a victim of Colombia's internal conflict really have? How much freedom is granted a rural resident with no job opportunities? Can one have agency when armed thugs with guns stand ready to take a cut if you are too successful? And yet, in between these extremes, some had more freedom than their structural positions suggest. Through *rebusque*, people move on, change cities, and try alternatives. They come back home. They leave. When a mining company packs up, or when a once valuable commodity like tagua becomes worthless as the winds of global markets change, women like Elisabet and men like Antonio look to articulate themselves to something else.

Precisely because the Colombian state has been so limited and fragile, people turn to self-help strategies to support their own lives without simply selling their labor power for slavelike wages on a labor market that is not of their own making. Stories of living through *rebusque* are stories of a creativity and optimism that are a counterpoint to alternative renditions that would focus on lack of choice, on lack of opportunities, and on the legacies of slavery, poverty, and war. To tell overly negative stories is to ignore the possibilities of life that shifting livelihoods on the precarious periphery offer. Mining might, sometimes, offer alternatives to entering the world of the poor slum dweller of Pereira, Cali, Medellín, or Bogotá and a circumscribed urban existence where money buys freedom and a lack of money does the opposite. There is a certain freedom from living on the curve of a river an hour from town on the edge of the jungle, which comes precisely from the fact that high-value export commodities give a little cash, which gives a little freedom.

Consider Antonio. While the structural forces were stacked against his community and family, he adapted. He spent the season before I met him working as coca picker in the south of Colombia. While I was there, we worked in his father's artisanal mine. For some, this physical labor—the chopping of coca leaves, the mining, or even the cutting of logs, hauling of timber, and digging of pits—elicits a certain horror. This horror has much to do with the fear of physical labor that accompanies many who live in bourgeois comfort. Hard work is low status, and it can be backbreaking.[50] This terror of working in the mud does not reflect Antonio's lived experiences. Take his mother Martina's panning: it was hard work, but it was *her* hard work. Sometimes people themselves looked for alternatives. The next year, Antonio left for the police academy. His career as a policeman did not last, however. In 2019, when we last chatted, Antonio was pumping gasoline in Quibdó.

TRANSFORMING VALUE ON THE RESOURCE FRONTIER

In scholarly writing about artisanal, small-scale, and large-scale mining, the focus tends to be on mine labor, working conditions, environmental impacts, and social movement opposition. Meanwhile, wider public and media discussions focus on illegality and criminality or profits and jobs. In the following pages, I add a different approach.

Two narratives underpin many critiques of resource extraction: production and accumulation. The first encompasses the widespread belief that resource economies are about the commodification of nature, for example, digging from the earth, logging trees from the forests, or mining minerals from the ground, among other activities. Investors, governments, communities, and scholars assume a project getting underway is imminent. A project will create jobs, say promoters. It will destroy the environment, say detractors. The second narrative sees capital as accumulating at extraction sites, transportation routes, and export locations. Value flows outward to corporations in the form of profits, stocks, and salaries; to governments in the form of rents, royalties, and taxes; and to communities in the form of employment, wages, and jobs. Behind many accounts of extractive economies lies an assumption that commodity production creates value that accumulates as profit. This characterization is an oversimplification, of course, but it is analytically useful because it focuses attention on the flows of value from a resource economy, rather than on the entanglements of a commodity itself, even as the materiality of that shiny yellow metal continues to matter greatly.

To explore gold in the jungles of the Chocó, this book dwells first on production, second on accumulation, and third on a narrative of transformation, which is inspired by (but different from) the emerging literature on financialization.[51] Transformation puts attention on mines and mining projects that serve to convert value between different economies, rather than to produce value in the form of profits, speculative or otherwise. By dwelling on production, accumulation, and transformation, this book develops a novel approach to a gold rush.

There are two critiques of the assumption of production. The first takes for granted *how* production happens. The second takes for granted *that* production happens. Both assumptions are central to an economic imagination based on resource development for commodity export, where projects are imagined as having impacts only after they come online. On the one hand, focusing on real or potential large-scale mines is to ignore actually existing mining and its impacts on local communities. There is a refusal to engage with the messy, contradictory, and everyday normalcy of life on a resources frontier where there are no simple stories. Stories of primitive accumulation and dispossession are helpful, but so too is a consideration of the potentialities of mining. To push back against the tendency to read all resource extraction in the same way is to show the importance of particularities. Ownership, governance, means of production, mining techniques, property relationships, traditional systems of mining regulation, and scales of operation all matter.

On the other hand, assumptions of production contribute to an underestimation of the ways multinational corporations are often not involved in production, as their processes of capital accumulation become forms of value transformation. For example, there is a lot of money to be made from the extractive industry that has nothing to do with producing actual physical commodities. In Colombia, where the informal economy is widespread, where there is a large-scale drug economy, and where there has been a war going on, it is also not enough to assume production because the extralegal economy of cocaine can play a role. The following pages show the need to dwell on processes of capital accumulation through production, and on processes of value transformation through illicit economies and speculation.

One way to develop a value transformation argument is to rethink a narrative of production. This narrative is visible when boosters and critics both assume that projects are inevitable and imminent harbingers of change to the corporate bottom line, national economy, local community, and environment. These assumptions are central to an economic imagination that sees resource development for commodity export as a benefit to the nation (or detriment, depending on one's perspective). Another way to reorient a focus on commodities is to consider resource extraction that never occurs yet that still engenders outcomes. Here, looking beyond Colombia is informative. Unbuilt mines in northern British Columbia have had significant impacts on the landscape through railways built to mines that were never dug.[52] Indeed, there is a growing literature on failure. Why do some schemes fail?[53] What are their unintended consequences?[54] And what do their failures do?[55] The insight that failures *do* things is suggestive. After all, failed economic ventures (unbuilt mines, plantations, or pipelines) all do complex things. There is a long line of business ventures that do not exist in a material sense yet have complex financial lives.

Marx developed the concept of fictitious capital to describe such ventures.[56] London merchants profited on the *idea* of trade with India. Trading houses could generate capital by buying and selling bills of lading for goods to be shipped to or from the subcontinent. Even when the trade never took place, the paper trade was profitable. While land, labor, and money became fictitious commodities in their own right when disembedded from deep social relationships through the creation of markets,[57] fictitious capital points to something different. The fiction created through an absence of trade is the speculative moment of capitalism.[58] With such speculation and financialization, capital does accrue, not by producing, trading, or extracting real things, but through financial machinations reliant on convincing narratives.

Such speculative ventures rely on the everyday labor of creating good narratives, not on successfully implementing a productive venture. The process is similar to what rural colonists in the Brazilian Amazon do when they invent paper land titles to legalize what had originally been illicit land acquisitions.[59] While a land rush has had a devastating impact on the deforestation of the Amazon, the rush has as much to do with accruing timber, cattle, or soya as it does with the accumulation of land through small (and large) acts of conjuring that register real land with fake titles. Brazilians call this process *grilagem*, which refers both to the small acts of paper fraud for small plots and massive scams with well over a million hectares.[60] While *grilagem* refers to fake land registrations, for example, perhaps through a premature aging of forged land titles using boxes of insects, conceptually similar processes of fraud, chicanery, and paper conjuring are common to other speculative endeavors and the resource industry.

One junior Canadian mining company operating in Ecuador promoted the significance of its subsoil claims to mineral wealth for its investors, even as it downplayed the scale of the project to community opposition groups and environmental organizations.[61] The corporate play was the accumulation of titles to future mines that junior exploration companies engage in on Canadian stock markets. The arrangement relies on a labor of paper production, which is undertaken by white-collar professionals to conjure narratives of future extraction. As is so often the case with such projects, even after decades, this mine has not opened and no minerals have been extracted, if they exist at all. Another example of paper conjuring comes in the corporate reports, legal titles, laws, regulations, and carefully crafted storylines that have helped create land as a commodity for investors in the global land grab.[62] These labors generate paper trails not merely to persuade investors by creating attention on a land project but also to convince the media and gain publicity to persuade potential investors.[63] While a company may never build a mine or land project, its paper performance can underpin attempts at speculative accumulation on the securities markets. Legal claims to remote places (e.g., tracts of land in Africa or subsoil deposits in Ecuador) help companies sell investors on modern-day stories of El Dorado. What underlines such speculation are narratives of production that assume projects will come online and narratives of accumulation that assume capital will be made along the way. While scholars have begun to focus on the profitability of the extractive sector through such financial speculation, as well as the value produced through commodity circulation,[64] what this book adds are the ways that paper conjuring can facilitate schemes of value transformation that are intertwined with the global informal economy.

THE INFORMAL ECONOMY, MONEY LAUNDERING, AND EXTRACTIVISM

The neologism "informal economy" described the creative hustle of the urban poor in Ghana in the 1970s, which Colombians would call *rebusque*.[65] The term called into existence its opposite: the formal economy. Rather than a separate economy, it was a continuum. Just as those living a precarious existence in the Global South survive using creative informal strategies, those living at the heart of neoliberal capitalist globalization in the Global North do something similar. Newspapers are full of accounts of fraud, speculation, financial crime, predatory lending, and tax evasion. The Panama and Paradise Papers suggest tax dodging relies on fairly common, if ethically and legally dubious, techniques of moving, hiding, and transforming wealth in a world where free trade has removed capital controls. While tax avoidance may be legal, the tools used by the world's wealthy (tax havens, financial transactions, and front companies) serve the global underground economy as well. Oxfam estimates put the global underground economy in the trillions, with at least $7.6 trillion held in tax havens.[66] The extralegal economy includes proceeds from tax evasion, social security fraud, and transnational organized crime. The last, amounting to 42 percent of the total, includes theft, arson, prostitution, loan sharking, counterfeiting, illegal gambling, human trafficking, and the trade in illegal narcotics, including cocaine. While the size of the global cocaine economy is impossible to quantify, the United Nations Office on Drugs and Crime (UNODC) offers estimates and a detailed discussion of the hundred-billion-dollar cocaine industry.[67] By considering how gold intersects with the extralegal economy, this book highlights the importance of the transformation of value from the cocaine economy through a gold rush.

Money laundering is a process to transform profits acquired illegally from drug trafficking into what seems to be legal, for example, turning illegal cash from drug sales into what appears to be a legal bank account. There are three broad steps:[68] First, placing dirty cash in a bank account to make possible noncash payments, which is important because most large financial transactions use checks, credit cards, or other forms of noncash instruments. Second, layering funds to create the appearance of a legitimacy that makes it difficult to trace the source of the cash, which is done via businesses with high cash turnovers, for example, casinos, barbershops, currency businesses, or jewelry stores. Third, integrating funds by inserting them into the broader economy using businesses that help to make the funds appear legitimate.

In one sense, such transformations are a classic topic in economic anthropology—the movement between two spheres of exchange. For the Tiv of Nigeria, particular goods were relegated to certain value categories, and moral sanctions were applied to attempts to transform valuables from one category to another.[69] In Lesotho, workers transformed wages from South African mines into cattle.[70] In the Trobriand Islands, multiple forms of money circulated in the form of male and female valuables.[71] In the US-Mexico borderlands, mineral specimens from Guanajuato, Mexico, were extracted, circulated, and used in different ways.[72] In Peru, conflicts over mining projects were conflicts over incommensurability, as some things (e.g., water from a reservoir versus a processing plant) were not interchangeable.[73] In a Mongolian gold rush, where the metal itself was seen as ill-gotten, polluted, and cursed, people got around the resulting cosmological conundrum by selling gold to traders who sold the metal to Chinese buyers in exchange for Chinese yuan. The traders then converted the yuan back to Mongolian currency at a currency exchange house, and this resulted in cash sacredly cleansed.[74] Laundering profits from the drug trade in northern Mexico relied not on virtual financial transactions but on the movement of physical cash through couriers into small bank accounts.[75] In each process, different techniques were used to move items of value from one economic sphere into another—what I call the transformation of value. From this perspective, money laundering is a process to transform value between two spheres of exchanges. The movement is achieved by constructing legal fictions that move value from an illicit to the licit economy.[76]

The profane processes of laundering drug cash in Colombia through a gold rush is a prosaic transformation whereby commodities facilitate value transfer between two ordinarily incommensurate and incompatible spheres of exchange. Along the way, some money is lost to the transaction costs of doing the laundering. Value from cocaine created in an illicit sphere of exchange is laundered into assets in the licit sphere of exchange. The global prohibition of high-value narcotics fuels a parallel system of trade and finance to support the transport and consumption and cleansing of drug profits. In this light, the method money launders use are chicaneries to move, obfuscate, and confuse the source of their profits. It is precisely the appearance of production or accumulation—through business, enterprises, and transactions—that enables the transformation of value between ordinarily incommensurate economies.

The recent neo-extractivist critique and the growing anthropological work on mining that addresses multinational corporations, activist networks, community opposition, debates over knowledge and science, and corporate social responsibility[77] might do well to engage with transformations of value, not just through speculation, financialization, and circulation but also through money laundering and the extralegal economy.[78] While a focus on production assumes a project will come online, and a focus on accumulation assumes profits can be made, a focus on transformation explores the flows of value associated with such projects. What this book adds is a focus on the ways that paper conjuring facilitates schemes of value transformation through speculation and through the global informal economy.

All of this matters in order to make sense of various scales, kinds, and narratives of mining. To consider mining that may not exist, this book dwells on actual mines and actual miners. This matters for those concerned with positive social change and improving the lot of some of the most marginalized in Colombia's most unequal department in an economy where there are few options because it is a question of strategy. If a mining project is imminent and bulldozers are about to transform a landscape, then particular strategies of resistance may be most appropriate. If, however, a mine can be tied to speculation, stock market manipulations, or other processes of capital transformation rather than accumulation through production, then the most effective forms of resistance might change. If a mine itself is merely a speculative scheme where profits are made from potentialities rather from actualities, then social movements and community organizations that wish to prevent a project may need to recalibrate their response. To understand a gold rush in the Chocó requires understanding a river and a place within a broader nexus. It requires understanding mine work alongside subsistence, *rebusque*, and economic fictions of both money laundering and speculation. This book offers such an understanding grounded in insights from the labor of mine workers to develop a novel perspective on production, accumulation, and transformation during a gold rush.

THE STRUCTURE OF THE BOOK: PRODUCTION, ACCUMULATION, AND TRANSFORMATION

This book is woven from stories about different mines over six chapters divided into three parts. The chapters reverse the flow of various tributaries as they descend from the Andes before joining a larger river that makes its meandering way toward the coast. In part 1, from the lowest reaches of one tributary, Martina, Pedro, and Don Alfonso combine subsistence household production with artisanal mining as source of cash embedded in a dual household economy. In part 2, from up the same river, Esteban, Geraldo, Jorge, Carlos, and others attempt to accumulate cash using heavy machines on a small-scale mine that is more fully embedded in the market economy. If the first two parts draw on participant observation working alongside miners on the lower reaches of the same river, in part 3 attention moves beyond ethnographic fieldwork to a river's headwaters. Here, a reading of newspapers and secondary sources suggests that the legal and extra-legal economies are processes of value transformation through money laundering by cocaine traffickers and stock market speculation by multinational mining corporations. Tracing the production, accumulation, and transformation of value in a gold rush over three parts shows the potentialities and ambiguities of gold. The conclusion returns to Pedro and Martina's village and their river to ask what happens after the gold goes.

How and why do artisanal miners earn cash by panning? In part 1, flecks of yellow metal dug from under the ground, pumped from the bottom of a river, or panned from a dry sandbar complemented the fishing, gardening, hunting, and out-migration of rural Black residents. From opposite directions, the first two chapters dwell on the same scales and techniques of artisanal production that embed mining in a rural, dual household economy of subsistence and cash where the metal itself is at the center of a place-based system of production.

Martina and Pedro, Antonio's parents, dig at their family mine to supply cash to support their subsistence livelihood strategies of gardening and hunting. In chapter 1, Martina and Pedro wield picks and shovels to excavate hillsides, just as their enslaved and escaped ancestors did over centuries. They see unearthing metals on their family mine as having a craft with its own intrinsic rewards. Their daily labors put the lie to common portrayals of artisanal mining as contemporary slavery. For them, gold does various things: it supplies money, it builds savings, and it promises upward mobility. It is at the core of their practice of a dual household economy, and it gives them a modicum of agency and the good life.

Don Alfonso, that spry elderly neighbor of Pedro and Martina, has spent a lifetime traveling from his village to highland cities to engage in migrant labor and petty trading. In chapter 2, Don Alfonso and I travel to Medellín to buy bulk merchandise to sell in his village. Following the route of the displaced, our trip is part of Don Alfonso's *rebusque*—as a coffee picker, a traveling laborer, and a petty trader. His life challenges assumed narratives of displacement, as the land, a mine, and his home in the village all gave Don Alfonso a base from which to attempt to find a living in the wider economy. The mine provided Don Alfonso with a fallback position to return to between forays to the city or to seasonal work. While he engaged in household production like Pedro and Martina, it was cash from his mine that allowed him to participate in an itinerant mobile livelihood strategy. Indeed, it was both his mine and his gardens that let Don Alfonso enter into the broader cash economy on—somewhat—his own terms.

From opposite directions, as Pedro and Martina mined and hunted and Don Alfonso and I traveled to Medellín, part 1 dwells on the same techniques of artisanal production, which are so important to the rural economy of Black communities in the Colombian Pacific. Theirs is a dual household economy—an inward-oriented subsistence production and an outward-oriented cash economy—which makes gardening, fishing, hunting, and outmigration all complementary to mining. Together, these productive activities are a package of diverse strategies that are the basis of an autonomous dual household economy. It is a combination of activities that gives marginalized rural Black families an economic basis for the household and a means to participate in a market economy. Their dual economy—with activities for household subsistence and cash generation—facilitates both a productive way of life and gives a mine its emancipatory potential. It is the mine that allows subsistence producers like Martina and Pedro and Don Alfonso to stay on the land. Far from a commodity curse, artisanal mines support what for Martina and Pedro and Don Alfonso and others is a good life. In part 1, production with wooden pans becomes a successful stratagem of some of the poorest and most marginalized communities in Colombia, a strategy that beats the alternatives.

What might the hope of a little cash make people do? In part 2, mercury slips down a sluice like drops of condensation sliding down a cold bottle of beer. It is this toxic, silvery heavy metal that traps flecks of gold dug from deep pits or dredged from rivers using machines. Such small-scale mines require at least a dozen workers, who earn a monthly wage and a share of every wash. Their scales of operations are different from artisanal mines; the goals of the owners and workers are different too. These outsider-owned small-scale mines become a strategy to accumulate cash for its own sake, rather than a complement to subsistence activities. It is a way to get rich quick. Despite the hope that an excavator mine engenders in the jungle for owners and workers alike, things rarely turn out as hoped. Wild dreams of accumulation end in naught.

Although Esteban and his extended family had—like Pedro, Martina, and Don Alfonso—mined their family land over decades, in 2010 the family brought in two brothers—José and Geraldo—with heavy machinery. In chapter 3, the family began to spend all their time digging a tunnel, which was when they called in the brothers with the excavators. They had many reasons, due to the intersections of familial pressures, profit sharing, soaring prices, access to the metal, and dangerous conditions. The small-scale miners and their machines fully inserted Esteban's family into the cash economy by unbalancing the family's dual household economy. Nevertheless, the quick profits he and his family had hoped for failed to materialize.

The excavator owners—José and Geraldo—and their employees—Carlos, Felipe, Meta, and others—were all outsiders. In chapter 4, these owners and their workers have their own stories and reasons for arriving from other regions of Colombia to the river. Each engaged in their own form of *rebusque*. Each came with different motivations and objectives to the same jungle mine. Neither owner nor worker was a mere stereotype of an outsider, and all came to the excavator mine in the jungle following worn but understudied human corridors from the city to rural areas as mine laborers working the resource frontier on their *rebusque*. These miners, muleteers, washerwomen, and cooks chased the boom times of illegal mining, even as the hoped-for bonanza turned into a bust. As with Esteban's family, these small-scale mine owners and workers had hoped to get ahead through mining. For these miners, those profits failed to materialize. Nevertheless, while the excavator operations that dotted the Chocó were illegal, the men and women who were owners of the machines formed their own organizations to contest their rights as small-scale miners.

From the perspective of landowning families like Esteban's and the hopes of small-scale miners like José and Geraldo and their workers, part 2 considers the expansion of the small-scale mining frontier and the movement away from a dual household economy. People from rural and urban areas attempted to accumulate cash through illegal and informal mining. Small-scale mining became one of various get-rich-quick schemes of *rebusque*, which were attractive to small-scale miners from urban shantytowns as well as to families who owned rural land. Much media attention on the industry demonizes the small-scale miners, while portraying artisanal miners as victims. Yet various informal *rebusque* strategies render this simplification to be inadequate, as all sides attempted to make a little cash. People embraced forms of precarious and informal labor as large machines offered landowners and small-scale miners a way to get ahead. Like Colombia's other illegal exports, gold was central to an economy of *rebusque*. Their *rebusque* may not have been legal, but it was moral for most involved. While the goal for both miner and landowner was to accumulate cash by bringing in mechanized miners who use dredges and excavators, and although the optimism was contagious, the land that Esteban gave to the machines ultimately did not give enough gold.

What can the failure of a mine do? In part 3, mines that produce gold only on paper or that are speculative ventures in the jungles of the Chocó are failures. These failures are no mere disaster but instead enable other processes. These global connections are gold-based money laundering by drug traffickers and speculative projects by multinational mining corporations, both of which transform value through mines said to exist in some form in out-of-the-way jungles. Both phenomena are connected in the ways that they transform rather than produce or accumulate value.

Visits to a river with no mines by myself and my girlfriend (now wife) Mercedes, stories told by an old mechanic, and my reading of online news stories all point to processes that connect out-of-the-way peripheries to global chains of value transformation. In chapter 5, cocaine and gold intersect through money laundering. Money laundering helps explain sometimes impossible production figures and implausible municipal registrations. Turning to thirty years of news reports, this chapter sketches a recent history of different money laundering techniques. It is the very materiality of the metal as a holder of wealth that enables traffickers to launder their profits from cocaine by smuggling precious metal into Colombia and passing the metal off as originating in small-scale mines. In this way, narcotraffickers transform cocaine profits into laundered money deposited in bank accounts. For the employees of such *lavaderos*, the goal is neither production nor accumulation but the transformation of cash from one form to another—even if the workers themselves may not know quite what is going on.

The endless stock market speculations of Canadian mining companies that prospect for open-pit megamines undertook another form of transformation. In chapter 6, the concerns of Ximena and other Black activists about one Canadian multinational exploration project in the headwaters of a river point to the impacts of mining projects during their earliest phase, before operations begin. What ultimately is likely to become a mine failure relies on paper conjuring to lubricate speculative extraction in ways that have little to do with production or accumulation, and much more to do with transformation through stories about mineral wealth in out-of-the-way jungles into investments on Canadian stock markets. Considering the mobile capital of Canadian junior mining companies shows the centrality of speculation to their industry. And yet, although no actual mining takes place, such processes have real consequences for Ximena and her neighbors living in the area of a proposed mine. To understand these multinational mining projects means understanding local histories.

Mines that produce little to no actual metal are part of broader processes—be it laundering money or the speculation of multinational corporations. Both processes show how the transformation of value rather than the production of gold or the accumulation of cash was important. These unexpected connections show how broader economic processes reshape places as extensive networks of contemporary capital through their ability to facilitate processes of value transformation.

Together, parts 1, 2, and 3 offer different accounts of shifting livelihoods during the same gold rush. While a high-value export commodity from the jungles of the Chocó provides emancipatory possibilities to artisanal miners, it offers *rebusque* and dashed hopes to small-scale miners, and it lubricates global circuits of money laundering and corporate speculation. For

As they work, artisanal miners sometimes leave behind terrace formations, which serve as retaining walls so they can dig deeper.

miners without much technology, producing gold is the core of the good life. For the operators of the excavators and owners of the mines, gold is the hope of accumulating fast money and part of a strategy of accumulation through *rebusque*. For the money launderer passing the metal off as if it comes from small-scale mining or the multinational corporation speculating on foreign markets with stories of potential mines, mines are ways to transform value.

    The conclusion leaves behind those local and global connections of production, accumulation, and transformation, and returns to the river where Pedro and Martina and Esteban and the rest lived. It asks what happens after the gold has gone and when a river has rights.

PART I

Production

Subsistence and the Dual Household Economy

CHAPTER ONE

Gold and the Household Economy

GUAPI, a medium-sized dog with short, spotted black-and-white hair, stood at the edge of the sluggish water and scratched, pawed, and whined. Did he want to give chase? Two rows of men fanned out on both sides of the slow-moving creek that fed the river a hundred yards downstream. Some stood waist-deep in the water; others bobbed in the current, circling their arms wide to keep their heads dry. Half a dozen pairs of eyes scanned the surface of the water for movement. In the shadows, the men saw the jungle reflected in ripples of olive brown. The mud, the damp vegetation, and the insects smelled musty, but the water had washed away the scent of Guapi's prey, and he whined.

A row of white dots, the spine of a paca, broke the dark water and then disappeared between the rows of men. The lowland paca is a giant rodent, the size of a small dog. Its legs are short, its body chubby, and its back distinctive, with rows of white dots. It resembles a large rat without a tail or a sleek groundhog. The paca resurfaced a few meters downstream before it dove deep again. The men in the water heaved forward, and Guapi threw himself after them in frantic chase, but in the water, the dog was at a disadvantage. The paca surfaced for air where the creek joined the river, having escaped between the dog and the lines of hunters. Pedro, wearing a hat made of reeds, left one of the lines of hunters and swung himself onto a long wooden canoe with two other men already in it. He moved the motor into position and yanked the machine to life. Javier, lankier than his brother-in-law Pedro, scrambled aboard the boat and then leaned out to grab the loose skin on the nape of Guapi's neck and haul the dog into the boat. Javier used a long pole to push the boat downstream. The putt-putt of the nine-horsepower motor then pushed the canoe into the river. Javier held a spear

Guapi rests, while Pedro and Javier watch Antonio dig.

with a barb as he leaned forward over the bow of the boat to scan the water with his eyes.

Both Pedro and Javier loved to hunt. They alternated between hunting, gardening, slash-and-mulch agriculture, rearing domestic animals, gathering fruits, and fishing. When they needed cash, they mined. Like Pedro, Black miners in the Colombian Pacific unearthed gold through mine work, which has its own intrinsic rewards. The metal offered Pedro and other miners independence, because high prices and money earned through their sales provided a source of cash to spend or save, which, in combination with other subsistence activities, made mining key to what Pedro considered the good life. Pedro and Javier worked their own land and made cash without wage labor and without a boss. For them, mining and subsistence production were part of what they liked to do. On the one hand, Pedro used mining to earn cash and have access to the market economy. On the other hand, he participated in rural subsistence production. In addition, he went to urban areas and helped his children migrate for education and work. The livelihood strategy worked because, with the metal, Pedro could make money to support other activities. With the exception of logging or migrant work, few tasks made much cash. Mining was rarely an all-encompassing activity, however. It was what Pedro and Javier might do for a few hours a day, most days of the week, after the almost nightly rains.

For Pedro, his wife Martina, Javier, and the thousands of other Black miners, producing gold really did matter. The gold the three produced using hand tools and manual techniques was emancipatory and central to a rural, place-based livelihood. Without their mines, the dual household economy on which Pedro and his wife Martina relied would fall apart.[1] For the two of them, as for many of their neighbors, cash from metal sales was one part of their household's economy. The cash from their mine complemented subsistence production. It was a way of life that was at once embedded in a cash economy accessed by selling gold and in rural subsistence household production that relied on a living landscape of people and mines and rivers and forests and animals. What they got from subsistence gardening and hunting was complemented by gold sales, which provided access to cash. Mining and subsistence production together formed their dual household economy. It was through mining using hand tools and manual techniques that Pedro found a modicum of freedom and the good life. The mine was one spoke in a wheel of interconnected livelihood strategies. Another spoke was hunting.

Pedro and Javier and the two rows of men in the river were hunting pacas. Pacas prefer the forests and hot lowlands of South and Central America. Across the Americas, the lowland paca has many names: the ponderous *Cuniculus paca* in its zoological taxonomy, the colloquial Colombian Spanish *guartinaja* in the Andean regions, and *guagua* in the Pacific. (*Gua* is pronounced *wa*. *Guagua* in the Caribbean is a bus; in the Andes, a baby.) These forest babies are browsers, vegetarians who pick at leaves, roots, stems, and fruit. They dig for tubers and they climb for avocados. They follow paths through the thick underbrush and burrow to hide. They live a nocturnal and solitary existence. Pacas are born in the forest, where hunters like Pedro look for them. Because their range is so large, pacas are not endangered, but they are at risk in many regions. If you were to picture a graph of their population, it would probably be, as is often the case, an inverse echo of the human population. The fortunes of the paca rise and fall as people go away and come back. Pacas face deforestation and hunting. In the Chocó, a wise paca heads for the jungle when the mines fall silent for the day. The animal is favored because its flesh is delicious when served in stew.

Despite being quick runners and fast swimmers, pacas are little match for dogs and hunters. The paca that had escaped into the river by swimming between the row of hunters had long whiskers, yellow buckteeth, a pale white stomach, dots on its shoulders, two lines of white dots close together on both sides, and four lines of dots on the brown fur of its back. The paca might have escaped because it had experience with hunters. The animal had evaded hunters and dogs the year before. Its hind foot was swollen from a cord that had dug into its flesh. Pain from the lame leg had not hindered its escape, however, and the animal had made it first to the muddy creek and then into the lowest reaches of that fast river where Pedro and his family lived, which itself was a tributary to a larger river that meandered its way to the coast.

GARDENS AND MINES

Thirty hours earlier, on a morning in late February 2012, the sun glowed red, the moon faded, and wisps of fog dissipated over the river that passed the village where Javier and Pedro lived. Birds, flying in tight formation, called over the steady sound of the Johnson engine. Pedro was a quiet man in his fifties with a measured manner, graying hair, and the gleam of a smile. He kneeled at the stern of his wooden canoe and controlled the outboard motor with his right hand. He wore a cream-colored T-shirt, jeans that were cut off just above his black rubber boots, and the same reed hat he wore the next morning at the hunt. On a string around his neck he wore a delicately painted little pendant charm with a figure of Mary and Child. Martina sat in front of him. She was late middle-aged and wore a dark shirt and gray shorts, a pink bandana pulled tight to protect her hair, and a pair of delicate gold filigree earrings. Martina was quiet, careful, and guarded. She carried a thermos of *agua panela*, a drink made from cakes of raw sugarcane, and four plastic containers of rice and fried cheese. Javier, Martina's older brother, stood in the bow of the boat and held a smooth wooden pole. Javier had gray speckled hair, and like his sister, said little. Between Martina and Javier sat Pedro's two dogs. Guapi, the macho, prize hunting dog with scratched paws, sat on his haunches. Troqui, a chocolate-colored basset hound, with a small body, short legs, floppy ears, and a droopy face, lay low.

Pedro maneuvered the canoe toward a gravel beach ten minutes upriver from the village, which was a five-minute walk to his family mine. Wood smoke and the smell of fried dough wafted by as the boat passed a village. A stand of sugarcane strode toward the forest on the opposite shore. Plantain trees teetered on an embankment the river had recently carved out. Banana trees came into view on the riverbank. The roots of an avocado tree, its branches heavy with promise, gripped the soil in temporary victory over the encroaching water. Gravel piles tumbled in slow motion into the river, while rocks teetered where they had been left when excavators had ripped them from what had once been forest gardens, creating a landscape of gravel where tenacious weeds gained a foothold. The river, torpid with sediment, drifted by; the boat neared its destination.

Pedro turned into the current as the river became shallow. He idled the motor and lifted it clear. Javier, with feet apart in the bow of the canoe, reached out over the water and wedged the tip of the pole between stones on the riverbed. He pulled his arms back, and, as the pole remained immobile, he levered the canoe forward through the shallow water. The prow crunched the pebbled shore of the beach. Javier jumped onto a stone, heaved the boat up the gravel, and tied it to a fern with a short length of rope. Pedro started into the woods, Martina carried her thermos and containers of food, Javier lugged two jugs of gasoline, and the dogs followed behind.

On the trail, water had pooled, creating a mud path through the forest. Pedro trimmed the branches with a machete as he went. The trail narrowed to go through two dozen plantain plants, half of which were wilted yellow and dying, and then formed a thin, dry channel that cut through a small rise as it entered Pedro's mine, where the three spent most mornings and some afternoons.

Imagine a space half the size of a basketball court, but narrower. A dry man-made channel cut along the base of a nine-foot-high cliff on the left-hand side. The channel sloped for twenty yards as it curved along the base of the cliff and gained a few feet in altitude. The colors of the mine were all grays and blues, but the forest encroached on the gravel in the lower right corner of the court to reclaim the mine as its own. At the top of the cliff, near where the centerline of the court would be, on the left, the roots of a tree reached into the air where the cliff top had fallen away. The cliff consisted of layers upon layers of sediment. Stones, pebbles, and clay were stacked together in a geological mishmash of horizontal patterns: a thin line of reddish soil struggled to support the greenery above, brownish-yellow clay extended for a few feet before it petered out into gravel, sand made another layer, and down near the base, rocks wedged themselves into the cliff amid the gravel and clay. A streak of sediment painted the base of the cliff a dark blue. The blue promised gold. The sediments were crushed under the weight of the cliff and had probably been left by the prehistoric stream that the miners were slowly following.

The channel sloped upward for a dozen yards along the base of the cliff until it disappeared below where the basketball net would be, and where another hillside met the cliff—this intersection was the mine front. On the other side of the channel, along the right-hand side of the imaginary court, was a large pile of small stones jumbled together. Pedro and his family had tossed stones onto the pile over the years as they mined. A fallen tree trunk, wider than the canoe, rotted at about the centerline, lying along the right-hand side of the court. Beside the trunk, a black plastic shelter protected a low bench, a small fire pit, and metal cooking pots. Martina went to start a fire in the pit and used a pot to heat water for that morning's breakfast of boiled plantains.

The plantains had grown in the stand at the mine entrance. Plantains are like bananas, but starchier, and they have to be cooked before they can be eaten. The plant is indigenous to the tropics of Southeast Asia, and yet through the Columbian exchange, plantains are a staple in the Caribbean, Central America, and South America. The cream-colored flesh can be boiled, fried, or roasted. Pedro picked plantains for their meals; Martina served them for breakfast, lunch, and dinner. She accompanied them with rice and fried cheese, sauces made using lentils and salt beef, canned tuna in brine, tins of bony sardines, or stew made from paca meat.

A handful of banana trees and woody shrubs struggled to grow out of the stone piles beside the shelter inside the mine. The shrubs—known as manioc or cassava in English and *yuca* in Spanish—thrive in backyards and on more marginal soils, where it requires little care. The *yuca* tubers are long, brown-skinned, white-fleshed, starchy, and inedible until boiled, fried, or baked. Martina prepared *yuca* boiled with salt for breakfast, as cakes baked in a clay wood-fired oven, as crispy morsels deep-fried in oil, or as an ingredient in stews made with meat and corn. Pedro planted corn using a slash-and-mulch technique in a plot ten minutes down the river. He slashed the underbrush with a long thin machete, let the vegetation rot for some time, and then scattered corn kernels in the cleared area. He waited for the rain and sun to germinate the kernels; the crop would be ready a few months later. A peach palm (*chontaduro*) on the edge of the river near the village had, to the consternation of everyone, stopped producing its bright red and orange fruit. While I found the fruit to have a disappointing texture, one that was chalky and dry, much like that of an overcooked potato, Pedro and his neighbors enjoyed peach palm fruit with sugar, honey, or salt. The fruit used to be plentiful, until it disappeared. Pedro suspected a fungus, while his father, Don Gabriel, blamed the fruit's demise on changes to the underground water flow caused by the excavators that had mined the jungles above the village on land owned by a neighbor of Pedro.

Across the river from the village and its single barren peach palm tree, Pedro had cleared the side of a hill to plant pineapples. He picked ripe ones for his family and his neighbors' kids. Pedro tended papaya trees up the river, and the unripe green ones were delicious when made into a jam on cakes of *yuca*. A cashew apple tree at one end of the village gave shelter from the sun, and twice a year it produced hundreds of pink-skinned fruits with purple and white flesh. Kids also sucked the sweet flesh around the seeds of giant gnarled, knobby guama pods, which were about three feet long and an inch around. They loved to shimmy up the thirty-foot sapote trees to pick the fruit with a green leathery skin and a bright orange interior. The tropical staple guava, used in jams and juice, exploded weed-like on the river's edge, which children gathered with plastic pails as the fruit was on the cusp of rotting. Sugarcane on flatlands near the river's edge produced the raw material for cakes of minimally processed brown sugar called *panela*, although Pedro bought *panela* in town. The *panela* was the basis for *agua panela*, that sugarcane tea made by combining boiled water with lemon, ice, and the *panela*, which people consume for energy in the heat.

Martina kept an herb garden that contained both kitchen and medicinal herbs; the plants grew in soil that was placed in a log that had been split in half and suspended between two posts. The soil was made from anthills picked clean of insects by hungry chickens Pedro kept for meat and eggs. The village had plots of lemongrass, bananas, lime trees, and *borojó* throughout. *Borojó* fruit the size of baseballs hung incongruously from slender branches and had a flesh the color and consistency of human excrement, yet when blended with sugar and ice made a drink that is thick and delicious and said to be an aphrodisiac. In season, Pedro's neighbor Don Alfonso would send his *borojó* crop by boat to town to sell to a visiting trucker who transported them to the city. Other than *borojó*, all the starchier crops and the fruits and herbs were for household consumption. They were not for sale.

It was produce from these horticultural endeavors that gave Martina and Pedro access to much of the food they ate. All the plants they grew, the fish they caught, and the animals they hunted were important in keeping the household going. But none of this subsistence production was a source of cash. Plantains, for example, while an important subsistence crop, were quite worthless. Pedro could earn no money from plantains, because the costs of getting the crop to market were prohibitive. Pedro said people used to sell plantains from their gardens at a market in the town down the river, but now produce trucked from the Andean interior was too cheap, and Pedro could not compete. To buy things he could not produce himself, like the basics—rice; salt; cooking oil; clothes and shoes; gasoline and diesel; salted soda crackers; cans of tuna and sardines; hard, dry, salty cheese similar in flavor to feta; and bottles of beer, juice, soda pop, and aguardiente, a liquor made from distilled sugarcane—Pedro had one reliable source of cash: his mine. His and Martina's household was a dual one: subsistence production on the one hand, with production from a mine as a way to enter the cash economy on the other.

Pedro left Martina to cook plantains at the hut with the plastic roof and hiked toward the mine front, where the channel disappeared and the two cliffs met and the ground had not yet been worked by Pedro, Martina, and Javier. From there, Pedro followed a black rubber tube to the right into the forest. Javier followed Pedro, carrying the two jugs of gasoline. The rocky path twisted ten yards or so into the bush, over a small rise, and past clumps of banana trees. A tube connected to a red gasoline-powered water pump dingy from use. The pump was six months old. A second tube connected the pump to a deep trench full of water. Javier poured the fuel into the motor, and then Pedro pulled the cord and started the pump. Pedro then dashed back to the mine front and picked up the tube, which ended in a metal nozzle from which poured a gentle stream of water. Pedro yelled to Javier, who turned up the pump. The stream became a torrent, which Pedro directed at an overhang of rock and clay and gravel that jutted precariously, high above the channel where they would soon be working. Pedro stood sideways and guided the hose in a figure-eight motion so that the water cut into the outcrop of gravel and clay. A web of fissures raced across the surface of the overhang, which melted away into a pile of sediment and sand that buried the channel below. Pedro whistled; Javier cut the motor. Martina left the cook fire.

Martina, as she did most days, walked to the mine front where the channel disappeared into the cliff a few feet up from where the overhang had been. She filled her wooden pan with sediment, then she took the pan to a puddle formed by dripping water, and then she swirled the pan to flood it with water. Using her knees for motion, she rocked the pan in her hands: this ejected the larger stones. Then the water carried gravel and sediment out of the pan and into the puddle. She panned until the motion had carried away the last of the sediment and the four, flat, sugar-sized flecks of yellow appeared. She said to me, "Almost nothing."

Mining is the core of what might be called Pedro and Martina's dual household economy. Pedro gardens, hunts, and fishes; Martina does her own work: cleaning clothes, gardening, and watching chickens. For both, mining is something different than subsistence production. Pedro might describe mining using the word "economic." For the rest, he would use the word *fijo*, for something stable, or *pancoger*, for "daily bread." The hunting with Guapi, the plantains, the gardens, the sapote, and the other fruit were not "economic" in Pedro's sense of the word. They could not be sold for cash, yet they were the basis of the subsistence component of their household economy. Pedro hunted because it was a source of meat, because it was fun, because it was something to do, and because it took skill. But hunting and gardening and other activities would not give him access to the cash economy. Plantains, limes, avocados, fruit, herbs, corn, rice, and sugarcane were all plentiful. Food, meat, and herbal medicine were easy enough to get, yet it was gold that had a market price that made it worthwhile. Mining was one of the few activities with a potential cash income. Mining complemented the *pancoger* of subsistence production because it gave cash. Without the metal and the cash it could be sold for, there would be no money to go into town, no generator for lights when the power went out, no music to listen to late into the night, no new clothes to celebrate the New Year, no nice hats for special occasions, and no cellphones to stay in touch with or show off a little. Without the mining, the dual household economy on which Pedro and Martina and others relied would fall apart.

The expression for a mine that produces—a productive mine as it were—is one that *da*, or gives. "Does the mine give?" Give gold, give cash, and give savings. In his mine, Pedro found his *ahorros* (savings). Martina's filigree earrings were her savings made in gold. She used the diminutive of gold to describe them: "*mis oritos*" ("my little golds"). Savings in metal took many forms: a shot glass full of gold dust wrapped in a slip of paper and hidden at home, a pair of links hung on a necklace, or a ring on a finger. Pedro did not just mine to sell directly for cash, as the metal itself was the form in which he stored his savings for the future.

Gold, still underground in a mine and not yet brought to the surface, was a similar form of savings. Pedro had his family mine, and the wealth still in the ground was his source of security, which he could draw on slowly over time. Thinking of metals as savings, like Pedro did, made the gold something positive and alive. It was meaningful. Even as mine work itself was hard for Pedro and many others, it was skilled work. Mining had a particular craft, and although it was difficult, it was far from terrible.

A Black activist I met in the city once described the techniques Pedro used as little better than slave work. Certainly, the techniques of sluices in the forest and wooden pans were similar to those used by the enslaved Africans who worked the same rivers centuries before. But Pedro would probably disagree, because he found the work rewarding and he was a skilled miner. He could read the soil, sediment, and landscape for signs of water left over from the biblical Great Flood. He knew how to find a mine by looking for light coming from the ground under a full moon. He tried new machines and new techniques. Sometimes, like the water pump, the machines enabled mining when it had not rained; at other times, like when he tried to use a metal contraption that divers use to vacuum up mud from the river, it didn't work. Mine work meant solving a multitude of problems: dealing with a dangerous overhang that might collapse, clearing the roots of a tree, repairing a cracked wooden pan using a strip of plastic cut from an oil container and held in place with a dozen small nails, replacing the handle on a scraper for mining, or protecting tired backs from the hot sun beating down by using the leaves of a tree. A full wash of the mine—the five days it took from starting a pit to finishing the final panning—would require that Pedro and his family solve dozens of these small challenges. The promise of the wash at the end was one recompense; so too the problem-solving of mine work itself. For Pedro, Javier, Martina, and the others, the rewards were fair, sometimes. The mine was not waged labor on a factory floor, and while Pedro had no benefits, no hourly wage, and no guarantees, he had the freedom to do what he wanted. With luck, he and Javier might make more than the minimum wage.

Javier climbed, as he or Pedro did most days, up the cliff to a sluice gate above the puddle where Martina had panned at the front of the mine. Javier heaved on a rope, which lifted the wooden gate, releasing an avalanche of brown water. The water swept the sand, clay, gravel, and stones from the cliff face. The water flooded into the pile of gravel from the overhang and washed it down the channel. Javier jumped down to help Pedro. Pedro anchored two wooden planks to the edge of the channel with clumps of clay. The planks directed water against the cliff base. The onrush of water washed the sand and gravel away. Large stones remained motionless. Pedro grabbed a metal spike, washed the handle in water to clean away any grit so that it would not cut his hands, and wedged the pointed end under a stone. Javier shoveled gravel away from the cliff edge. The water from the sluice washed the sediment down the channel below the cliff and out of the mine into the plantain grove. The spray soaked the two men. When the water slowed to a trickle, Javier climbed to the top of the mine and closed the sluice gate. The flood of water stopped, and then everyone cleaned the gravel from the channel for ten minutes until the reservoir behind the sluice filled up. Then Javier flooded the mine again. He flooded the mine three more times, before Martina served late breakfast.

Pedro and Javier sat on wooden planks in the shelter, and Martina poured them *agua panela* from the plastic thermos. The three scooped rice and salty, hard, deep-fried white cheese from the plastic containers, ate boiled plantain, talked, and joked. At the mine, they tried to stay in good spirits. Pedro stood to pick some yellow, sweet, finger-length bananas, which he ate as Martina washed the empty containers.

Breakfast over, Pedro climbed the cliff to the sluice gate. He paused to look at the water, then frowned because it had not filled again. To investigate, he hiked along the trench that went higher into the forest. The trench, which was maybe three feet deep and two feet wide, followed an incline from the cliff that was the mine front into the woods for two hundred yards. Pedro followed a path beside the trench, and the burble of a trickle of water accompanied his footsteps. Insects buzzed around, and Pedro slapped at a few until he stopped at the trailhead, where the trench ended with a second sluice gate. The second gate controlled the water flow from a large reservoir. The gate was closed. Pedro opened the sluice gate, and water began to slowly fill the trench. Pedro watched, and his face settled into another frown because there was so little water in the reservoir.

People tried not to be frustrated when they worked, because when they did, terrible things happened. One reason for Pedro's ordinarily good spirits was that his mine was remarkably productive, and prices in 2011 were the highest they had been since the 1980s. Pedro's was but one family at one mine, and Pedro did not have brothers and sisters and nephews and nieces to support. This gave him the liberty to do what he wanted. The three chose to work together, and while it was a stable labor arrangement, it wasn't necessarily permanent. Javier, especially, and even Martina, might have taken their labor elsewhere and worked at another mine. They stayed, though, and the three divided profits from the mine. The mine gave them each an income that was just above minimum wage. It was the basis of their household economy precisely because it was good money and they had no boss; they were their own masters.

The situation was good, in part, because neither Pedro and Martina nor Javier had large families to support with their labor. Pedro and Martina's children had grown and gone. Miguel, their eldest son, worked in a mine camp down the river; their youngest son, Antonio—who months before had looked out over the landscape of an excavator mine with me—sometimes came to work at the family mine, but he had left the year before to study at the police academy. And while their daughter Eva and her common-law husband Carlos often came to the village, and Carlos sometimes worked with Pedro, Carlos too had left to work as a washer on an excavator mine that had recently opened near the village. On Saturdays, a gaggle of their grandnephews would come to play at the mine. A photograph might suggest child labor, but really the children were at play. The work of Pedro, Martina, and Javier was hard, but it came with the possibility of cash, and without a time clock, outside rules, or a boss. Pedro preferred mine work to construction or other things in the city.

Pedro's neighbor Don Alfonso once asked me if I preferred being called *Míster* or *Señor*. Don Alfonso elongated the "i" of the English salutation to pronounce it "meester." His question regarding the use of *Míster* or *Señor* came from experiences during his youth, when the American engineers of the Chocó Pacífico Mining Company dredged rivers. At the time, there had been well-paying, unionized, waged labor available. A few old men still received—in 2011—a small a pension from what was left of the long-defunct company. Although the men of Don Alfonso's generation might have dreamed of good employment in their youth, the generations that followed had no such fantasy. Pedro, Martina, and Javier came of age in the 1980s and 1990s, when the mining company had already imploded, the guerrilla wars were worsening, and any stable waged work in the forest was a fantasy. Wages might be good, but there were none to be had. In any case, a job would take their freedom and make them reliant on someone else. Men and women like Pedro and Martina made their own decisions about their mines, their gardens, and their time.

Pedro had experience with other forest products for faraway markets. There had been a timber boom in the Colombian Pacific from tropical hardwoods when Pedro had been a younger man. Pedro and his neighbors bought or borrowed chainsaws and worked as itinerant loggers. They had roamed the forests to bring timber to the rivers and float the logs downstream. People who lived on other rivers still logged to make a little cash. When Pedro was younger, he did it because the price of gold was too low. He stopped when the trees were gone, and gold prices were higher. His chainsaw rested unused in the back of his house. Pedro preferred mine work, because mining is easier on the back. One reason was the weight. In early 2012, the price of gold was the highest it had ever been. An ounce of gold paid far more than an ounce of waterlogged wood hauled from the forest to a river and then floated to a lumber mill in the town downstream. Moreover, logging is a special hell: carrying a heavy chainsaw all day, fighting the bugs, and slipping on the rain-sodden trails only to watch a buyer in a lumberyard make all the money with illegal environmental licenses and few scruples. Pedro loved the forests to hunt in, but only on his own terms, when it had not rained, and when the hiking was easy.

Miners need rain. The fact that they live in some of the most humid and rainiest forests of the planet makes their work possible. Water from the reservoir in the woods above Pedro's mine filled the trench. Pedro used the water to wash the mine. The heavy rains and reservoir water made the work easy. The trench that Pedro had made was one of a network he had dug in the forest over decades. The trenches channeled water for the mine from a reservoir. Pedro had not dug the reservoir, however. Excavators had. The reservoir was on a lot owned by neighbors from another village. The neighbors had fled rural violence to the city ten years before. While many people who were displaced to the city never came back, that family had come back years later with outsiders and an excavator to dig. The heavy machinery had dug the reservoir as a water supply, and the excavators had stayed for three months until the earth was exhausted and the neighbor's mine stopped giving. The machines left behind the large reservoir. Torrential downpours filled the reservoir most nights, which gave Pedro water. But since there had been no rain for days, the reservoir was almost empty that morning. Pedro turned to walk down the trail. The three miners washed the mine a few more times until the reservoir ran truly dry. Without water, Pedro and Javier could only work with a water pump, which was expensive because of the cost of gasoline.

Pedro and Martina and Javier ate their lunch, and then motored back to the village. Pedro tended a garden in the afternoon, Martina washed laundry in the river, and Javier fished with a line from a dugout canoe.

"What will we do tomorrow?" I asked Pedro.

He shrugged, "Mine. It'll rain tonight."

HUNTING IN THE MORNING

By dawn the next morning, it had not rained. Pedro, fresh from bathing in the river, packed a bag and sat sharpening his machete.

"I'm going hunting. You coming?" he said.

Five minutes later, Pedro used a long wooden pole to punt his dugout canoe up the river. He stood in the back, and his two dogs, Guapi and Troqui, sat in front. Indigenous boat builders had carved the canoe out of a single piece of wood twice the length of a man. The cuts the carvers had made in the wood were still visible. Pedro had bought the canoe cheaply years before. The Black and Indigenous communities who lived in the same watershed sometimes had an easy antagonism, because the Black miners had the money to buy canoes from the Indigenous carvers, yet they paid far too little.

Everyone, it seemed, learned the knack of being a *panguero* as a young child: feet wide, knees bent, and body ready. The *panguero* performs what looks like a dance, body, knees, and feet flexing against the sway of the water to stay upright. A paddleboarder on a calm ocean performs a choreographed dance to the same rhythm, but, without the fins a paddleboard has, a narrow dugout canoe is anything but stable. A better comparison: traversing turbulent waters while standing on a kayak. When I first tried, I overcompensated, lost my balance, tumbled into the water, and capsized my young teacher, one of Pedro's grandnephews. The dugout, shallower than Pedro's other boat, displaced little water, which made it perfect for a stream.

Pedro turned from the river into a stream. He used it as a waterway into the jungle. Hiking was much harder and slower than traveling by boat. Pedro used his *canalete*, a hand-carved tapered wooden paddle, to keep the prow with the current. Tendrils of mist clung to the forest. The stream, which was just narrower than the length of two men, was a few feet deep, at its deepest. Sunlight filtered through the canopy to dance on the sandy stream bottom, where tiny fish seemed to give chase to the light. Ripples broke on a stone, drops fell from a leaf, and water gurgled past. The air was cool and damp, not yet warm from the day. In the forest, it rarely grew hot, because the green canopy of the multistoried forests kept the air humid. Trees, leaves, branches, stems, fronds, and foliage melded together, and a blue butterfly flitted above the surface of the stream.

Pedro followed the stream, and soon the air quieted and the sky receded. Pedro beached the canoe on a sandbar, in an area where he said the pacas were fierce. Pedro scrambled ashore. Guapi leaped into the water; Troqui paused, looked around, and flopped after them. I stayed in the canoe. Of the two dogs, Guapi was in charge. Where Guapi was fast, domineering, and scarred from seven dozen run-ins with pacas over his six years, Troqui was a year old, timid, and slow, and had never caught anything. Pedro sometimes had to throw Troqui into the water or push him into the woods. Pedro dismissed Troqui as *baboso*, a lazy, stupid drooler, but he still tried to train the animal to be a hunting dog like Guapi. Pedro and the dogs were off: Pedro, after the sound of the dogs, the dogs after the smell of the paca; and the paca—wherever it was—after freedom.

Running in the jungle takes as much skill as canoeing; it is easy to get disoriented and lost. Trees close in, distance is impossible to measure, and direction loses meaning. It is hard to go fast. Pedro ran after the two dogs, "falling" through the jungle with a two-foot machete slicing through the cover, the gravity of one descent pushing him up the next rise, a tricky technique to master. But he could not keep up with the animals. I could follow how Pedro was doing by the sounds he and the dogs made in the forest. He communicated with the dogs using a long, sonorous *cahoo* sound with a modulating cadence. Shouts did not travel far in the jungle, but the *cahoo* did. Once, when an eleven-year-old boy got lost for three hours during a hike, everyone fanned out and called out *cahoo* to find him. No yelling, no words, just *cahoo* and then a pause to listen for a sonorous reply. Pedro cahooed, and Guapi barked. When Guapi had cornered the prey, his bark would turn to yips.

For Pedro and Martina, the paca would be meat for a week. Paca was also served at La Paila de Mi Abuela (My Grandmother's Pan), a restaurant in Quibdó famous among middle-class, social-movement, NGO urban types wanting a taste of *chocoano* home cooking. The second-floor establishment was a project run by displaced women, supported initially by the Canadian International Development Agency. The food was delicious, featuring dishes of yellow rice rich with fried cheese, *longanisa* (smoked blood sausage), *mondongo* (diced tripe soup slow-cooked with vegetables), and every now and then, a rich and meaty stew made of paca. The stew sold quickly because the gamy meat was popular. The meat of a wild paca has more flavor than that of a domestic one, Pedro explained. Pedro had once caught a paca with a cord and tried to domesticate it in an unused chicken coop. The pregnant animal did not like captivity, chewed through the cord, and escaped a few nights later, much to Pedro's frustration. His experiment in domestication had ended in failure.

Pigs fattened with plantain or left to forage on small islands in the river were another source of meat. For Easter Week or Christmas Day, Pedro's neighbor Esteban butchered a pig early in the morning, packed the flesh in banana leaves, sold some around the village, and ate the rest as a special meal with his family. Esteban's wife, Valentina, mixed the blood with rice and herbs and stuffed them into the cleaned intestines of the pig to make *morcilla* sausage. Until the fish stopped running up river to spawn, fish were more often Pedro's source of protein. Pedro and Javier would relax by casting a line in the late afternoon to catch *bocachicos* and other fish that used to come up the river in January.[2] People caught the fish by the thousands in nets strung across the river or in wooden traps spiked with rotting flesh. Women salted the fish, spread them out to dry on all the flat surfaces in the scorching January weather, and waited. When dry, the fish would last for months in the tropical heat. All of that was in days gone by, before the fish stopped running, probably because the rivers carried so much sediment from mine runoff. Pacas and armadillos and other forest animals provided meat when the pigs were fattening and the fish were not running. Still, Pedro hunted for more than caloric intake. Just as the NGO crowd in Quibdó enjoyed their home-style cooking and stew, Pedro liked to hunt.

Pedro ran following the sound of the dogs; he ran for the thrill of the hunt; he ran to train the new dog, Troqui; he ran because it hadn't rained for days and the forest was easy running; he ran because there was no water and he couldn't do mine work; and most of all, he ran for the paca. The dogs followed a ridge through the trees on the hill above the boat. Now and then, Pedro would let out a slow *cahoo* as he moved across the forest landscape. The greenery enveloped the stream, while higher up, the vegetation was less dense and the running was easier. Still, Pedro sliced at the vegetation that got in his way by chopping at the base of the plants. It easily fell to the steel blade because it was flimsy, all watery and fast growing. Climbing the rise, Pedro jumped over fallen logs covered in sharp spikes. He was careful to never touch the branches or trees and kept his balance by shifting his weight rather than grabbing vines or trunks of trees, lest insects or fire ants or snakes bite him and leave painful, even deadly, welts. He moved fast, but the dogs had gone farther and faster. The sounds the three made kept moving, and there were none of the rapid yips Guapi would make when he caught a scent.

Pedro hunted with dogs because he liked the chase, the chance to run, and the challenge to try to outthink the animal. It sometimes escaped: throwing itself into the water to lose its pursuers, or going underground and hiding in a burrow. If the animal sought refuge in a burrow, Guapi would scrabble frantically with his claws like a drug addict waiting for his fix—that's how Pedro described it. Pedro would make a spear from a nearby tree to flush the animal out. If that did not work, he would dig the animal out. Hunting was fun, but the food was important. Fishing was getting harder every day, and Pedro did not keep pigs. The paca was a source of meat for his family that would last for a few days. Was it necessary? Maybe not, as Pedro did have other supplies, such as canned food that sometimes came to the village as flood relief from the government. But when it had not rained, he liked to hunt, and the meat was good, boiled to make it last or cooked in stew.

When Guapi's barks changed to yips, Pedro knew that the dog had caught a scent, and so he ran to the cornered paca.

Pedro walked back to the canoe with the plump animal over his shoulders and a machete hung in its leather holster on his belt. The dogs cavorted behind him. Pedro stepped into the canoe, Guapi jumped after him, and then Troqui, who tried to follow, fell into the water. Pedro grabbed Troqui by the neck to pull him aboard. Pedro returned to the village just before noon and gave the paca to his sister-in-law, who put it on her back step for later butchering. The dogs sniffed at the blood while the kids played nearby and Martina looked pleased. As Pedro sat down to a lunch of salt beef and lentils, two men arrived, Pedro's eldest son Miguel and a *paisa* from Antioquia. Both worked at an excavator mine camp half an hour downriver. They had seen a paca near their camp. "Could Pedro come with Guapi?" "Yes," Pedro said, leaving his lunch and taking both dogs.

HUNTING IN THE AFTERNOON

Pedro, Javier, and Pedro's other brother-in-law Mauricio took the motor canoe with the dogs. Javier wore a pair of black rubber boots, green soccer socks, black tracksuit pants, and a yellow work shirt from a construction project in Bogotá. He had a little Holy Trinity charm—a silver cross on a pendant—around his neck. He dozed in the front of the boat, tired from spending the morning in his garden, or fishing. Mauricio sported a goatee, mustache, dark glasses, and a Niño Jesus pendant wrapped around his wrist like a bracelet. He carried a purple apple-cashew fruit in his hand. His other hand held a small plastic bag—lunch? Mauricio must have grabbed both before he left. He wore no shirt, but he did have a white cloth with a cartoon design thrown over his shoulder. Beside him, Mauricio had two machetes and a beaten-up umbrella; the latter was for shade and had probably been bought from their neighbor Don Alfonso, who might have brought it back from one of his trips to the city. Miguel and the *paisa* used the boat they had come up the river in. Miguel wore a black T-shirt with yellow lettering, blue jeans, and black boots. The dark-skinned *paisa* sat on a small wooden stool in the boat and was dressed in a cream-colored T-shirt, a green baseball cap turned backward, a machete in a leather holder attached to his belt, and, on his left wrist, a watch—fake or real gold, one never knew. Guapi stood tall in the bow, facing Pedro, who was piloting the boat.

The sky was gray, but there was no rain. The boats passed each other and made long S curves as they headed down the river. After a few minutes, a quarter of the way into trip, the boats motored past a heron perched on a tree trunk several feet below plastic bags that had caught in the trees. The water was low.

The boats then passed nine people on a sandspit formed by mine runoff in the river. The people were mostly a family who had come up from a nearby village to pan the river bottom. There were five women, three men, and one *paisa* man. They worked the sediment for gold by filling a low sluice box they had hung at an angle on stilts on the sandspit that had appeared in the middle of the river. They were using a *mazamorreo* technique, which involved panning directly in the river. Most observers who visit the Chocó and its rivers write about this technique because they see it as they travel on boats: groups of men and women (mostly women) working the river bottom when the river levels are low. The technique is marginal, however. The women would find a little gold, but it was difficult to extract. It is often not worth the time. The *mazamorreros* were from towns or neighboring villages, and it was what people might do when the river was dry and they had no land of their own. For many people with no land, panning the river was one of few options. They would work as *mazamorreros* in the few weeks when there was no rain. None of Pedro's neighbors worked as *mazamorreros*, because they had their own mines and land. When it did not rain, they did other things. Troqui barked as the canoe passed the men and women who were working the spit of gravel in the river, perhaps left behind by one of the excavator mines.

The excavator mines were about every mile along the length of the river, with excavators and a half-dozen workers each. These so-called "small-scale" mining operations were anything but small. The central canteens had food and a place to sit, workers stayed in makeshift huts made of wooden planks and green tarpaulin, and the mines were the size of six football fields carved into the earth where there had once been forest. On weekends, some of the workers came to drink at the two bars in the village that Pedro and his neighbor Esteban kept. Pedro's bar, at one end of the village, had billiards. Esteban's bar, at the other end, had a gravel dance floor. The destination of the two boats was the beach near the mining camp where Miguel lived and worked, near where a small tributary flowed into the river.

The boats slid onto the beach under the shade of a banana tree. Troqui jumped ashore, his tail straight. Was he coming into his own as a hunter? Pedro tied a blue rope around Guapi's neck and chest. Guapi strained, tail straight, ears back, and body forward to catch the scent. Pedro held the rope and a machete in his right hand. Most of the men carried two-foot machetes. Water droplets glistened on the metal barrel of a rifle hung on Miguel's shoulder. The gun would not be needed, unlike the machetes, which were used to clear a way through the forest. The dogs and men ran. Where was the paca? On the island, on the mainland, or in the jungle? The hunters turned inland and followed a stream through banana gardens, past sugarcane and into the bush. The mostly dry streambed seemed like a well-worn trail. The *paisa* was in front, Miguel behind, Javier and Troqui next, and behind them Guapi, pulling Pedro forward. Another man—a boy really, barely out of adolescence—joined them. He wore a soccer shirt in the colors of the Barcelona Football Club, with the name José and the number ten on the back. The hunters ran quickly up the stream, and then stopped to look at the cause of the commotion. Preserved in the sand, as if it were concrete, the delicate five-fingered paw print of a paca.

Pedro released Guapi, and the dog disappeared in a blur of white into the undergrowth. Pedro looked into the jungle. The sun was higher. Pedro gave instructions.

"Wait," he said, pausing to think and listen. Silence. Where to go? There was a bark as Guapi caught the scent of the paca and ran. The men followed. The boy in the Barcelona shirt leaped into motion like a football player in full sprint. Pedro dashed ahead of the boy. Pedro was older, but faster. He carried his hat and machete in his right hand and the leash in his left. It was too much, so he headed for the tributary and the boat.

Mauricio punted the long boat with a blue-bottomed hull, yellow trim, and Johnson motor along the far side of the tributary. The white cloth with the cartoon was draped over his back as protection from the sun. Pedro yelled over the water, then waded in up to his chest. In his right hand he still held the machete, the leash, and the hat; in his left hand, he held a plastic bag wrapped tight around his battered cell phone. He crossed the tributary and left the phone, the hat, and the leash in the boat. He continued wading through the water and peered at the edge of the river.

Guapi and Troqui stood on the muddy gravel beach. They did not follow Pedro into the water. They stayed in the shelter of the trees beside some flowers and paced. Troqui put a paw in the water; he seemed surer of himself that afternoon. Guapi scratched and pawed at the edge of the water and howled with his tail low. Was he impatient? Frustrated? The paca was somewhere, but Guapi did not know where. Mud oozed around his paws, and he could smell nothing. Five minutes passed, then five more. I stood beside the dogs, waiting.

Mauricio moved the boat up to another bank; a man, who had arrived from somewhere else, stood in the bow with a wooden spear made from a tree with its branches removed and a point sharpened with a machete. The six men, two dogs, and I searched the water for movement. Pedro waded up to the bank, near the dogs, with another spear. The water was muddy with sediment and green with leaves and the reflection of trees. The current moved slowly. Javier joined Mauricio and the other man on the boat. He too carried a long spear. Miguel, now without the gun, waded along the same bank of the river with a machete held low in the water in his right hand and a spear in his left. He looked at the shore and the shadows. Up and down the tributary, men peered into the mud. Wading deeper, some men treaded water; others swam. The water slowed them down. Some leaves hung from trees far out over the water, while other leaves floated by. The shadows on the shore offered many places to hide. Was that movement in the mud? Miguel went to investigate. Nothing. Was there movement in the water in front of the boy with the Barcelona shirt? The mud was thick and the water green with the sunlight. Was that a curve of an animal's back in the water, or just a tree trunk at an angle? The boy with the Barcelona shirt and a spear sharpened at both ends waded until he was in up to his waist.

Then there was a twist of movement—the curve of the back of the paca in the creek. Guapi howled and threw himself into the water, but he was too slow. The line of hunters in the water rushed after the animal from both sides of the river, but they were also too slow. The paca escaped through the middle of the two rows of hunters. Mauricio punted the canoe to the beach.

Javier, now in the water, threw himself into the boat. It took two attempts to get in, and then the water in his boots gushed into the boat. Javier moved to the bow, a spear hung low in his right hand with a steel tip and that deadly metal barb; this was no spear made quickly with a machete in the woods. Mauricio paddled the boat into the current, and then Pedro climbed in, positioned the motor, and started the engine. Javier pulled the dogs into the boat, and I followed as Pedro revved the motor and gave chase.

The paca swam through the water just ahead of the boat. The current pulled it away, its back curved, dolphin-like and graceful in the water. The paca dove and surfaced thirty feet away. Guapi threw himself into the water. The dog gained distance. Two heads were silhouetted against the water as the paca headed back to shore. The current shifted and the water became shallower at a stone beach. Guapi began to gain more. The boat beached itself. Javier jumped into the shallows with a spear in his right hand—he moved faster than Guapi—and thrust the spear into the water where the paca was. It skewered the animal under the water.

Two pacas in one day: Pedro and Guapi and Javier and the rest were a team. Pedro might not have killed the second one, but he had piloted the boat, he had trained Guapi to follow the scent, he had directed the hunt, and he had shown people where to go.

Javier heaved the paca into the boat, and then the blood came. Red mingled with the water. Javier threw Guapi into the boat and climbed in himself. The dogs got close to the dead animal, sniffed at its blood, and lapped at the wound. The five fingers on each paw of the paca were long and delicate, its back-right foot was purple from an old cord that had cut into swollen flesh, and Pedro declared the animal was one that had gotten away the year before. Pedro turned the boat back to the mine camp. Once there, Pedro held the animal high in his hands and walked to the kitchen canteen. The dogs followed close on his heels, trying to get another taste of the animal. Pedro shooed the dogs away. Most workers at the mine were young Black men. Were they neighbors from the river, or had they come to work at the mine camp? A *paisa* passed Pedro a large plastic bowl, where Pedro put the animal. Miguel brought a three-month-old puppy to taste the blood of the paca, which, I thought, seemed overwhelmed by the smell. A teenage girl passed by with cups she had washed in the river. Someone put water on to boil.

Mauricio and Pedro played with their phones. Pedro made a call. He was sitting on an aluminum pipe from the excavator mine. Mauricio made a call too. There was a signal here, unlike in their village. Javier rested, lost in thought. Pedro stopped looking at his phone to chat with another older man about the excavator mine. The man wore a black-and-white striped shirt that matched his hat; on his wrist was a gold watch. He had brought in the excavators to mine his family land.

"There is gold there, yes?" Pedro said.

"That will give money," the man replied.

"It might work," Pedro said.

The Barcelona boy took a knife, poured boiling water into a plastic container, dribbled water onto the body of the paca, and used the sharp edge of the knife against the grain of the animal's fur. The boiling water and the knife blade pulled the hair away from the animal's skin. He continued to pour boiling water over the dead animal until he had removed all of the fur. When the animal was hairless, he put it over the gas burner to sear the skin. The blue flame mixed with the light coming through the tarpaulin of the kitchen and made the white skin of the scorched animal turn an extraterrestrial green. The boy took the animal down to the river and butchered it. He removed its front and hind feet, and then its head. He put everything in a blue oil drum that had been cut in half and cleaned. He removed the intestines, the organs, and half the flesh of the animal—the meat was muscled, with little fat. Miguel held up what I took to be the animal's gall bladder before he threw it into the river. Half the meat was for Pedro, and the intestines were for Guapi. Pedro trained Guapi with the feet and the head of the butchered paca. Pedro explained, "You get them addicted to the head, like training dogs in an airport to find cocaine." Guapi had cornered eighty-eight pacas in six years. Once a *paisa* had offered Pedro two million pesos ($1,111) for Guapi.[3] Pedro had laughed.

We returned to the village with half of the meat in a blue container. Javier lay in the bow of the boat, asleep. The dogs sat in front of him. I was next. Mauricio sat behind me. Pedro took the motor. The sky was an arresting array of blue streaks and high clouds. It had not rained in days. We had left the village just over three hours earlier, we had hunted two pacas in one day, and Pedro and I had not had lunch yet. It was time to eat and relax, watch television, doze in a hammock, or sit by the river as the sun went down.

THE EMANCIPATORY POTENTIAL OF PRODUCING GOLD

As the moon rose on a Friday evening in March 2011, almost a year before the two-paca day, Pedro and I sat on a bench near the dock by the village and watched the water. He stretched his arms wide to embrace the water, the hills, and the forest lit by the setting sun and said, "We are in the glory, man." He was content from our day's labor at his mine.

"Life is hard, but in the city, nothing comes easy. Food is difficult. Here, you can always pick plantains, hunt pacas, or mine gold."

"Have you ever been to the city?" Pedro asked me after a long and poignant pause.

Rural families like Pedro's often went to the city. Pedro had family members who had lived in Quibdó. Indeed, Pedro had a home in the city where his three children had stayed when they went to high school. He often went to the city to sell what he mined and buy supplies, and he was building a second home there to rent out for an income when he stopped working at the mine. His neighbor Don Alfonso did much the same thing with a one-story brick building in a slum overlooking Medellín, Colombia's second largest city, which was a day's bus ride over the western range of the Andes in the department of Antioquia.

Pedro, like everyone in his village, had lived in the city. He had fled to Quibdó when the guerrillas had occupied the village, stayed for a month, and killed a neighbor in 2001. He had also fled downriver to Quibdó when a massive flash flood had washed away the entire village in the early 1990s. While many families had scattered for good in those moments of forced displacement, the people I knew had come back and rebuilt. Pedro and Javier and the others had come back after the flood and the war because life was easier on the river and because food and gold could be had.

While spending more time with Pedro and Javier and Martina and their neighbors digging and hunting would undoubtedly add nuance to an understanding of their strategies to find food and money, describing a day at his artisanal mine and a day hunting pacas is enough to see that it was a good life. The freedom that Pedro found raises uncomfortable questions for those who think of panning either as a form of resource extraction disconnected from the places where it occurs or as a vestige from earlier ways of mining by enslaved men and women. One facet of gold is that for some rural residents like Pedro, Javier, and Martina, who made a living combining hunting and fishing and everything else, provided there was a little gold to be had, times were good.

The two days of mining and hunting described here were not unusual. Pedro and his family repeated these activities most days, over the year, weather permitting. What was central—for both the subsistence livelihood of gardening, hunting, and fishing and the artisanal mining—was the way Pedro combined a diversity of activities. This meant that a week at the mine with no rain or a week when the mine gave no gold was as much a problem as a fungus ravaging a plantain crop, as the river pulling an avocado tree into the water, or as the attempt at paca domestication that ended with a destroyed chicken coop. Although such failures might be destabilizing for a time, they were not life altering, precisely because Pedro had other ways to produce both food and cash. He could always do something else. For Pedro (and others), mining was the good life because it enabled a dual economy in which he mixed mining for cash with rural subsistence production. For him, it was part of a livelihood that included engagement with urban spaces yet that mostly emphasized place-based activities in the forest and on the river. Gold was key to the family income, because with the metal, the family could make money—few other activities except maybe logging or migrant work gave cash. Mining, for Pedro and his neighbors, was a task that he might do for a few hours a day, or sometimes all day long. Producing gold was one of many interconnected shifting livelihood strategies, and a source of money and savings that ultimately offered Pedro a certain amount of freedom.

On the river, Pedro was a skilled hunter with a prize hunting dog. He had his own boat and his own canoe, and no one told him what to do. In the city? He would be just another middle-aged man looking for work, less certain of how things were done, and discriminated against for the way he talked or dressed. Gold, precisely because it was a high-value export commodity and an international symbol of wealth, let Pedro change how people saw him. With their mine, Pedro and Martina had a steady enough income and the basis of an autonomous household economy. Without the cash from the gold, life would be hard because there were few ways to make money. But with the cash from mining, Pedro could choose to continue to live in the forest a free man.

It is no coincidence that the rural Black residents I knew called themselves free men and women, or *libres*, and not *afrodescendientes* (Afro-descendants) or *afrocolombianos* (Afro-Colombians) or *negros* (Blacks) or even *campesinos* (peasants). Most of the men and women I knew were the descendants of former enslaved peoples. After all, the Chocó is a former slave society. The mining terms people use today are similar to those found in the colonial and republican archives; the men and women were just a few generations removed from chattel slavery. Pedro's neighbor Don Alfonso said he remembered his grandfather as a slave with a ring in his nose who worked for a family from Cartagena that owned the mining rights to the river. The remains of the slave mine workings were all over the jungle: the curve of a hill shows slave mine tailings, and people told stories of cave-ins from old slave workings. Pedro's father Don Gabriel, at ninety-six the oldest man in the village, said he learned to be a traditional healer from a man born free in Africa who had roamed the forests of the Chocó making herbal remedies. The descendants of those manumitted and runaway enslaved peoples built their own independent economies based on their mines. For them, producing gold was their independence, just as it is today for Pedro and others. For the descendants of escaped or freed enslaved men and women who scattered into the riverine valleys of the Colombian Pacific, gardening and fishing and hunting and gathering provided subsistence, while gold gave them cash and autonomy. While gold might have let Pedro's ancestors buy freedom, it meant Pedro had no need for a boss.

The emancipatory potential of artisanal mining is evident in these practices of mine work and other quotidian activities. In the months I accompanied Pedro and Martina to their mine, we worked hard, but with optimism. The work was ordinary: it was difficult but not bad, and it put gold at the center of a way of life. It was the realization that there are pleasures in mine work that helped me see how Pedro experienced what was, for him, the skilled labor of mine work.

All was not positive, of course. In the forests and rivers of Chocó, *libres* like Pedro were free from the state, to an extent, but they were not disconnected from wider conflicts that had shaped the region over the last thirty years. Although mining takes place out on a periphery, where the Colombian state is crumbling or never quite arrived, the mines were by no means isolated. When the state did come, it was often the military intent on rooting out guerrilla forces. Soldiers stole pineapples from Pedro's gardens and threatened to conscript teenagers in the village. I heard accounts of the army accusing children on other rivers of being members of guerrilla groups, killing them, and reporting the deaths as deaths from combat. The paramilitaries too had their presence. Moreover, the municipal governments were incompetent at best, and more than likely corrupt. The state regulations that existed against small-scale mining were often twisted to make the lives of artisanal miners like Pedro more difficult, even as they were used to give a patina of legitimacy to the exploration operations of multinational mining corporations that claimed mining title to much of the whole region.

Still, while Pedro was caught between guerrillas and the state and paramilitaries and mining companies, he was able to muddle along with his mine and gardens. Maybe not by escaping conflicts or avoiding the war totally, but certainly by keeping a low profile, minding his own business, and being lucky. His mine and garden were each a kind of refuge, even if, as a refuge, they were fragile. Mines and gardens had been the same for his ancestors when they had come up the river a hundred and fifty years earlier to escape slavery.

Producing gold offers an emancipatory potential to its miners, precisely because it provides rural Black men and women with a source of cash when

Antonio (top right) watches as Pedro and Javier work the family mine.

the rest of the economy does not. Spending time learning to mine on a river in the midst of a gold rush makes this clear. Give a person a mine, a forest, a river, and a little land to garden, and they would want for nothing. Gold offered a certain freedom because it was a source of cash, because the descendants of a former slave society had no master, and because the state did not stop them. The mine work was hard, of course, but the work was also meaningful. For Pedro and Martina, their mine was the basis of their household economy and their freedom. However fragile and dependent they might be on staving off the ever-present possibility of disaster, gold and pacas were the good life. If they found the good life on the river, others sought it in wider economic circuits of the cash economy and *rebusque*.

CHAPTER TWO

Gold and the Cash Economy

A FEW weeks before Christmas 2011, Don Alfonso, Pedro's spry elderly neighbor, and I went to work his family mine. While Don Alfonso worked artisanally, his technique was different from Martina and Pedro's. For one thing, he did not dig, because he was too old and too tired. Instead, he let the water wash down a trench in the jungle from a reservoir that an excavator had carved into the landscape above his mine three years before. The water pulled sediment from a cliff into the long trench he had dug. At the bottom of the trench, Don Alfonso had placed wooden sticks parallel to each other. The water carried sediment over the sticks, and the heavier metal settled down through the spaces in between. By raising and lowering a wooden gate he had built at the mouth of the reservoir, he let water rush down the trench. It was the rush of water that pulled away sand and gravel and almost infinitesimal yellow specks. When the water had slowed to a trickle, he would collect the sediment under the sticks. His panning technique was bad, I thought. He lost much of the richest material from the pan. Still, that day we mined eight *tomines*, or one *castellano* (the colonial terms still in use), which weighed 4.6 grams. The metal was worth 600,000 pesos ($330) at the time. I know this, because I bought the gold from Don Alfonso that day to make two rings and a pair of earrings.

About a month before that day at the mine, I had slumped, as on most nights, on a plastic chair in Pedro's living room, too exhausted to bathe. Pedro, refreshed from a swim in the river, watched the seven o'clock evening news from a hammock. His four young nephews lay on the cool concrete floor in front of him. Javier, his brother-in-law, looked through an open window. Mauricio, his other brother-in-law, leaned against the doorframe. Martina, his wife, was in the kitchen. Antonio, Pedro's son, had long since left for the police academy. Don Alfonso, who lived a short walk away at the

Don Alfonso pans barefoot and in shorts for comfort.

other end of the village, supported himself on the windowsill. We all watched the ten-inch television just audible above the whir of a gasoline-powered electric generator, the hum of a freezer, and the steady drum of rain on the corrugated metal roof. Watching the seven o'clock evening news was the nightly ritual. That day in November 2011, the broadcast was nonstop coverage of the hunt for Muammar Gaddafi and the wars in the Middle East. For once, the newscast had nothing to say about Colombia's civil war, which by 2011 was already forty-seven years old.

"War is terrible," Pedro said. "Thank God it is not like Libya here."

How dangerous that war in Libya looked on the small screen! In this village, in one of Colombia's poorest and most peripheral departments worst affected by the armed conflict, danger always felt somewhere else, yet never too far away. The images on the television painted the civil war in Libya as much, much worse.

"Where's Libya?" Don Alfonso asked aloud.

"On the Mediterranean, in North Africa, somewhere west of Egypt, not far from Saudi Arabia," I replied.

"I've been there," Don Alfonso said.

"Where? Libya?"

"No. Saudi Arabia."

"What?"

Don Alfonso did not reply; the news continued; I was wide-awake. Don Alfonso in Saudi Arabia? How? After the broadcast, I walked with Don Alfonso past a dozen or so buildings to his home at the other end of the village. I asked him about the time he had gone to Saudi Arabia.

"I went coffee picking in Valle in the 1950s when I was eighteen," Don Alfonso replied. "I knew we had to leave the plantations when we found bodies of dead peasants hidden in the rows of coffee plants. A friend and I traveled to the Pacific coast and the city of Buenaventura. My friend found work on a merchant steamer. I stowed away until we got out to sea. We sailed to many places, and one of them was Saudi Arabia. I didn't like Saudi Arabia though. They said you knew a woman loved you by the way she wore her veil when she looked at you, but I never understood the women there. I was on that boat for two years. Then, we went back to Buenaventura, and I came home."

Don Alfonso did not just mine like Pedro or pick coffee or travel to foreign lands; he also ran a small store. His store consisted of three shelves on the back wall of the front room of his house; they held gum, soap, salt, sugar, batteries, cooking oil, soda crackers, toilet paper, blue single-blade razors, cheap black flashlights, sticks of deodorant for men, transistor radios that may or may not have worked, surprisingly well-made umbrellas imported from Asia, blocks of *panela*, and small, neon-red bottles of cleaning fluid. His customers were his neighbors and the dozen or so workers in the excavator mine who had come to live in the village. The rate of return from his store was, sometimes, better than that of the miners. Bubblegum, Don Alfonso and I calculated in my notebook, earned an incredible return. It cost 10,000 pesos ($5.50) for a jar of a thousand or so *chicle* bubblegum candies bought in Medellín. Don Alfonso sold each piece of bubblegum for 100 pesos (5 cents). A hefty profit, we guessed. Hefty, that is, until children from the village started to buy the bubblegum with coins they stole from the shelf in Don Alfonso's front room. The trick was a neat one. The children used the same physical coins over and over again to buy more and more bubble gum. When Don Alfonso realized that the children were buying candy with his own money, he installed skinny, split tree trunks as wooden bars down the middle of his front room to prevent the children's illicit black-market candy exchange. Even so, the store had him bored. He needed stock.

Don Alfonso and I conceived of a trip to the city of Medellín over the Andes Mountains in the department of Antioquia as a solution. There and back again, as cheaply as possible. In Medellín, the second largest city in Colombia, he would buy wholesale for the store. I would front some of the money for the bus ticket and merchandise. He would buy the return tickets, pay me back when he had the money, and explain the trip to me as we went. I also wanted to buy a Christmas gift for the children in the village: a soccer ball made of leather that would last on the rough gravel of the pitch left by an excavator mine downriver. When I was not around, Don Alfonso would fund his trips to Medellín or Pereira, another Andean city, with sales from his mine. Don Alfonso called these shopping trips to buy wholesale his *rebusque*.

Along with mining and his gardens, Don Alfonso lived through *rebusque*. He moved. He tried one thing, and when that failed, he tried another. Don Alfonso did a lot of *rebusque*. So did others. A teenager from the Pacific forests left for a few years to look for work before coming back. A young woman moved from her village to find work as a domestic servant for a white, middle-class family in an Andean city. A young man worked in the city and returned home to visit on holidays. Don Alfonso and his neighbors all had their own forms of *rebusque*. Indeed, even the excavator miners who came to the river to find work were on their *rebusque*. They all survived through a *rebusque* that emerged in the everyday encounters between rural miners like Pedro, Martina, and Don Alfonso and the migrant miners who moved to the river to work on excavator mines. *Rebusque* took many forms. Rural Black people moved between cash-making activities excavating gold, cutting timber, and migrating to the city for work. Although neither Pedro nor Don Alfonso saw growing plantains or hunting pacas or their subsistence activities as *rebusque*, the other activities were. The miners who came to the forests of the Pacific followed well-worn yet unmapped corridors between the city and the countryside. It was the promise of fast cash that lured those miners, along with the muleteers, the washerwomen, the cooks, the traveling merchants, and the construction workers on their *rebusque*. Don Alfonso did the same, going the other direction. In the Chocó, gold was not just a high-value commodity mined in a tropical forest destined for markets in the north, it also let Don Alfonso engage in his *rebusque*.

It was what he mined on days like that December morning that ordinarily gave Don Alfonso the cash he needed to go shopping in Medellín. Don Alfonso relied on a dual household economy of subsistence production and mining like Pedro, and he used his mine to fund his *rebusque*. More so than Pedro, Don Alfonso habitually entered into the wider cash economy. Indeed, Don Alfonso always had. Ever since he had been a young man and gone to Saudi Arabia, he had gone over the Andes to the Eje Cafetero, or Coffee Axis, of western Colombia to look for work by picking coffee or by engaging in petty trading. For Don Alfonso, his rural village and his gardens and his mine were a fallback position from which he could venture forth. Although he engaged in household production—having herbs and a forest garden—it was his mine that allowed him to participate in these wider networks connecting the Chocó to other parts of Colombia through *rebusque*. For Don Alfonso, the cash from the panning provided him the modest capital to travel to Medellín. Like Pedro, he relied on cash from gold sales, but unlike Pedro, he relied on gold to engage in a creative, mobile, shifting livelihood strategy of *rebusque*. From opposite directions, both men relied on the same scale and techniques of gold production. Yet in the case of Don Alfonso, his was a place-based rural economy linked to the wider circuits of temporary and contingent out-migration of *rebusque*.

THE *REBUSQUE* SHOPPING TRIP OF DON ALFONSO

Vomit dribbled along the grooves in the floor of the bus from Quibdó to Medellín, past rows of seats, away from the driver and a glass partition with an image of Our Lady of Mount Carmel, the patron saint of truckers, bus drivers, muleteers, and other travelers. The woman who had thrown up into a black plastic bag missed again, and her vomit congealed in the puddle in the aisle. As the driver's assistant poured cleaning fluid from a neon-red bottle into the mess, the smells of puke and cleaning fluid and diesel fuel from the ancient bus mixed. Don Alfonso and I contorted to get comfortable in the last seats at the back, a metal rod dug into my left thigh, and as the bus lurched around potholes, I too tried not to vomit.

While there are no roads to his village, Don Alfonso routinely took the bus. He took a boat to town, then a bus to the city, and then a bus to look for work or to buy things in Pereira or Medellín. Other people left their homes in the forest to trade, look for jobs, commute to university classes, or visit children. People from the city came the other direction to work as miners, loggers, cooks, and coca pickers. To assume that Don Alfonso and his neighbors just lived off mining for cash and gardening for subsistence in the village would be to miss the everyday connections between remote communities and large cities. Bus tickets from Quibdó, the capital of the Chocó, to Medellín, the capital of Antioquia, cost a quarter of the cheapest flight. If a bus took most of the day, a flight took less than an hour. Those who could afford to fly did so. NGO employees, public servants, mine owners, and visiting academics—we flew. For us, by air, Colombia was a small country. For the rest, by bus, the country was vast. Buses were a slow and uncomfortable way to travel, but they made for good fieldwork.

Later that morning, our bus crawled past a handful of soldiers sheltering on the porch of two farmhouses. The soldiers talked to a farmer, drank from small cups, and left their automatic rifles leaning against a wall. Nearby, a green-clad figure slept in a hammock pitched under a rain-lashed plastic tarp, while a machine gun pointed at our bus from a metal tripod on a hillock overlooking the road. The owner of the machine gun, a teenaged soldier, chatted on a cellphone in the rain. Soldiers who charged their cellphones at small farms caused problems for the farmers from the guerrillas. Don Alfonso watched the soldiers from behind the security of the bus window.

Our bus was not stopped that morning, but checkpoints by the army and the guerrillas are a common feature of bus travel. The armed conflict between left-wing guerrillas and right-wing paramilitaries and the Colombian armed forces has claimed hundreds of thousands of lives and displaced millions of people from their lands.[1] In 2011, few observers could have imagined the peace accord negotiated (from 2012 and 2016 in Havana, Cuba) between the Colombian government and the Revolutionary Armed Forces of Colombia (or FARC) guerrillas. The low-intensity war arrived in the Pacific region in the 1990s,[2] as cocaine traffickers used remote rivers to access drug routes to the Pacific and the Caribbean. The military, the guerrillas, and the paramilitaries all profit, in their way, by producing cocaine or by extorting drug producers. By 2013, newspapers were reporting that armed actors were profiting more from illegal mining than they were from cocaine.[3] Gold was becoming the main moneymaker for some armed groups.

Observers and journalists writing about artisanal and small-scale mining in Colombia tended to dwell on a narrative of violence that emphasizes the role of armed actors in an illegal mining sector.[4] They ignored the quotidian interactions between soldiers, paramilitaries, guerrillas, miners, and the communities in which they operate. They took for granted state laws that rendered mining an illegal part of the underground economy. The relationships between outside miners, communities, and armed actors were more nuanced than simple coercion. While in the village the war seemed far away—like watching the soldiers from behind the false security of a bus window—Don Alfonso and his neighbors were cautious. After all, they lived in a mining region in the midst of a territorial war for control of coca and gold.

A bus on a narrow road through a jungle may make for good research, but I squirmed in the last seat by the window, where I could not sleep or do much of anything but watch through the glass. Where were we? I checked my phone, which did not help my queasiness. The maps of this part of the Chocó were poor. Digital maps, for example, displayed roads that did not exist. A tourist guidebook, targeting middle-class urban motorists, would have led a hardy day-tripper to the wild, helter-skelter dirt track between Condoto and Nóvita and the limits of the road system in the south of the

Chocó. Some roads had been paved half a dozen times on paper, and yet, according to a cynical joke, no tree had ever been cut. In their maps, the Geographic Institute Agustín Codazzi, the state agency in Bogotá charged with mapping Colombia, put the curve of a river out of place, located Don Alfonso's village miles from where it was, and gave a decade-long afterlife to places that have long since disappeared under the teeth of an excavator or the force of a river. In the institute's library in Bogotá, the hand-drawn elevation maps depicting the contours of the landscape showed blank pages for the area around Don Alfonso's village.

Hours before, while still in Quibdó at seven o'clock that morning, Don Alfonso and I had yelled "¡Nos fuimos!" ("We've left!") from the back of the bus. It took another hour for the bus to actually leave for Medellín. We were giddy, even though we had not moved, and the day had started badly. The plan for the trip was to spend as little money as possible, but we got the worst seats on the most expensive bus, and it was my fault. My girlfriend Mercedes bought the bus tickets for us on the evening of the day before, after I had called her that afternoon in a panic. She bought the last seats on the most direct bus to Medellín from Quibdó. Each ticket cost 66,000 pesos ($37), and Don Alfonso was angry. He complained that we should have taken the Quibdó-to-Pereira-to-Medellín bus because the tickets were 55,000 pesos ($30). The difference of 11,000 pesos was a lot of money when Don Alfonso's margins were so tight. Later that morning, our bus pulled out of the terminal to head north through Quibdó and onto the Medellín road that climbed into the Andes following the Atrato River. The higher the road got, the smaller the river became below us.

"Do you know what those are?" Don Alfonso said, pointing out the bus window to the white crosses beside the road.

I did. The crosses marked a road accident. Had the accident been the one when a bus had fallen into the valley below and killed fourteen people on board?[5] I imagined so. Our bus rocked on its suspension on the road that followed the Atrato River into the Andes. Two roads connect the Chocó to the Andean interior. The Quibdó–Medellín Road, which follows the Atrato River northeast into the department of Antioquia, and the Tadó–Pereira Road, which follows the San Juan River east into the department of Risaralda. Processed food, commercial goods, mine equipment, gasoline, and diesel fuel are trucked along the roads into the Chocó. Little wonder things in Quibdó cost so much more than in the Andean cities. The high prices meant that Don Alfonso could do the trip himself and make a little extra with the spread in prices between Medellín, Quibdó, and the store he kept in his front room.

Mid-morning, the bus stopped at a roadside restaurant overlooking a forest valley. The restaurant had a house attached and a small store. Flowers spilled from pots, chickens scratched the dirt, and the mist drifted across the valley. The menu was stewed beef, fried fish, or fatty pork rinds (*chicharrones*) accompanied by rice or fried plantains (*patacones*). Don Alfonso declined my offer to buy him breakfast, but I was hungry, despite my nausea on the bus, and I ordered pork rinds, fried plantains, and sweet milky coffee.

"Too much cholesterol," Don Alfonso said, poking me in the ribs.

"Leave me alone."

"You're fat."

The bus driver, having brought a few dozen passengers, ate first and for free, and the other clients (a road repair crew in bright clothing, a handful of soldiers, and travelers) ate their food as it came. The server, a white woman in a spotless dress, brought fresh fruit juice. Over a day, she would see travelers heading to or from the Chocó. She also ran a small store beside the restaurant, which sold cooking oil and bags of rice and other basics. Did travelers buy bags of rice and cooking oil? Maybe. But the forests in the valley below the restaurant, as far as the eye could see, were the territory of Indigenous Embera Katío communities who live between the two highways. Those forests are the frontier where three departments—the Chocó, Antioquia, and Risaralda—met. Our bus passed maybe half a dozen Indigenous settlements between Quibdó and the border between the Chocó and Antioquia. The communities had fled thirty years of conflict over mining in their territories. In 2011, two multinational mining corporations—one Canadian and one South African—had projects in the area, which raised the specter of further displacement from a mine. When the driver finished eating, we boarded the bus and soon left the jungles of the Chocó behind.

"These mountains give money. I used to be able to pick 180 kilograms of a coffee a day," Don Alfonso said as the rainforest landscape receded and we entered the Coffee Axis. The wet forests gave way to a dryer climate and row after row of dark green, shrub-like coffee plants advancing up the hillsides, which growers have domesticated into a monoculture landscape. We passed dozens of squat houses sitting among the rows. Don Alfonso explained how to grow and harvest coffee. Small farmers make money from coffee in Antioquia, but not in the Chocó, Don Alfonso complained. Almost as if to support his complaint, the bus entered a well-appointed town with red brick buildings, wide streets, parks, schools, and dozens of hardware stores and cooperatives that sold supplies for coffee producers—an ordered contrast to most of the towns in the Chocó.

Don Alfonso had spent the decades since the 1950s in *rebusque*, moving back and forth between the village and the coffee lands when the dry periods came and there was not enough rain in his reservoir to mine in the village. Sometimes he went to plant and other times to harvest coffee at a farm owned by a friend he had met while coffee picking in the Cauca Valley as a young man. Don Alfonso met his wife, who was from Manizales, the capital of the department of Caldas, on one of those trips to pick coffee. He brought her back to the village with him when they were young. Don Alfonso's wife died a few years before I met him, but he grinned as he told me about her in her youth, with her long, straight hair that hung down to her waist.

"We had children," he said. "One was a police officer in Medellín. All *paisas*." The roads between the Chocó, Antioquia, and Risaralda and the biography of Don Alfonso mark not only an ecological and economic frontier between three departments but also a racialized one. The Chocó is Black, while Antioquia and Risaralda are white or *paisa*; in between is Indigenous. *Paisa* is an identity at the heart of a subnational regional identity founded on ideas of whiteness, hard work, and Catholicism and centered on Medellín.[6] In the Chocó, where the population is 90 percent Black and 5 percent Indigenous, *paisa* refers to any white or *mestizo* outsider, Colombian or otherwise.[7]

It has often been said that Colombia is a country of regions.[8] It has also been said that the regions have been racialized as ethnic and racial identities are ascribed to geographic and ecological areas. Peter Wade, an anthropologist who has written about blackness and race in Colombia, makes this argument.[9] While the Chocó is populated by Black and Indigenous communities, it is also a region whose geography is described in racialized terms as dark, wild, and dangerous. The Chocó, in the imagination of urbanites in Medellín and Bogotá, is a dangerous place, a place that easily gets cast as an aquatic, wild tropical jungle between the Andes and the Pacific, where a drug war has raged for decades, where armed paramilitary and guerrilla groups fight each other over jungle, and where, in 2017, teenagers were murdered by machete, the guerrillas had released a kidnapped politician, and paramilitaries were retraining.[10] But flip the perspective to that of Don Alfonso, who took a bus over the mountains to the coffee lands and then to a city fraught with urban dangers. From his perspective, the Chocó was a world away from Antioquia, yet it was home.

Nancy Appelbaum identifies a parallel process in the way race is regionalized in her work on the Coffee Axis,[11] which, in her account, is imagined as *paisa* in ways that ignore the histories of the Indigenous and Black peoples living there. Another way to think about these two places is neither as a region racialized nor as races regionalized but as peoples and places in motion, at least since the mid-century convulsions of La Violencia, which put millions of people on the move. The Chocó has been at once the source of displaced men, women, and children fleeing to Andean cities, and a place where *paisas* go to work or settle. Don Alfonso, with his trips to Saudi Arabia as a young man and those between the jungle and the Coffee Axis, is an example of this *rebusque* movement. Contemporary accounts often focus on the permanent migration from the Pacific to the interior cities but ignore people, like Don Alfonso, who move back and forth. Not all movement is permanent, after all.

The bus stalled in a traffic jam entering Medellín and crawled past hundreds of shipping containers stacked high in a storage yard beside the highway. I imagined the containers had arrived on boats from Asia to the Pacific port of Buenaventura, then traveled by train and truck to Medellín, and then to the storage yard. Sometimes, when thinking about globalization, the focus is on new technology, instant communication, and how finance moves from northern metropoles to the capital cities of the Global South to the rural extractive enclaves in ways that skip the spaces in between. The shipping containers served as reminders that the movement of physical stuff matters too. Gold, as a high-value export commodity from the forests of the Colombian Pacific, has both a physical and a financial component.

Gold can become a financial instrument, seen as safe haven for investors, alienated from its own physicality. Yet it was as a valuable substance that Don Alfonso found it useful. For him and others, gold mattered because it was an important, high-value export commodity. Producing gold mattered, because gold, like blood diamonds and cobalt and some other minerals and gems, was expensive, fungible, easy to transport, and liquid anywhere in the world. Gold was a form of commodity money whose value came from the physical activity of shifting the earth, moving water, burning mercury, exchanging it at buying and selling houses, shipping it to refineries in Medellín, and selling it on global markets. While planes sometimes fly gold from the Chocó to Medellín, most physical goods come to Quibdó on trucks and buses.

Our bus continued on into Medellín on its way to the southern bus terminal. Medellín is a narrow city that fills the bottom and sides of a long valley, with modern skyscrapers in some areas, and extensive slums in others. The first thing Don Alfonso did when we got to the bus terminal was to buy the return tickets to Quibdó via Pereira for the next evening. The plan was to spend the night in Medellín with Don Alfonso's son Diego and Diego's wife, who lived in one slum far to the north, shop the next day, and catch the overnight bus back. The second thing Don Alfonso did was call his daughter-in-law on a battered, second-hand cellphone.

"Have you cooked dinner?"

He paused to listen.

"Cook something."

Don Alfonso, it turned out, had two reasons for the trip. First, to shop with me. Second, to collect rent from Diego and Diego's wife. In one of the *comunas*, the favela-like slums high on the slopes above Medellín, Don Alfonso had built a small house with the share of cash he received when he and his family had let an excavator operation come onto his and his extended family's land three years prior. The excavators did not stay long, but Don Alfonso's share of the profits was enough to start to build the house. While Don Alfonso was still healthy, he planned to live in the village. When he was too old to live in the village, he would move to Medellín. Don Alfonso rented one apartment in the house to Diego and his wife and the other to a neighbor from the village. While Diego did take care of the house, he still owed Don Alfonso three months' back rent. Don Alfonso and I had come to collect 450,000 pesos ($250).

We caught a bus from the southern terminal to the city center, which was decorated with Christmas lights, and we passed stalls selling multicolored tube lights. Don Alfonso made a detour and asked the price. The next day, he would buy some to sell in the village. We paused near a statue by Fernando Botero, a famous Colombian artist, in Botero Park, an area that used to be an open-air market until the people were pushed out to make way for urban public space. Don Alfonso asked me to take a picture of him with the giant bronze statue of a horse. We walked by food stalls where women sold hamburgers—fried beef patties with bacon, onions, green tomatoes, and Cornish eggs—slathered in white mayonnaise, yellow pineapple sauce, pink mayonnaise, yellow mustard, and red ketchup, with crushed potato chips sprinkled on top, all squeezed into a steamed bun wrapped in tinfoil. The result was a Colombian exaggeration of American fast food.

We caught another bus and headed north toward Don Alfonso's house. A busker came on the bus to ply his trade. Don Alfonso pointed out the window to a tall and slender dark-haired woman standing silhouetted in a doorway of an apartment building, wearing heels and a miniskirt and halter top, with one arm crooked behind her back and the other at her waist. Was everyone working? *Rebusque* describes all of it. The stalls selling Christmas lights, the street sellers who had food stands with the *paisa* interpretation of American fast food, the buskers on the bus, and the woman in the doorway.

Tube lights and tinsel decorated the window in the front room of the apartment Don Alfonso rented to Diego and his wife. Outside, the neighboring red brick houses on the narrow concrete street were resplendent with yellow and blue and white lights that cast an electronic glow. Don Alfonso's daughter-in-law served food, his three grandchildren played on the floor, and he and I sat on plastic chairs against the wall. The walls were made of hollow red bricks, which Don Alfonso hoped one day to cover with cement and paint a pastel color. It was a single-story house, with a fringe of metal rebar sticking out of the unfinished roof in an optimistic nod to a future second story. The house was built without city permission on an informal subdivision with dubious property title. (Don Alfonso later asked Mercedes, my girlfriend and a lawyer, if she could help legalize his informal property deed. She said it would be very complicated.) Beside the television, Diego fiddled with a small electric box, trying to fix a string of Christmas lights as he chatted with me.

Diego explained how he had left the village for Medellín in 2004 because of violence from the guerrillas and the lack of work. He worked in construction as a laborer, commuting two hours each way. He left for work at five o'clock in the morning to start at seven o'clock; he stopped at six o'clock in the evening to get home by eight o'clock. As we talked, he complained about minimum wage, little overtime pay on holidays and Sundays, and no job security if he arrived late, refused overtime, or could not travel to new contracts. He said he would be building a bridge until the New Year, then he would take a two-day holiday before taking another contract to build a bridge a day's bus trip north. He said he dreamed of education, qualifications, and a raise. When I asked about night school, he answered, "When?" He had to be ready for overtime and work on Sundays. He earned 900,000 pesos ($500) a month, paid every two weeks as a steady income. The salary was good compared to the village, where a miner might stand to make more money but with less certainty.

Late the next morning, Don Alfonso and I caught a bus and rode down to the city center. In the dense commercial streets of El Hueco, men and women sold things from wooden tables, street carts, small shops, and ground-floor stores of large skyscrapers. People sold coffee, gum, books, wallets, antiques, clothing, magazines, knick-knacks, secondhand cameras, Italian-style stove-top espresso makers, and, I was once told, assault rifles and hand grenades. I had seen the cameras and bought the espresso maker but never looked for the weapons. Don Alfonso had come here for the wholesale prices on bulk packages of inexpensive merchandise for his front-room store.

"They will charge me more if a *Míster* comes," Don Alfonso said by way of asking me not to actually go shopping with him. I was foreign, which would raise his costs.

We split up: he shopped alone, and I did other things. I went to a bank, I wrote emails, and I had my shoes cleaned by a man who charged me 12,000 pesos ($6.66), three times the regular price. When I complained, the man showed me a price list. Don Alfonso had been right.

I called Don Alfonso in the afternoon, but he could not understand me on his cellphone. He said he was shopping at the corner of Calle 46 and Carrera 51; I headed south ten blocks, scanning the crowds. I gave him a call and said I was on the corner of 46th and 51st; he said he had gone to Berrio Park and the church where he had left me in the morning. When I got there, he was not there. I sat down at the fountain and thought about the city. Don Alfonso appeared and sat down beside me; I apologized for getting lost.

"Let's go for lunch. I'll pay," Don Alfonso said.

We went to the nearest *paisa* restaurant, which specialized in *bandeja paisa*—a large plate of beans, rice, ground meat, chorizo sausage, fried eggs, fresh avocado, and lettuce, with tomatoes, onions, a lime-and-salt dressing, and a footlong piece of *chicharrón*. I said I was not hungry, but Don Alfonso insisted. Instead of a *bandeja paisa*, he ordered *mondongo* (tripe soup). I asked for the same. The soup was too salty and too expensive (18,000 pesos, or $10). Don Alfonso had not wanted to spend that much money on a bad lunch. By then, I had lost count of how much I owed him and what he owed me. Don Alfonso had not. He offered to buy food for that day and the next on the trip back to Quibdó. I agreed; Don Alfonso did not want to be in my debt.

"We should look for a football," I said.

We walked for a long time, first in one direction and then the other, before we found a store that sold sports equipment. Which football to buy? I bought an expensive one, embarrassed by the price but hopeful that it would last on the rough gravel pitch in the village.

Don Alfonso led me to the store to pick up the things he had bought. It had plastic toys, a cash register with cardboard products for children, and cheap, colored Christmas ornaments. The store sold in bulk, and at the back, shelves were full up to the ceiling with black plastic garbage bags. Don Alfonso's name was written on masking tape on two of the bags. I realized then that what Don Alfonso was doing was normal. Many people came to

Medellín and then went home to sell what they had purchased. Don Alfonso took the two bags he had filled up earlier in the day.

Purchases complete, we waved down a taxi to take us to the bus terminal. I got in the front and gave directions, while Don Alfonso got in the back. The taxi driver was a woman, the second woman taxi driver I had ever met in Colombia. To make conversation, I asked her about the work.

"The company I work for employs five hundred men and three women," she said.

"Do you work nights?" Don Alfonso asked.

"No. But I work a lot to pay for the car."

I asked about the taxi.

"A family friend lent me the money. I only have to pay back 50,000 pesos [$27] a day. The loan has only a small interest."

"Is it a *gota-a-gota* loan?" I asked, thinking about my own interest-free loans to Don Alfonso versus the usurious drop-drop (*gota-a-gota*) loans of a loan shark.

"No! God, no," she said as she took her hand from the wheel and crossed herself. "With *gota-a-gota* loans, the payments keep going up: 50,000 pesos a day, then 60,000 pesos, then 70,000 pesos, and you can never pay it all off. I have to pay back 50,000 a day, but there's no interest. Or just a small amount of interest. I don't know. It's more manageable than *gota-a-gota*. *Gota-a-gota* is horrible. It just grows and grows and never gets paid."

"When did you start driving a taxi regularly?" I asked.

"I worked in clothing design for twenty years. I designed and made clothes to sell in El Hueco. It was stressful, but I liked it. I did it all: designed the pattern, bought the material, provided the instructions to the seamstress, made sure the workers made the clothes to the right specifications, delivered the clothes to the shop, solved the problems that came up, made sure the clothes arrived at the shop, dealt with people when things didn't arrive, and worked with the buyers and suppliers. Now, I have nothing to show for it but this unpaid for taxi bought on borrowed money."

"I worked in coffee all of my life," Don Alfonso said from the back seat, "I've got nothing to show for it either. You never get ahead."

"It is harder today. There's a lot less money circulating than before. The money is illiquid. No money to buy. The government has been cracking down on coca and mining. People have no money to buy anything. I have a friend who brings T-shirts in from Panama because clothes are cheaper there. In Panama, people make the clothes on boats. The bosses pay them badly, and they don't pay any taxes. The workers get no time off and they have no benefits. How can people compete with that? I ask you, are their clothes better quality? My friend brings them in through Buenaventura. It's probably illegal; I don't know. But it's much cheaper. Now, I drive a taxi."

As we arrived at the bus terminal, she said to Don Alfonso, "You should go buy jeans in the south of Medellín, where clothes are even cheaper. They will put whatever logo you want on the jeans: Diesel, Levi's, Tommy Hilfiger, or whatever. You can buy jeans for 20,000 pesos [$11] and sell them for 70,000 pesos [$39]."

We found a bench in the bus terminal to wait. The first thing Don Alfonso did was to empty the two black garbage bags onto the floor and repack the contents—transistor radios, tube lights, batteries, soap, and other things—into plastic bags, which he redistributed into his backpack, a shoulder bag, and a striped carryall. He made it look like normal luggage. When he finished, the bags did indeed look inconspicuous.

"The garbage bags are too dangerous," he said. "They make you a target. This is for safety: to prevent robbers and to not raise suspicions from soldiers. Do you want dinner? We should eat. Who knows when we'll have lunch tomorrow?"

We ate, we waited for hours, we went to find our bus, and we took our seats. As the bus left Medellín for Pereira at eleven o'clock at night, a child screamed from where he lay, with his leg raised on pillows above his body a few rows in front of us.

"He should be in a hospital," someone yelled.

"We were, in Medellín, but they sent us back to Quibdó," the mother snapped.

On the trip, the child cried with each bounce of the bus. On the road between the two cities at night, there was nothing I could do. So I took two travel sickness pills that put me to sleep until I woke, groggy, at seven o'clock in the morning. Don Alfonso pointed out the window: a landslide had slid down over the road, and the bus stood frozen behind a long line of trucks, cars, and jeeps in the San Juan Valley between Pereira and Quibdó. As the morning became afternoon, we bought fresh cheese from a farmer beside the road. Later, we worried about food, delays, and the cost. But by evening, excavators had cut a narrow track through the landslide and the traffic began to move.

A little later, a group of soldiers stopped our bus. The young men climbed on board and told the passengers to dismount with their bags. Don Alfonso pushed the bags with his shopping under the seat in front of me with his feet. Was I his decoy? I took my shoulder bag out with me. Don Alfonso glared at me. Would the soldiers make me unpack the bags under my seat in public? Would they find a way to disguise a demand for money in the process? Did Don Alfonso have money? Did I have any cash left? Would unpacking and repacking our bags let others know what Don Alfonso was carrying and make him a target? How could I explain that the dozen packages of blue razors and sticks of deodorant under the seat in front of me were for Don Alfonso's store? Might the soldiers think the supplies were for the guerrillas in the jungle? At that moment, beside the highway, with the forest all around, I felt scared. I thought about the war, and I thought about this not being Don Alfonso's first trip. The soldiers took my identity card, radioed to check my name, asked who I was and what my business was. I explained: Canada and research. I told the truth, and I had the correct papers: a foreign passport with a research visa and a letter of support from the Black community where I was working to explain my project. Don Alfonso, with no passport, a rural accent, and no letter, was in a more precarious position. After checking my identification and opening a couple of other people's bags, the soldiers let us go. The bags under the seat in front of me remained unchecked.

The bus stopped in a small town for 20 minutes in the dark before we continued until the road was blocked again, this time by a truck carrying metal rebar that had crashed into a fuel tanker. Would we have to wait until the crash was moved? No, our driver found a way. We continued, passed other checkpoints, where more soldiers looked at our bags, and finally got to the Istmina–Quibdó Road. The bus turned toward Istmina, and Don Alfonso and I got off to wait for a bus to the Quibdó. We arrived at midnight. I stayed in the city a few days. But the next morning, Don Alfonso caught another bus and then a boat to get to his home in his village by the river.

FROM SUBSISTENCE TO *REBUSQUE*

I returned to the village briefly, from Canada, almost two years later, in September 2013. Don Alfonso rested in his hammock in the late afternoon shade of a tree and we talked.

"What was Saudi Arabia like in the 1950s?" I asked, because I still did not believe what he had told me two years before after watching the news about the hunt for Gaddafi.

"Why such interest, Daniel?" he said, avoiding my question.

I changed the subject to ask about his trips to Medellín and Pereira. Had he gone again?

"I'm too old and slow now," he said as he claimed that he would never go to Medellín or Pereira again, because when he had gone by himself a few months before, things had gone badly. On that trip, some teenagers had stolen all his stock, and he had barely been able to make it back to the village. He had lost all the money he had invested in the trip. The trip was a disaster, so much so that he swore he would never go again.

Don Alfonso's and my bus ride to Medellín was just one trip, not that different from other trips that I had been on with him. Not that different from other trips he did by himself. Our trip that November of 2011 puts the Chocó into the wider context of the region, and it shows glimpses of Don Alfonso's way of life, in which mine work and *rebusque* work co-existed, while having a stable rural subsistence base allowed him to engage in other activities. It was a shifting livelihood whose purpose was not so much getting rich but getting a little cash to have a good life. Don Alfonso had many strategies: a house he rented in Medellín to Diego and Diego's family, a lifetime of moving between the village and the Coffee Axis to pick coffee, a store he kept in the front room of his house, a stint as a stowaway going as far as Saudi Arabia, a forest plot where he grew fruit to sell, a home garden with plantain and lime and fruit trees and herbs, and his mine. Don Alfonso combined rural subsistence production with urban rents and migrant labor and mining. He lived through a *rebusque* in the cash economy with diverse strategies, and yet for him, producing gold at his mine was central. His mine provided a base from which to access the wider economy on his own terms.

For Don Alfonso and for Pedro and Martina, the cash produced by mining complemented a wider system of production. When Pedro and Martina and Javier went to the artisanal mine where they have been working for decades to dig under the ground using wooden pans and sluices cut into the jungle that were fed by the nightly rains, they were undertaking work that complemented their fishing, gardening, hunting. Their savings were literally in the form of gold, and it was this that complemented their subsistence activities. When the family went with picks and shovels to their mine, they did something that their ancestors had done before them, and they did work that required deep knowledge of the landscape.

Furthermore, mining had its own intrinsic rewards. The two days in March 2012 with Pedro, mere weeks before I left the field for Canada, and the bus trip to Medellín with Don Alfonso render mute the portrayals of artisanal mining as contemporary slavery. For Pedro and Don Alfonso, cash from their gold sales was integral to their livelihoods. Gold was a source of money, a way to save a little, a way for Pedro to send his son Antonio to the police academy, and a way for Don Alfonso to fund trips to the city. For these artisanal miners, actually producing gold from the ground gave a value that was the core of their economic practice, which gave them a certain agency,

Don Alfonso waits with his wholesale purchases.

despite the adversities that accompanied uncontrolled mining. It was by producing gold that Pedro and Don Alfonso were able to attempt to enter, somewhat on their own terms, into the wider cash economy that predominates in Colombia. While Pedro made fewer such endeavors than Don Alfonso, he did use cash from his mine to build a home in Quibdó, which he hoped in turn to rent for cash. In 2017, Pedro rented that house to his son Antonio. For Pedro and Don Alfonso, the still-functioning rural subsistence economy and the production of gold using artisanal techniques was what gave them each the cash to enter into the broader economy on their own terms.

If Pedro spent his time in subsistence production with mining as a complement, Don Alfonso moved, as he often had, from a rural household economy to the city—to look for work, to shop, to charge rent to his children, and then to come back to the village. For Don Alfonso, subsistence production complemented his *rebusque*. Both Pedro and Don Alfonso relied on what might be thought of as a dual household economy. To different degrees, both mixed gardening, fishing, and hunting with mining and temporary out-migration and itinerant work as a source of cash. Both employed diverse strategies. It was this diversity, along with their base of a bit of land at the bend of a river on the edge of the jungle, that gave the two a livelihood and a source of cash to access the wider economy. For both, producing metal from the ground using artisanal mining techniques was emancipatory. Far from a commodity curse, what they extracted using manual techniques supported what was for them the good life. From different directions, both Don Alfonso and Pedro adopted the successful stratagem deployed by some of the poorest and most marginalized communities in Colombia: subsistence production alongside a high-value export for cash. This shifting livelihood of gold mining and subsistence and itinerant work beat the alternative of displacement to the city permanently. Subsistence activities and producing gold in the lower reaches of a river are ways of mixing household subsistence production and artisanal mining to enter the cash economy. Actually producing gold mattered greatly to Pedro and Don Alfonso. But what happens when things become unbalanced, when a family begins to rely wholly on accumulating cash through small-scale mining?

PART II

Accumulation

Rebusque *and the Cash Economy*

CHAPTER THREE

Family Mines and Small-Scale Mining

ESTEBAN ducked to enter the tunnel one morning in April 2011. Gravel and pebbles peppered the walls, and blue-gray powder caked his skin. The tunnel produced gold for Esteban and his family, enough to buy clothes and a refrigerator and a generator and other things. Yet barely four months later, the tunnel was gone. Four large excavators had replaced the labors of Esteban and his family. Applying the term for the machine to the men who ran them, Esteban and his neighbors called the owners and operators of the excavators *retreros*. The word comes from *retro*, shortened from *retroexcavadora*, the Spanish for excavator. The *retreros* on Esteban's land were a dozen workers and two owners, brothers José and Geraldo. Both brothers were middle-aged *paisas* from the Lower Cauca mining region of Antioquia. José was a heavy-set man whose nickname was from a word meaning death, in reference to a deadly mine accident in the area. Geraldo had lighter skin and an exercise machine in the house he rented in the village. The brothers owned two excavators each, employed all the workers, and let Esteban's family, his neighbors, and people from nearby towns and villages come to pan for a few hours at a time. Esteban and his family, however, thought of themselves as co-owners because it was they who had invited the *retreros* to work their land and because it was they who received a percentage of every wash.

If Esteban and his family had cash from the sale of gold from their tunnel and access to their own gardens and other subsistence activities, why had they sought out the *retreros*? Why give up a tunnel that was producing? The family had several reasons: kinship and familial pressure over customary property rights, a profit-sharing regime that differed between the *retreros* and the Black miners, gold prices that were high and rising, the problem of accessing metal everyone was sure was under the ground, and the risks

Marco empties water and Esteban fills a wheelbarrow in the tunnel at Esteban's family mine.

inherent in digging too deep. Considering these reasons complicates two assumptions: The first is the idea that cash from mining complements household subsistence strategies and is the core of a dual household economy and the source of the good life. The second is the idea that *retreros* and Black communities had a coercive and violent relationship. In the case of Esteban and the family mine, the reasons for inviting in José and Geraldo matter both because the outcome was worse than either side expected—Esteban and his family received less than they had hoped for, and the *retreros* never recouped their costs—and because stories of coercion do not explain the rush of *retreros* into the Chocó.

José and Geraldo's excavator mine was a little further upriver from the village where the tunnel had been. It was there that both Esteban and his extended family and later the small-scale miners with their machines had attempted to get rich. For Esteban and his family, who received a small share of what the *retreros* mined, the excavators were a way to accumulate cash quickly. For the outsiders, it was a chance at a lucky strike. The scale of mining was much larger than Pedro and Don Alfonso's, however, because it involved excavators and pumps and heavy metal. The labor relations were different, too. Bringing in the outsider-owned machines was an attempt to accumulate cash by fully entering the market, rather than merely as a complement to other subsistence activities. While Esteban and his extended family had mined their family land over decades, it was when they started spending all their time at the tunnel, and later when they brought in the small-scale miners, that they inserted themselves fully into the wider cash economy. The attempt, for a time at least, unbalanced their household economy in an effort to accumulate cash. In the end, the mine was less lucrative than the family had anticipated.

What of the distance between the hope for that little cash and the reality of a mine that did not give, between the good life and the reasons to bring in excavators? If the share of gold that Esteban's family received from the *retreros* was less than the share the family had thought they would gain, why bother to invite José and Geraldo and the *retreros* in? The question is compelling, because the *retreros* practiced a form of mining that reshaped landscapes, removed thin soils, cut down forests, and filled the river with sediment.

Bringing in the *retreros* was no mere miscalculation on the part of Esteban and his family, however. Across the Chocó, thousands of hectares of rain forest have been given over to the barren gravelscapes left by the excavators. Black miners gave up their land all the time—the end of the land was literal. The earth was removed, flushed over a miner's sluice, and washed down a stream into the river.[1] In some cases, *retreros* mined land from under people's homes, and even erased villages from the landscape. The process was one some people joined eagerly. Thus, when Esteban's family converted their customary right to an artisanal mine into a share of a *retrero* mine, the story was not one that Marx might have called primitive accumulation. In Marx's rendering, the expropriation process was violent. In the case of Esteban's family mine, the process was not violent but voluntary.

In November 2010, a Catholic priest explained to me his theory of the invitations over coffee in a small town not too far from Quibdó. The priest, a *paisa* who had spent decades working with Black communities, outlined why he thought people were inviting in the *retreros* despite the obvious negative consequences. He described what happened. The *retreros* came, set up mining camps, cleared trees, altered the flow of rivers, employed migrants, and added mercury to their sluices to trap the gold. The *retreros* vaporized the mercury with blowtorches to separate out the gold. It was this that created a toxic mercury gas that settled into people's hair and clothes and homes, where the poisonous heavy metal had the worst health impacts.

"The Black miners rent their territory to exploit it, either by mining or logging," the priest said. "As the saying goes, 'Del ahogado, el sombrero.' [From the drowning man, his hat.] Black miners say, 'Before I die, if they are going to take all of this, I will rent my territory so that *retreros* can work it, and I can get a little bit before I die, because the legal businesses are going to come finish off everything. Although *retreros* exploit me, they will give me a little. If you fall into the water while wearing a hat and you are drowning, then we will exert ourselves to save you, even if all we can save is just your hat. That is how the people are.'" While the common Colombian expression the priest used means taking something from someone in a life-and-death situation, I read the priest as making a subtle point: Black miners saw a future threatened by the inevitable expropriation of outsiders, and for them, the *retreros* were a chance to get something before it was too late. To complete the metaphor, if a Black miner were drowning, the *retreros* would give the miner a chance to at least save a hat for himself. From this perspective, the *retreros* were the best of a bad situation. Still, the priest thought the Black miners would face violence if they opposed the *retreros* on their land, as armed actors would pressure people to let in the *retreros*.

Landowning families like Esteban's brought in small-scale miners in the hope of accumulating cash. This chapter addresses the artisanal miners turned co-owners, while the next considers the *retreros*—owners and workers alike. For some Black families like Esteban's, small-scale mining was *rebusque*. It was a get-rich-quick scheme attractive to the rural family, and to an extent, it demonstrated their agency in attempting to navigate the boom in mining. Both that Constitutional Court decision over the rights of the Atrato River and much media attention to the small-scale mining industry demonized small-scale miners, while portraying artisanal miners as victims. Examining the decisions of artisanal miners like Esteban and his family shows things to be much more complicated. He and his family embraced the large machines, as this offered the possibility of getting ahead and accumulating a little. Yet, although the optimism was contagious, as people hoped to make a lot of money, the result was frustrating. Small-scale mining proved to be a precarious and marginally profitable activity. Yet it is only by understanding why Esteban and his family saw the *retreros* as positive that the decision to bring in the excavators can be seen as a chance to get something before it was too late. For Esteban's family, the machines were a logical choice.

KINSHIP AND PROPERTY RIGHTS

That April morning when Esteban went into the tunnel, he wore rubber boots, khaki pants, an orange T-shirt, a wide-brimmed straw hat, and no helmet. Mud spattered the watch on his left wrist. Water made small echoes as it dripped onto the bedrock floor and flowed beside a black hose to a depression at the tunnel entrance where Esteban's elder son Marco worked to empty it using a five-gallon plastic fuel jug cut in half. Esteban followed the tunnel to the left. A pair of candles cast a circle of light, and Esteban's eyes adjusted to the shapes of other workers.

All were members of his extended family. Ernesto, Esteban's seventeen-year-old nephew, filled an old wheelbarrow with a mixture of material taken from the bedrock floor and pushed it out of the tunnel to a pool not far from the entrance, where he would pan. With Ernesto outside, Esteban began to fill another wheelbarrow. When that wheelbarrow was full, Marco came to push the wheelbarrow out. Marco joined Ernesto by the pool where Sofía, Esteban's mother (and Ernesto's and Marco's grandmother) helped work the wooden pans. Esteban's uncle used a pick and a scraper and his hands to fill pans with material from the walls. Esteban's brother worked past the last of the candlelight, where the temperature seemed to rise from an underground source. His work was hard to follow. He crouched and dug at the wall and loosened stones by raising a metal bar high and smashing its tip into the tunnel wall; he then scraped the loosened material into a pan. Then he would stop and take someone else's job: bailing water, filling the wheelbarrow, pushing the load out, or panning. Each family member took a short shift at each task, except for Sofía, who just worked the pan with a dexterity learned over a lifetime. To answer my question, "How long have you mined gold here?" Sofía replied, "I have worked the mine for forty years. I raised my kids here. Now, I collaborate with my grandsons."

Evidence of the age of the mine was all around: walls stacked with stones, a long trench carved into the bedrock, and a channel cut through solid rock. The tunnel was newer, however. Sofía and her grandson Ernesto had begun the tunnel only months before. Ernesto had been in a Quibdó high school but dropped out to come back to the village and work below the hill using wooden pans and scrapers. The old woman and her grandson had begun the tunnel when they hit a vein, which brought in Sofía's children, her brother, and everyone's families. As the tunnel got deeper, Esteban, his brother, and his uncle began to negotiate with the *retreros*.

Esteban and his brother had tried to bring different *retreros* onto their family land in 2008, just as many of their neighbors up and down the river had done. Those *retreros* had dug a large reservoir and stayed for a few weeks but then left because they found too little. While Esteban and his family used the reservoir to provide water for their mine, they still saw the excavators as a way to remove the entire hillside down to the tunnel and work the bedrock to extract the metal. So they tried again with José and Geraldo. The two *retreros* brought their machines and workers from a village downriver—Leidy's village—where they had worked for three years. At that mine, the four excavators had transformed a dozen football fields of jungle into a vast expanse of holes, gravel, sand, and water. From the air, that mine must have looked like a brown scar on a green landscape.

Four months later, Esteban, Marco, Ernesto, Sofía, and their extended family used picks, shovels, and shallow wooden bowls at the same location where the tunnel had been. With the tunnel gone, the family was excited. The four excavators had removed the hillside down to the bedrock where the tunnel had been. It took the machines a week. It would have taken the family a lifetime. The excavators used the same principle as Esteban: dig down to the bedrock and wash. The scale of their operation was vastly different, however. Esteban and his family used a combination of water, gravity, picks, shovels, and a small water pump to separate the earth that they would then sift using wooden pans and centrifugal force. The four excavators were accompanied by two powerful water pumps made from old truck motors, seven metal sluices, a two-story metal contraption called a classifier, hundreds of yards of aluminum pipes, and liberal dollops of the toxic heavy metal mercury. One excavator could move in a week what one artisanal miner working with hand tools might in a lifetime. The scale of deforestation, erosion, sedimentation, and mercury contamination was incommensurably larger from the excavators than from the tunnel of Esteban's family.

Esteban's neighbor Pedro, who mixed artisanal mining with subsistence production, thought it a bad idea to bring in the *retreros*. One might assume he was opposed purely for environmental reasons. For example, the holes left over from the excavators in the mercury-contaminated landscape were filled with water and populated by *paludismo*-bearing mosquitoes. Evidence of excavator mines could be seen along the entire river: wide-open gravel spaces where once had been forest. Miners who use hand tools leave little permanent ecological change. Pedro, nevertheless, thought that bringing in excavators to work a productive mine was a bad idea for a simpler economic reason: Why not keep profits for yourself? Why give a mine over to the *retreros* and let them take the bulk of the profits? Pedro once also brought in *retreros* to mine a piece of land that was his, because the plot was no good to him for either gardening or mining and he thought he would try his luck with the machines. Despite any doubts they may have had, Pedro and Don Alfonso and all their neighbors saw the decision as a matter between Esteban and his family and the *retreros*.

A kinship-based customary property regime explained both the shared belief that the decision to bring in *retreros* was up to Esteban's family and the reasons why Esteban's family made the decisions they did in the first place. Most recent scholarship on the Colombian Pacific has focused on the collective territory of the *comunidades negras*, or Black communities. These communities were created by constitutional reforms in 1991 and Law 70 in 1993, which granted Black communities culturally based collective territorial rights.[2] Through the 1990s and 2000s, the Colombian state began to recognize Black communities with inalienable legal ownership to what were called their collective territories. Dozens of communities across the Pacific region came together to claim land rights. Although the state granted collective land title and surface rights to these *comunidades negras*, the state kept subsurface mineral rights to itself. While Black communities claimed collective territorial rights to hundreds of thousands of hectares, they had no mineral rights.

Rural activists—in some areas connected with the Catholic Church or with nongovernmental organizations—mobilized into communities and won legal titles to the territories where rural people had long combined subsistence production and mining. Across the Chocó and the wider Pacific lowlands, such organized Black communities claimed a form of collective ownership known as a *título colectivo*, or a collective land title. Although Esteban, Pedro, Don Alfonso, and all their neighbors were Black and rural and lived in the collective territory of one such organized Black community, they all understood and practiced property ownership in a different way than the collective title created by the 1991 constitution.

Indeed, a tension existed between what was a legally recognized collective title and the practical customary lot ownership based on kinship. Esteban and his family practiced the latter, within a territory legally recognized as the former. Extended families owned gardens (sugarcane, corn, fruit trees, and perennials) and mines. These lots were discontinuous and distant from each other, perhaps to reduce the risk of crop failure due to diseases or floods, or as a reflection of the history of family labor opening mines and planting gardens. A family's lots might include a stand of fruit trees on one bend of the river, an island with avocados, a slash-and-mulch swidden field for corn, a slope planted in pineapple, a flat area for sugarcane a mile or so away, and a family mine demarcated from a neighbor's by a stream. A family could trace its claim to a lot based on the ancestor (the father, mother, grandfather, or grandmother) who first cleared the bush, planted trees, or opened the mine. This labor-based property regime created an intricate, if invisible, grid of ownership that mapped human relationships with trees, gardens, and mines onto the landscape. This invisible grid of customary property rights was not reflected by state surveys, which had legally extended collective title to the figure of the *consejo comunitario* (community council), rather than to the extended family.[3]

Nevertheless, the collective titles were hard-won by rural activists and served as a hedge against displacement from over fifty years of internal conflict and land speculation fueled by the illicit business of cocaine trafficking. Yet, in practice, the everyday life of the rural households I knew best revolved around family-based customary ownership of lots consisting of mines and gardens, rather than collectively held title to a larger territory. This ownership of a lot did not extend to a spouse through marriage, but did to male and female children. Lots existed by customary practice, as everyone recognized each extended family's claims. Of course, people might disagree over who owned what or over how large a lot was, as customary lot ownership had no maps or deeds, and people demarcated their lots using local knowledge of geography and soil conditions and kinship relations over time. A ridge or a stand of fruit trees might mark a lot boundary, or a stream could divide two lots. One leader of a legal Black community I knew, which represented dozens of communities, told me he hoped to conduct a survey of these informal boundaries of lot ownership using GIS software, in other words, an internal cadastral survey.

The existing customary land tenure system was widespread among the families living on the river, although many families had moved to the city over the last two decades. Half of Esteban's village had left by 2011. Some families escaped flooding, others fled violence from the state or guerrillas or paramilitary forces, and others left to find work. People went to nearby towns or to the Andean cities of Cali, Medellín, Pereira, and Bogotá. These families, despite their absence, still maintained a claim to their lots. Some returned to plant crops or pick fruit or mine, and some never came back. Still, those who remained in the village respected the land of the absent families. Esteban said, for example, "It is not my family's" to explain why he stayed off a neighbor's lot, even though its owners had long since moved to the city.

The *retreros* created a tension between the community councils, with their legal title, and families who lived on the land. Black community councils, which represented dozens of villages and held legally recognized collective titles to tens of thousands of hectares, might vociferously oppose the *retreros*, yet village and family politics complicated the formal opposition. A collective title might provide legal protection from outsiders interested in logging or mining, but the dynamics between different households in an extended family group were the most salient to a decision of whether to bring in *retreros*. Esteban and his brothers decided to bring in the *retreros*, just as a family who no longer lived in the area came back from the city with an excavator to work their land. It was the lot owners, rather than the legally titled Black communities, who negotiated with the *retreros*. The state recognized community councils as controlling land, yet the decisions about particular lots were made—informally—by the extended families who had customary rights to particular places. Absent family members who lived in the city might want to participate in the decision, because, unlike Esteban's, Pedro's, and others' families, who only shared the gold among a mine work group itself, the *retreros* shared the metal with the members of the extended family who owned the lot. The key difference: profit with or without labor.

PROFIT AND LABOR

"What will you do when José and Geraldo come?" I asked.

"Nothing!" Marco, who was almost eighteen, said with a grin.

The exuberance with which he answered the question demonstrated the contrast between labor-based profit sharing and lot-based revenue sharing. In the former, Marco would have to work hard underground, bailing water. In the latter, he would receive a share from the mine and had to do nothing. Money for no work.

In late 2010, Esteban and his wife and their two sons worked together in a small group at the top of the hill far above where Ernesto and Sofía were still panning. Esteban's family worked at the top of the hill, where there was no obvious rich gravel to exploit. The family used a water pump to wash gravel from the hillside over a sluice. The water pump as a technique was a marginal venture, because costs were high and the profits were barely worthwhile. For this reason, Esteban put off my early overtures to help. He did not want to pay me for my dubious labor contribution. I offered many times to come work the next morning with him, instead of working at Pedro's mine, where I spent most of my time. But Esteban only agreed to my offer when he realized that Pedro did not pay me and that I did not want a share of anyone's mine. Profits were divided based on labor: Esteban worked with his immediate family and shared the gold with them. He wanted to limit the number of workers, and therefore limit who could claim a share. He would have felt obliged to share the gold with me, and so he refused my help. When Sofía and her grandson Ernesto worked far below Esteban's family at the bottom of the cliff, using just pans and shovels, they only shared the profits among themselves. When the four households came together to mine the tunnel, the venture worked out because the tunnel gave plenty.

Retreros neatly redefined this labor-based profit-sharing arrangement because they paid the co-owners (the extended families that claimed customary ownership of a lot) between 10 percent and 16 percent of the gold mined before operating expenses, which included wages, diesel, repairs, taxes, and extortion monies to the armed groups. All family members who had a share of ownership of a lot could claim a percentage of what the *retreros* paid. It was this share of profits based on lot ownership and not labor contribution that had Marco so excited. The same principle applied to absent family members who lived in the city, which explains why some pressured their family to bring in *retreros*. The absent family wanted to receive a share of the profits from the *retreros*, because they would get nothing from the tunnel.

People who moved to the city to escape rural violence or find employment as domestic workers, security guards, or construction workers rarely came back to do mine work. While a family in the city did not make a living mining, they often brought *retreros* onto the family lots for a few months. When the mine was exhausted and the land was flushed over a sluice, the family would go back to the city and not have to deal with the environmental and health consequences from the mercury, the malaria, the depletion of fish stocks, the disruption of gardening, or the exhaustion of the deposit. The claims from an extended family in the city to the profits from an excavator mine would dilute the potential share of each individual miner, because dividing the 10 percent paid by the *retreros* between a hundred family members would result in a small amount per person. Don Alfonso, for example, complained about the time when his brothers, who no longer lived in the village, had brought in the *retreros* for a few weeks. He only got a few *castellanos*. He could have made that by himself, working alone, for a few weeks.

Although *retreros* paid the family members a share of the profits, it is difficult for me to describe how the division of gold took place. Since miners were sometimes wary of letting me watch them, I felt reticent about asking too much about the mechanics of profit sharing. José once used a metal spoon to scoop out roughly what he said was the share of a week's wash for Esteban's family. To me, the calculation seemed unfair and imprecise, even if their actual agreement was a specific percentage. Yet months later, when

I asked Esteban directly about the incident, he said the spoon was not how their share had been calculated. When Esteban divided his family share of work in the tunnel, he carefully weighed the grams of metal on the small scale he kept in his house. He was just as meticulous when he weighed gold that he had bought from a neighbor.

The division of gold brought tensions, of course. Family members with a claim had to be physically present in the village. This meant that many long-term city residents might come back to the village for a few months when the excavators came. The family members wanted to ensure that they got their "percentage" of the profits, suspecting they would get nothing if they were not physically there. Pedro, too, became suspicious. He normally only mined in the morning, but with so many people around, he spent extra-long days at the end of the wash cycle to extract the gold from his mine. He did not want anyone else to take his metal from the mine at night. Esteban's family, for their part, distrusted their neighbors and the *retreros*. Before the *retreros* arrived, Esteban flooded the tunnel every night to prevent someone from panning for gold in the darkness. After the *retreros* arrived, Esteban and his brother built two separate huts so they could watch the mine at night and make sure nobody else was working it.

The *retreros* were supposed to pay money to the community council for permission to cross the collective territory. The council had hoped to negotiate better conditions of entry: the machinery could only enter the mine far away from the village; the animals could stay anywhere but in the community; the mine workers could stay in rented houses in the village; and the council would receive permission money of 2 percent from each wash instead of 300,000 pesos ($160) a month. As the village's council discussed the matter, it soon became clear the challenge would be to have someone physically present at each wash to claim the percentage for the community. The foreman could call a wash at any time, and it would be impractical for someone to drop what they were doing and get up to the mine. The council compromised: Esteban would claim the village's share because he would be at each wash anyway.

The *retreros* also let Esteban's family and neighbors and people from nearby communities come and pan at the mine front for short periods every few days. This panning, or *bareque*, as everyone called it, was hotly anticipated. People came from nearby towns and villages to work the rich gravel above the bedrock opened by excavators. This gave the *retreros* a legitimacy with locals, who, as *barequeros*, could make a small income. In a symbiotic twist, the *retreros* actually learned where the gold they sought to mine was physically located based on where the *barequeros* congregated the most.

Esteban's family brought in *retreros* for a share of the profits without labor, while the community council and his neighbors hoped to benefit from their share of the profits and the *bareque*. Nevertheless, Esteban and his family also had another reason. The heavy machinery let the family access the metal they thought was under the ground while prices were high.

SAVINGS IN GOLD

Months after the *retreros* arrived, gold prices broke records, reaching an all-time high of $1,921 a troy ounce on September 6, 2011.[4] The price was reported on the seven o'clock television news each night and became a regular topic of conversation. Esteban and his neighbors spent more and more time at their mines. Gold sales were one of the few ways to make money, and everyone who could sold gold. People went to nearby towns on Sunday mornings to sell to shopkeepers who displayed scales in their storefronts; the old, the infirm, single mothers, and others who could not afford the cost of travel to town traded with their neighbors. The most successful miners also bought from their neighbors and traveled to the regional cities of Istmina and Quibdó to sell at dedicated *compraventa* buying-and-selling shops. These buyers would sell to Medellín-based refineries. Most *retreros* sold in Istmina, or directly in Medellín. At each step, as the metal moved up a chain of buyers on its way to international markets, the intermediaries took their cut.

Esteban and his neighbors thought of gold as a form of *ahorros*, or savings. Esteban kept dust folded in paper envelopes and hidden in safe places. His savings consisted of these *oritos* and, most importantly, the metal still underground in the mine. When Esteban needed money, he accessed his savings by mining and then selling his gold. He could grow his savings by leaving the gold in the ground as metal prices rose.

"Money comes easily and goes easily," a late-middle-aged neighbor of Esteban told me. "People should melt gold dust from the mine and save the metal in solid form to prevent it from evaporating and disappearing. People spend money quickly. If they did not, it would just disappear. If people try to store cash as paper money, it will just evaporate. Stored in its metal form, gold will grow. If you want to store cash, you have to store it in a hot place, in an oven. If you do not, then when you go to open the box in which you stored the cash, the bills will have wilted and disappeared. If you wait long enough, all the bills will have evaporated. People should store gold as a metal because it will not disappear. Gold grows. It keeps longer."

By 2011, Esteban seemed to be working hard to withdraw his savings. Esteban and his family wanted to access their savings still in the ground while prices were high. The fastest way they could do that was with the *retreros*. A miner might take decades to finish a mine; an excavator could do it in months. I think that Esteban, like many artisanal miners across the Chocó, wanted to take advantage of the soaring prices and turn his savings into cash, because he suspected the boom would soon turn to a bust, just as it had for other export-oriented resource economies in the past. The forests of the Colombian Pacific have long provided high-value commodity exports for global markets; miners have worked the gold-bearing alluvial gravel for centuries as prices rose and fell. Before World War II, people combined mining with gathering tagua, a hard seed nicknamed "vegetable ivory" destined for the export market. In 2012, a handful of stores in Quibdó sold handicrafts made from tagua as part of development projects funded by foreign agencies.[5] In the 1980s and 1990s, itinerant loggers removed tropical hardwoods.[6] And the Chocó has now emerged as an area for growing coca and smuggling cocaine. Each of these commodities brought a temporary export boom until the raw materials dried up, or demand withered, or the market collapsed, or the state started criminalizing the producers. Esteban's family, like the absent families in the city, saw the *retreros* as a way to quickly withdraw their savings from the mine and take advantage of the high prices in 2011. They saw the outsiders as a way to accumulate cash quickly. The machines were also a way to access what the miners could not access any other way.

ACCESS TO GOLD

Early in 2011, Esteban and his immediate family used a motorized water pump to work the top of the hill above where the tunnel would be. They did this because Esteban could not dig a reservoir higher up. The only way he could mine was with a pump connected to a thick, black rubber tube, which drew water from a large rain-fed reservoir the size of an Olympic swimming pool at the base of the hill. This basic technique was common up and down the river. The pump provided a powerful jet of water, which let Esteban wash gravel and sand over a sluice. The machine, of course, was more expensive than rainwater, considering the cost of gasoline and repairs. However, Esteban's family could not have worked any other way. Quite simply, the water pump made it possible to mine the hillside high above the actual level of the water.

New techniques often created an opportunity to mine gold that was hard to get at. For example, one was free diving to mine the river bottom. Ximena, who is from a village almost half a day away (and who features in chapter 6) explained the procedure. When she was a young woman, she carried stones on her back and dove under water. The added weight let her reach the river bottom, where she gathered mud in a pan before she ran out of breath and surfaced to wash the material on shore. Some women never resurfaced; they drowned underwater trying to get the rich mud. Ximena used an old word—*zambullir*—to describe this diving technique.[7] The technique was old, and women divers have given way to men with air compressors. The machines let men dive down to access mud deep below the riverbed.

Not far from Ximena's village, a burly, muscled man walked the short distance from his home to a clear, running stream one morning in 2011. The man was a diver and carried diving gear: a peeling gray wetsuit, a belt, a black diver's mask, a thin breathing tube, and a chewed-up mouthpiece. He stopped at his minidredge, a contraption made of a metal platform about six feet square attached to four large, orange, floating fiberglass pontoons. Like Esteban's water pump at the top of the hill, the minidredge allowed these divers to access what was too deep to reach with hand tools. In the area, there were dozens of similar dredges on streams and rivers. Each had a water pump, a long sluice box, and a small gray air compressor. The compressor forced air into a pressurized diving tank connected to a diver working under water. Two people operated the dredge: one underwater and the other on top to control the motor and air compressor. In the morning, one man crouched in the cool water and used a thick tube to vacuum the riverbed. After lunch, the burly man took a turn in the hole. What had been ankle deep had now become deeper than the man was tall. His feet floated on the surface, where bubbles popped as he worked in the underwater pit.

There are many techniques to access inaccessible metal. If Esteban and his wife and sons had persisted in using the water pump to wash away the hill, it might have taken them decades to reach the tunnel and the bedrock. The tunnel was one way to access gold, and the excavators, in a sense, were merely another technique to open a mine down to the bedrock and access the metal that everyone knew was there.

"Black miners say, 'The gold is finished. We have to go deeper,'" the same Catholic priest who had told me about the drowning man and his hat said to me. "The excavator can reach where the artisanal miner never can. For this reason, the miner opens the door to the excavators. The miner says, 'The excavators can get to where we cannot with our own methods. We cannot die while there is gold there.' This is why the excavators have had such a resonance here. 'If the *retreros* get it all out now, then we don't have to ask what have the *retreros* left us. They got everything out. They left us poor.' If the *retreros* come back, the miners would fall again, because the artisanal miners feel they have to get the gold out." (By "fall," the priest meant fall into the trap of the *retreros*.)

The logic was simple. The *retreros* let Esteban and other miners access their metals. While some miners used low-tech methods, such as shovels, scrapers, pans, metal spikes, and sluices carved into the forest, methods that have not changed much since the Spanish colonial period,[8] the excavators offered a more efficient technique to access what people knew was there. The method used by the *retreros* was also safer than tunneling underground or diving under the water.

DANGER AND SHIFTING RISK

Esteban worried about landslides, falling stones, and the tunnel caving in. The family worried that the deeper the tunnel, the greater the danger. By negotiating with José and Geraldo, Esteban's family wanted to shift the danger of digging the tunnel onto the *retreros*.

People told stories of dangerous mines all the time, especially while drinking. Esteban ran a bar in the village. The bar was a wooden-framed building with large black speakers for music and a roof of palm leaves and plastic tarp. Esteban had bought the speakers with his share of the *retrero* gold. Esteban also bought an outboard motor for his boat, a freezer, and a television. Esteban sold beer and liquor on credit to the workers employed by José and Geraldo. The workers paid their drinking debts to Esteban when José and Geraldo paid them their wages. By Christmas 2011, the workers had not been paid for months.

One evening in Esteban's bar, his late-middle-aged neighbor from the village was sipping beer, playing dominos, and speaking about the tunnels of his youth. He explained that when he was a younger man, he had mined deep underground in a tunnel like the one Esteban and his family had been digging. The technique was digging a *gauche*, or tunnel. The man told a story about how he had once accidentally extended his tunnel into an existing one, which must have been left by his "ancestors." That older tunnel had gone under the river, and it had long since flooded. When the man breached the wall of the earlier tunnel, water flooded into his newer tunnel. He almost drowned but managed to escape by crawling quickly backward to the surface. Such accidents were common. Miners were buried alive or crushed by a gravel embankment that gave way and trapped everyone below. I heard many stories of tunnels caving in and trapping entire families.

While we sat on a porch in the village drinking beer, Luis, a middle-aged friend of Esteban from the next village up river, told me a similarly disturbing story about working underwater with a minidredge, since our conversation had turned to diving underwater when two miners passed by carrying a homemade minidredge made from a battered oil drum. Luis and his business partner had co-owned a dredge. The two worked in the river, and one afternoon the partner took an extra shift underwater, two in a row. The man had said he needed the extra money to send his son to school in Quibdó. Luis let his partner take the second turn underwater. The two were using a suction tube and diving gear, and as they got deeper into the riverbed, the partner began to branch out horizontally underneath the river. Things worked well, until a fallen tree floated over the diver, snagged its branches on the hole, trapped the partner underwater, and snapped his fragile breathing tube. The partner, still underwater, drowned in seconds.

"If my partner had not taken the extra shift," Luis said, "it would have been him talking to you, not me. You should never take someone else's spot in the mine. I should have died underwater. Terrible accidents happen when someone gets greedy. I have never been diving since."

"People behave strangely for gold, especially young people," added Pedro, who had been listening to us talk. "Gold and hard liquor have the same result. People lose their restraints. Sometimes, when many minidredges mine the same spot, it gets dangerous. If a dredge is doing well, one miner might murder another; they can kill someone quickly. They can put poison in an air tube; they can even cut it. People might call it an accident, because how would anyone know? Mining is a dangerous business."

The stories of mine accidents help explain the fear Esteban and his family had of an accident while mining in the tunnel. They had long since lost their inhibitions about working deep below the ground, and they worried it would soon be their turn. Were they taking dangerous risks? Were they mining too hard and tunneling too deep? Esteban's family invited the *retreros* onto their land because it shifted the risk onto the outsiders. Working deep underground, in a poorly ventilated and pitch-black tunnel lit with only a few candles, they saw the excavators, quite reasonably, as a safer alternative.

FROM THE DUAL HOUSEHOLD TO THE CASH ECONOMY

The invitation Esteban's family extended to the *retreros* proved far less lucrative than they had hoped. José and Geraldo, the owners, complained about paying everyone: the percentage to Esteban's family as co-owners, the 2 percent fee to the village's local Black community council for the its permission to let the machines pass through its territory, the extortion money to the various paramilitary and guerrilla groups in the area, the bribes to the police and soldiers to be left alone, the royalties to the municipality so they could sell the gold legally, and the wages to their own workers. Their operating costs—food and repairs and machinery and diesel—were high. Geraldo also lamented his high-interest *gota-a-gota* debts to moneylenders. The mine where the tunnel had been ultimately produced much less than Geraldo and José needed to cover their mounting costs. The tennis-ball-sized hunks of gold mixed with mercury offered tantalizing hopes, yet no profit. By September 2013, the *retreros* had unceremoniously fled. José and Geraldo and the workers had packed up without warning one night, leaving behind four excavators to rust in the forest because they owed money to the guerrillas. They had never paid the 2 percent to the community council. The brothers still owed Esteban's family some money. Some of the *retrero* workers even owed Esteban money for drinks. The mine where Sofía had worked for forty years had been exhausted, and there had been less under the ground than everyone had hoped.

Two years later, in September 2013, when I asked Esteban what he thought about having invited José and Geraldo to come to mine his family lot, he scowled and refused to answer my question. The excitement he had shown before the *retreros* had come was long gone by the time they had left. Still, although the relationships between Esteban and his family, the community, and the *retreros* were fraught, they were far more complex than simple coercion. Esteban's family had seen the *retreros* as an opportunity to withdraw their savings and accumulate cash. For the family, it was the particularities of how they mined that helped explain why the family saw the *retreros* as an opportunity. Although the techniques Black miners used varied (Pedro dug pits and used a sluice, Don Alfonso used a reservoir, Esteban and his family used a water pump and tunneled under the ground, their neighbors used a minidredge, Ximena worked underwater with a stone, and divers used masks and an air compressor) and although people used different words (*barequiar*, to pan as a group; *catear*, to prospect; *lavar*, to wash; *guachear*, to tunnel; *bucear*, to dive; and *bombear*, to use a water pump), for some artisanal miners, the *retreros* were just one more way to mine.

Taking seriously the reasons that Esteban and his family brought in the excavators—kinship, profits, savings, access, and danger—shows how and why the family came to embrace a different scale of operation. Small-scale mines were not merely a get-rich-quick-scheme but a strategy that made sense to artisanal miners with a productive but hard-to-access mine. Although the excavators were comparatively massive and operated at a scale different than that of an artisanal miner, they fit within the logic of an artisanal miner. It would be easy to demonize the small-scale mining industry—and indeed the exploitation that occurred around the Chocó from the mid-2000s certainly warrants some demonization—yet Esteban and his family saw opportunities and possibilities in those same excavators. It would be simplistic to see Esteban and his family as mere dupes, because it was within their system of mining, land tenure, and labor that the family saw in the *retreros* an opportunity.

As for Pedro and Don Alfonso, for Esteban and his family, mining was merely one of many ways to make a living. Yet the family began to rely increasingly on the profits from their tunnel and spend less time gardening and raising animals. It was not the outsiders that forced Esteban and his family to specialize in activities to earn cash, but the tunnel and the *retreros* accelerated this specialization. The extended family came to rely first on their tunnel for accumulating cash and later on the *retreros* and a share of each wash. It was as they became co-owners of the small-scale mining operation that Esteban and his family inserted themselves into a cash economy, which unbalanced the other activities of what had been a dual household economy. By becoming—and seeing themselves as—co-owners with the *retreros*, the family began to focus on accumulating as much as they could

Panning in an excavator mine pit

from the mine, rather than seeing it as a complement to subsistence activities or as their savings. From the perspective of Esteban and his family, the expansion of the small-scale mining frontier and the move from a dual household economy at first seemed like a positive step.

Engaging in mining to make cash was the plan, and yet the family's transition into the cash economy was unsuccessful. The mine failed to produce enough gold. By 2013, with the excavator miners having left, Esteban and his family had returned to gardening and raising pigs. They opened a new mine in another area. His son Marco, for his part, moved away, first to do military service and later seek employment in Quibdó as a security guard. Although Esteban may have been attempting a move away from a rural subsistence economy in a strategy not so different from Don Alfonso, ultimately he had to fall back on the river and the land and the forest. All of this is to suggest that Esteban and his family had some agency on the resource frontier. They bet their family mine, because it made the most sense as a way to accumulate cash, and they lost. If this was how Esteban and his family experienced the *retreros* who came onto their land, how did José and Geraldo and their workers experience their time at the mine?

CHAPTER FOUR

Rebusque on the Precarious Periphery

"Fast money," the dirt-bike driver called back at me over his shoulder as we wove through the traffic. Stick out an arm at any intersection in the bustling capital of Quibdó and someone will stop to give you a ride. The two-wheeled unregulated taxi service is the fastest mode of transport. Dirt-bike-taxi drivers, mostly young Black men from the Chocó but also a surprising number of young men from other parts of Colombia, have created an anarchic rapid transit system that takes passengers throughout the city for the price of a cup of coffee—if there's fuel. If there is no fuel, because a guerrilla checkpoint or a landslide has blocked the two roads into the Chocó, the price of a dirt-bike-taxi ride increases fivefold. Without fuel, the informal transit system grinds to a halt, the lights go out in communities that rely on generators for electricity, and the powerful excavators shudder to stop in the *retrero* mines.

"How do you make any money?" I had asked the dirt-bike-taxi driver.

"I came here from the Caribbean," he replied. "I took a loan and bought a dirt bike. With luck, I'll give two dozen rides a day. I'll pay the daily quota on the loan, I'll buy fuel, and I'll have some pesos. It's easy here because of the fast money."

"Fast money" refers to the velocity at which money circulates in a boom economy and the dream of getting rich quickly and accumulating a little cash. The dream of fast money, which brought the migrant dirt-bike-taxi driver to Quibdó, is not that different from the dream of the *retreros* who came to work in José and Geraldo's mine on Esteban's family land. Others came for their share of fast money by hawking cheap imports on the street, selling knockoff designer clothes, laboring in construction, cutting tropical hardwoods, picking coca, or working on any one of the other hundred or so excavator mines. While some people, like Don Alfonso, left the Chocó for

Carlos stands atop a classifier.

rebusque, many came to the Chocó on their own *rebusque*, working in mines like the one José and Geraldo operated on Esteban's family land.

The work in an excavator mine transforms the landscape. Miners remove the forest, carve down under the earth, and pour the subsoil over a sluice. A *retrero* mine might employ half a dozen to a dozen or more men and women. What were the motivations of the sprayer, the driver, the assistant, the muleteer, the foreman, the cook, and the cleaning lady employed by José and Geraldo? What was their work? These workers cleaned clothes, fed everyone, directed the operation, carried fuel, did odd jobs, handled the excavators, and washed. José and Geraldo paid his workers a regular wage, while the workers themselves claimed a share of the gold each time the mine did a wash. The workers came for the fixed salary and the possibility of making it big from their share of the profits. There never was the big lucky strike that José, Geraldo, their workers, and Esteban's family had hoped for, however. Instead, José and Geraldo and the workers found just a little on Esteban's family land. By Christmas 2011, the two brothers owed their employees months of back wages. Still, why did each *retrero*—owner and worker alike—come to the mine and choose to stay when there was so little gold? One answer is that a mine offers a peculiar hope. A Catholic priest, the same one who put to me the story of the drowning man and a hat while sitting in a church in a small town, explained it to me thus: "Miners have hope; they always have hope. If I go to the mine for an hour, I might come back rich. I might work a little and find a lot. It could happen at any moment." An excavator mine is a little like a lottery ticket: there's always next time.

When José and Geraldo and the workers came onto Esteban's land, they each did so for their own reasons. The motivations were many for the *retreros* at the one end of an informal, unauthorized, illegal mining industry where the mine was their *rebusque*—a creative strategy and an attempt to make a little cash. Yet, as small-scale mines were by and large illegal, some miners formed cooperatives of mostly excavator owners to attempt to resist multinational corporations and the Colombian state's attempt to criminalize their way of life. The cooperative claimed to represent *retreros* who wanted to stay on the land despite a mining code that criminalized mine work, multinationals that claimed the land, and a military that impounded and dynamited their machinery. While the Colombian government described *retreros* as the financiers of the armed conflict, *retreros* themselves contested this portrayal. They attempted to legitimize their status through internal regulations, profit-sharing agreements with Black community councils, and other strategies reminiscent of social movements. These *retrero* organizations resisted the label of "illegal," preferring "informal." For these informal miners, the expansion of a small-scale mine, like the one José and Geraldo and their laborers worked, offered a chance at quick cash. For them, gold was one of various get-rich-quick schemes that were attractive to the workers, who often came from urban shantytowns. People embraced what was, at best, a precarious and informal labor alongside large machines because it was better than the alternatives.

REBUSQUE

One could survey the world of work in Colombia from opposite vantage points. From above, mines and plantations and industrial enterprises dot the landscape.[1] From below, a dense web of street sellers and day laborers and ordinary people dependent on a shifting livelihood of *rebusque* expands across the country. *Rebusque* offers a way to think about the ways people eke out a living, through even the most unstable, temporary, informal, and illegal strategies. But *rebusque* often implies its opposite: permanent formal employment in a factory or a foreign-owned mine. In mid-twentieth-century Colombia, young men and women could find stable work in the booming textile industry in Medellín. Company unions and paternalistic employers created a rising standard of living.

The factory jobs did not last, however. The textile industry, once the pride of Medellín, imploded because Colombian companies could not compete with foreign textile manufacturers, and the companies that survived automated their equipment and fired their workers.[2] In parallel, foreign-owned mines operated in the Chocó, the Lower Cauca, and Nariño. For example, the Pato Consolidated Mining Company, Canadian owned for a long time, worked on the Nechí River, which flows into the Lower Cauca River. The Chocó Pacífico Mining Company worked in the San Juan region and built a company town; in Andagoya, it employed hundreds of people in a segregated workforce. North Americans and foreign employees had their tennis courts and screened-in porches on one side of the river; on the other was the Black town, where men could find union jobs with good pay and later pensions from the mining dredges. In the 1970s, gold production declined, and the company struggled. In response, the Colombian government gave the formerly US-owned Chocó Pacífico to its workers in 1978. The company soon went bankrupt, and many opportunities for formal employment evaporated.[3] If the 1980s brought factory closures to Medellín and bankrupt mining companies to mining areas, it also brought a cocaine boom and with it the importance of *rebusque* as a way of life.

The Medellín Cartel and the infamous Pablo Escobar began to ship cocaine north to the United States in the 1970s. The money flowed back to Medellín, which has experienced a cocaine-fueled construction boom ever since. Contraband flooded into many aspects of Colombian life, which brought opportunities for other kinds of work, for better and worse. In the 1980s and 1990s, violence in Medellín spiraled out of control. The image of young men on the backs of dirt bikes from the slums overlooking Medellín became synonymous with fears of mobile *sicario* assassins fighting Escobar's war against extradition. The city's homicide rate spiked to 349 per 100,000—the highest in the world at the time. The state responded, and by the 2000s, the national government had militarized the country under its policy of democratic security.[4] City governments struck deals with various armed groups and instituted urban public renewal policies that created public spaces and emblematic infrastructure projects in long-ignored slums. The investment in public and tourist spaces closed informal opportunities for people to sell lottery tickets in the street, to make and sell food from homemade stands, to beg on buses, to run stalls in open-air markets, to drive dirtbike taxis, and to engage in other forms of *rebusque*, which became harder in the city.[5]

Rebusque is often translated as "the informal economy," which references economic anthropologist Keith Hart's article on periurban livelihoods in Ghana in the 1970s, an article cited some 2,500 times.[6] But those who live through *rebusque* do not describe themselves as living "informally." Interpreting *rebusque* from the perspective of the *rebuscador* (the person who survives through *rebusque*) means accounting for the differences between *rebusque* work and a world of formal work, with salaries, pensions, and workplace safety laws. Flip the perspective to that of the day hustler, the street seller, and the mine worker, and the question of formality becomes less relevant.

In a country where many people do not have formal employment, *rebusque* is not on the edge of the formal economy, nor can it be subsumed by the formal economy. Instead, *rebusque*, seen from below, encompasses and surrounds the formal sector. *Rebusque* becomes the dominant economy, and the formal economy is merely a normative project.

Rebusque is the word for a way of making an income common throughout Colombia. It describes how the landless and the displaced and migrants survive through self-help strategies on the urban and rural economic peripheries of Colombia. It is obvious that workers using *rebusque* have no organized unions, no legislated working conditions, no job security, no old-age pensions, and no health insurance. What is less obvious is that formal employment is becoming the exception everywhere: from service sector workers in the Global North to contract academic instructors. It might be said, around the world, that most people most of the time live in a world of *rebusque*, whatever they happen to call it. In the end, the *rebusque* in José and Geraldo's mine was a kind of work that contrasted with more permanent work. Their *rebusque* was a way of life, honest work, a rural phenomenon, and a moral way of life. *Rebusque* is the work of people who do not have something permanent and who creatively try to find themselves a life through hard but honest work on the rural and urban periphery with shifting livelihood strategies that may or may not be illegal and yet are moral and licit. To understand *rebusque*, consider the strategies of the *retreros*, owners and workers alike, at the mine on Esteban's family land, which illustrate why and how, through the use of *rebusque*, people stay at mines without much gold.

AN OWNER'S DISPLACEMENT

José washed for gold on a sun-drenched Saturday afternoon in July 2011. He wore the plastic wraparound sunglasses, blue sports T-shirt, red gym shorts, and gray knee-high soccer socks of a younger man. He bent over the sluice, a large rectangular steel box maybe nine feet long and three feet wide and a foot deep, at the bottom of the classifier, and in his bare hands he held a spoon to collect mercury. José owned two of the four excavators that had opened out the tunnel in Esteban's family mine. The machines worked in pairs: one excavator ripped gravel and stones from the ground, and the other dumped the material into the two-story classifier made of sluice boxes stacked at angles like a rusty steel game of snakes and ladders. The classifier had an opening on the top to receive stones and gravel. An old truck motor forced a high-pressure stream of water through a pipe and into the opening, where the washer, in this case Pedro's son-in-law Carlos, who had moved to the village in 2011, aimed the stream from the pipe so as to wash the stones and gravel into the classifier.

In 2008, José had come to mine on the river and join his brother Geraldo, who had arrived years earlier. Geraldo had left the Lower Cauca in Antioquia for the Chocó in 2004. He moved to get away from government repression and paramilitary extortion of the mining sector.[7] He opened a *compraventa* shop. At the time, Geraldo bought gold from miners who came in from their camps to sell their metal, which Geraldo then sold on to refineries in Medellín. Geraldo had been an intermediary, who soon began to make high-interest loans to gold miners who needed cash for fuel or machines. When one big loan went bad, Geraldo repossessed an excavator. Since Geraldo could not sell the machine, he turned to mining and asked his brother José to join him. The gamble went well for many years as prices rose higher, until the brothers arrived at Esteban's land, where the metal became scarce just as the price of gold began to fall.

Liquid mercury the color of silver spilled around José's black rubber boots and pooled in the classifier. José used a spoon to scoop the dollops of liquid mercury and gold caught in a metal grill at the bottom of the sluice box. This way of collecting gold was ingenious. The sluice box rested at a twenty-degree angle, the water and sediment and gravel flowed over a metal grillwork at the bottom of the sluice, the little yellow flecks bonded to the much heavier drops of mercury that nestled in the holes in the grill, and the water washed away the stones and gravel, which left behind gold and mercury in a buttery yellow amalgam. Once José had spooned all the liquid mercury and the amalgam into a bowl, he poured the mixture through a dishcloth stretched tight over another plastic bowl. The mercury dripped through the cloth, leaving behind a solid mass. José removed the dishcloth, twisted it around the mass, flicked the cloth-wrapped ball of metal into the air, and glittery drops of silver mercury fell to the ground, leaving a solid, misshapen, yellowish lump inside the cloth. José would later use a blowtorch to vaporize the mercury in the lump; the flame would turn the mercury into a gas, which would settle on the hair, skin, and clothes of José and his neighbors. José did not use a metal crucible as a protection, and he boasted that heavy metal poisoning did not worry him. He claimed he had experienced no ill effects in twenty-seven years as a miner. After José vaporized the mercury, all that would remain would be a lump of gold, maybe the size of a tennis ball: the product of the excavators working Esteban's mine after five days of work.

Before the *retreros* arrived on Esteban's family land in May 2011, they had spent the previous three years working a mine above Leidy's village down the river. Like most excavator miners, the *retreros* lacked the mining titles, the environmental assessment reports, and the technical studies mandated by the state. In the eyes of the law, almost all the *retrero* mines were illegal.[8] Newspapers estimated, in what might be hyperbolic magical realism, that eight hundred excavators and fifty dredges worked on three hundred and fifty illegal mines on the San Juan and Atrato Rivers.[9] The reports might also have been a simple statement of fact. There was a gold rush, many miners had come from the Lower Cauca, and the Colombian government had arrested mine workers, levied fines on the owners, and dynamited machinery. *Retrero* operations were everywhere, and everywhere they were criminalized. Many miners like José and Geraldo had come to the Chocó to run away from the state and the paramilitaries in the Lower Cauca. In the late 2000s, the Chocó was a relatively calmer place for them to work than the Lower Cauca, strange as it sounds. Judging by the traffic, many miners loaded their excavators onto flatbed trucks and hauled them over the Andes and into the jungles of the Pacific region in 2011.

Millions of Colombians have moved around for similar reasons, leaving their homes to escape violence. These are internally displaced persons, refugees who never left their own country. In 2011, estimates were that Colombia had over four million internally displaced persons, the most in the world outside the wars in the Middle East.[10] Although there are fundamental legal distinctions between people forced from their homes because of a war and those who leave to find work (the former have no choice in the matter, the latter do), daily life often blurs the boundary between the displaced person and the *rebusque* migrant—not least because displaced persons often survive through *rebusque*. Language matters. There is a difference between "Me desplazó" (It displaced me) and the reflexive "Me desplazo" (I am moving). In the former, the displaced person has no choice in the matter as they escape war, while in the latter, the person who is moving has a choice about the when, where, how, and why of the move.

While this distinction carries important legal weight—the forcibly displaced *desplazados* within Colombia can claim some state support—the distinction has moral weight too. Many people do not to want to identify themselves as victims of forced internal displacement. I suspect José and Geraldo, despite the fact that they left the Lower Cauca to escape violence from paramilitary extortion, would not describe themselves as "forcibly displaced persons." They would say they had decided to leave, rather than that they were forced to leave. My guess is that most excavator owners would share this understanding. Of course, their migration to the Pacific is not the same as a family who left one region for another to escape a death threat with few possessions and less money. For one thing, Geraldo brought enough cash with him to start a cash-for-gold shop; for another, the workers who had come in similar conditions found work, even if it was unstable, underpaid, and dangerous. Many saw themselves as making the decision to come, even when they left violence behind. *Rebusque* and internal migration and forced displacement can be hard to disentangle. People turn to *rebusque* or are displaced, and then they follow the same invisible networks of internal migration across Colombia, the same ones Don Alfonso and I followed on our trip to Medellín.

Geraldo watched from behind dark sunglasses as José finished the wash in the bottom of the classifier. Geraldo frowned. A ball of gold and mercury the size of a small tennis ball would not cover his costs. He was losing money with each wash. By April 2012, Geraldo was complaining about costs; he often had an easygoing manner with me but was in a dark mood because the mine was not producing. He had to pay 16 percent to Esteban and his family as co-owners, 2 percent permission money to the village's Black community council to travel through the territory, protection money to the paramilitary forces and the guerrillas present in the area, taxes to the municipality, money to the police and soldiers to leave him alone, repairs for the machinery, food for the workers and the cooks, diesel fuel, and everyone's wages. In total, it cost Geraldo millions of pesos (thousands of dollars) a day to keep the mine running. The mine did not produce enough, and Geraldo had debts piling up. Geraldo had not paid wages for months. The mine offered tantalizing hope, but production was rarely enough to cover costs. By September 2013, when I visited the village more than two years after that wash on an afternoon in July 2011, Geraldo and José had fled. The two brothers left the excavators rusting in the jungle because they could not pay the 2 percent to the community council, the money to Esteban and his family, the extortion to the guerrillas, the back wages to the workers, or, to bring it full circle, the money Geraldo owed in *gota-a-gota* loans to the gold-buying-and-selling houses that had become his loan sharks in a nearby town.

A WASHER'S PERMANENT JOB

Rebusque is what one does outside a *fijo*, or a stable, permanent employment—at least, this is how people described *rebusque* to me when I asked directly. Like the informal economy, this definition is a negative one. *Rebusque* becomes a complement to a *fijo*. A *fijo* might consist of salaried employment as a teacher, a petty official, or a company employee with a pension, but it might also consist of a regular income from a mine, or a small business with a steady clientele, or a productive forest plot. *Rebusque* contrasts something fixed and permanent. Just as those with a *fijo*—a teacher, a public servant, a soldier, or miners and horticulturalists like Don Alfonso and Pedro—might look for their own little side hustle, people who survive through *rebusque* look for their own permanent *fijo*. An official might engage in *rebusque* by selling favors or pocketing part of the municipal budget, a police officer might accept bribes from an excavator mine, a guerrilla might charge protection money to the *retreros* in his territory, or a soldier might assassinate teenagers and claim them as combat kills.[11] *Rebusque* becomes both what one does when there is nothing stable enough for a *fijo*, and what one does besides a permanent job as a side hustle. *Retrero* workers, despite regular wages, nevertheless engage in *rebusque* when they receive a share of every wash to complement their monthly salary.

Mud streaked Carlos's T-shirt and jeans and boots just after midnight on a Saturday in September 2011. Carlos was a fastidious dresser normally, but the spray of the mine had covered him in mud. He carried a flashlight in his left hand and a round wooden bowl to pan for gold in his right. He climbed into the mine pit by jumping from stone to stone lest he lose a boot in the mud. The pit was the size of a house, with sloping gravel banks gouged into the earth by the teeth of the orange excavator, which loomed from above on a gravel bank. A tungsten floodlight, which hung behind the cab of the machine, illuminated Carlos deep in the pit—raindrops shimmered as if frozen midair, while Carlos bent forward to fill a wooden bowl with sediment, which he then swirled to check for gold. When he finished, he looked up and made a hand motion to Juan David, the driver of the excavator: "No gold."

Carlos had come to find a steady wage at the mine. He planned to use his pay from the job as a washer to build a house for his family and a garage to repair dirt bikes. His hope was not to make fast money, so much as a little cash that he could turn into his own steady work from the garage. His job as washer was the hardest. Carlos did not check for gold most of the time. Instead, he stood on a wooden platform perched on top of the classifier. A lamp hung above his head and illuminated a sloping metal tray the length and width of a man lying prone with an opening at the bottom end: the maw of the classifier. An orange excavator dumped stones and gravel into the maw, and Carlos washed the material down into the classifier using a high-pressure stream of water. Washing was simple enough, but it required both practical skill and physical stamina to work most of the night.

Carlos had tricks to keep up with the excavator. He steadied a black, six-inch rubber tube with his left hand, and he aimed a metal nozzle with his right hand to direct the water into the maw in a slow, sideways figure-eight motion. It was like painting with a fire hose a few feet from a concrete canvas. The water pressure forced the hose skyward, so Carlos tied it down with twine and fought with all his body to aim it into the classifier. The figure-eight pattern cut away the material from below, so the gravels could wash down into the classifier. Carlos had about a minute before the excavator driver, Juan David, made the next dump. If Carlos did the figure eight too slowly or too quickly, the sediments and stones would build up. If he aimed the hose at a stone at the wrong angle, the jet of water would ricochet directly into Juan David's face. To control the flow of the water and to prevent this ricochet, Carlos used his index finger on his right hand to adjust the flow of water from the nozzle; the water pressure slowly peeled away the skin on that finger. He wore an apron made of a black plastic to protect the rest of his body from the spray. The shaking was the worst. Waves of vibration invaded his spine as the water on stone and stone on metal rattled the classifier. Inside the contraption, after Carlos had washed the material into the classifier, more streams of high-pressure water washed the material through the sluices. A metal grill separated stones from the other sediments and ejected them out behind the classifier. A thick, gray sludge flowed over the sluice boxes layered one on top of the other, and the heavier but invisible specks were trapped in the mercury-laced bottom of the sluices. The sludgy sediment flowed out of the classifier and into a stream that made the half-mile trip to the river.

Carlos had first come to work on the Esteban's river four years before. At that time, there were six dozen excavators working the length of the river, and Carlos found a job as an assistant at a mine. That first season, he had met Pedro's daughter Eva, and the two had begun a relationship. Eva never graduated from high school, and four years later, after she had given birth to twins, she was studying to finish her high school diploma through a distance education program. Carlos and Eva had initially moved to Carlos's home about three hours distant, but by 2011, with the twins, the couple moved back into Pedro and Martina's home so that Eva could finish school while her mother looked after the children and Carlos made money. At first, Carlos worked with Pedro at the family mine, but soon he got a job in the excavator mine, which promised better cash.

Carlos preferred working at night. He called it *más sabroso*, or more pleasant. There was no hot sun, the night air was cooler than the daytime heat, which sometimes neared 100 degrees, and the darkness gave the workers some freedom, because the foreman Andrés—whose extroverted wife from Antioquia I befriended—was in town getting fuel and Geraldo and José were asleep. There were more opportunities to take breaks, the tempo of work was slower, the workers set their own rhythm, the assistant might dawdle on checking the motor by the river, the dinner break might extend a little, and in the hours before the sun rose at the end of the night, everyone found a spot to nap for an hour. The sunlight gave the workers less freedom, because Andrés could watch everyone.

From his perch during the day, Carlos could see everything: the midmorning fog floating over the landscape; the green forests stretching into the distance; the Andes silhouetted against the sky; the muddy trails cut into the earth; the gray stones over an expanse the size of a few football fields; the weeds that struggled out of the gravel; the two excavators that worked in the middle distance, leaving teeth marks gouged into the hillsides; the streams that carried tailings to the river; the reservoir filling slowly with water pumped by a truck engine by the river; the aluminum pipes that snaked to the classifier; and the lumbering excavator that dumped gravel into the classifier maw below his feet.

Carlos had found unregulated and illegal employment at the mine. As a mine worker, Carlos did not have the social security payments, the union membership, the taxes, or the bank account that came with legal employment. The mine was, for him, a supplementary activity. He saw it as a step toward something else—the work as a washer was what he had to do to open his mechanic shop and create a more stable, permanent income for himself. The goal was the garage, which was why Carlos worked the night shift as a washer to save money. His work was hard and dangerous. As one of two Black workers at the mine, Carlos got little respect. But José and Geraldo promised a good wage, at just over the minimum monthly salary of 600,000 pesos ($333). Despite having a monthly wage, the job was also a form of *rebusque*, because it complemented a stable, reliable income in the future from the garage and a rural subsistence that Carlos and Eva had access to through Pedro. Teachers and community leaders do something similar when they sell clothes, colognes, or perfumes from mail-order catalogs. The mail-order sales are a little extra income, their *rebusque*. Carlos working as a washer was similar, because the job complemented his other activities, and because he saw it as temporary. The job indeed proved to be temporary: Carlos lost it a few weeks later.

Andrés fired Carlos not because as a washer he was slow or careless, but because he had asked to be paid. The work as a washer was harder than working with Pedro, where Carlos cleared maybe 300,000 pesos ($166) a month. In the *retrero* mine, the twelve-hour shifts were steady: one week on the night shift and one week on the day shift. The problem? José and Geraldo owed everyone months of back wages. Working six days a week for just above minimum wage was one thing, but doing it and not being paid was quite another. Carlos complained to Andrés. Andrés got angry. Carlos lost his job.

Carlos, unlike the other workers, had alternatives. He and Eva relied on Pedro's gardens for food. And, after being fired, Carlos went back to work at Pedro's mine. He could wait for his back wages from José and Geraldo. After things calmed down, Carlos went to talk with Geraldo. Although Geraldo had no money to pay everyone, he agreed to pay Carlos for the months he had worked. While ultimately, Carlos never did get the regular salary he wanted; his stint as a washer at the mine complemented the kinship-based subsistence activities he had access to through his father-in-law Pedro's mine.

A DRIVER'S GOOD LIFE

Rebusque is a way of life. What does the etymology of *rebusque* suggest about its meaning? The prefix *re-* comes from the Latin for "sending something backward" or "repeating"; in Spanish it may mean "intensifying" and "opposition" or "resistance." The word *busque* comes from *buscar*, or "to search." Together, *re-* and *busque* could be rendered in English with the literal "re-search," as in a cyclical, creative, and intensive search. Not a scholarly inquiry, of course, although perhaps not that different. As a noun, *rebusque* is the "temporary work that someone does to complement stable work," and the "casual and ingenious solution to a difficulty." As a verb, *rebuscar* means "to search with zeal and sacrifice to solve a problem" or "to find a good job." *Rebuscar* can also become *rebuscársela*, as in *rebuscarse la vida*, which colloquially means "to ingeniously solve the daily difficulties of quotidian survival" or "to contrive to confront and overcome daily difficulties."[12] *Rebusque* is often translated as "gleaning," in the sense of collecting the fruit and grain left in a vineyard or fields after the harvest. While gleaning does describe the *barequeros* who pan an excavator mine, which is their *rebusque*, the word "gleaning" is not the best word for *rebusque*, because it implies surviving on the dregs of capitalist accumulation. This sense misses the core ingenuity and creativity that is part of *rebusque*. A gleaner has little option, while a *rebuscador* does. Unlike gleaning, *rebusque* takes place not simply after an extractive process has worked over a landscape but also before or alongside. *Rebusque* is a way of life and something that people might do to find a life. For those with few options, *rebusque* offers a shifting livelihood strategy.

Juan David, young, muscled, and quiet, began to move the orange excavator just after Carlos had signaled no gold in the early hours of that Saturday morning. The *paisa* driver had stopped for a few minutes to wait for Carlos's signal. All night, the orange, Japanese-built machine stretched, bent, dug, grasped, lifted, twisted, and then dumped gravel into the classifier where Carlos sprayed it with water. The cab squatted on rusting caterpillar treads, and its engine thundered a wall of noise into the night. Juan David controlled the powerful hydraulic system of the excavator, which let him move the boom and bucket with a deft flick of a joystick that controlled the machine. He could pivot the machine 360 degrees and dig deep into the earth all while sitting on a comfortable seat in the cab, where he was dry and could watch videos on his smartphone—Juan David kept the skin on his right index finger. He slowed and paused work at about four o'clock in the morning as the rain pounded on. He would sleep in the cab, while Carlos, the assistant Meta, and I slept in the shelter as best we could. The night shift ended as the sun rose, and we walked back to the village to shower and sleep.

The excavators often worked in pairs. During the day, a second yellow machine owned by Geraldo and driven by an older man worked beside Juan David. The yellow machine, which had been built a decade earlier than the orange machine, broke down a lot; the orange machine Juan David drove was only three years old or so. The yellow excavator squatted on a platform lower than the orange excavator, dug into the earth, and dumped the material onto a pile. The orange machine pivoted on its mobile caterpillar treads to lift material from the pile and dump it into the classifier. The two machines repeated this digging and dumping motion hundreds of times a day. While the machines destroyed forests and contaminated the land and water with mercury and diesel, they provided work.

Why did Juan David come to work? He had left a *comuna* in Medellín for the excavator because it was better than what he could have hoped for in the city. Juan David might have tried urban *rebusque*: begging, street performing, singing on public buses, selling cheap goods on the street, hawking fruit, selling fried snacks, or making hamburgers. He might have joined a street gang or tried to find a poorly paid job as a security guard working the night shift for minimum wage, but instead he moved to the Chocó, like so many others, and found work at the mine. Juan David had come for the pay, and for the chance to make much more. As a driver he earned a million pesos ($555) a month and did not have to pay for food or housing. Juan David found mine work boring but not too difficult. Machines broke down and accidents were common, but as the driver, he had it good. The position was respected, and people aspired to be the driver, because the driving was easier than the other tasks. Juan David stayed because it was hard to leave the promise of steady pay and because there was that ever-present possibility of striking it big. Like the others, he would receive a share of each wash as a complement to his salary, and he saw in the mine a strategy to make a living, a form of upward mobility, and a way to earn some fast money.

Stories of fortunes made in an instant were common. A musician in a nearby town, I once heard thirdhand, had made an incredible amount of money in a few weeks from the excavators. The wash at the classifier was the complement to Juan David's wage, and he hoped it would be large like in the stories. But his share of the wash mostly turned out to be a small amount of extra cash each month. The unexpected windfall never came. His share of the wash increased his wage just by a couple hundred thousand pesos ($110). The potential of a bonanza kept Juan David and others at the mine, because mine work had an allure that street hustling in Medellín did not. Juan David wanted the big strike to buy an excavator, yet his dreams kept falling through. And anyway, José and Geraldo owed everyone back wages.

AN ASSISTANT'S HONEST WORK

Rebusque is honest work because it is hard work, irrespective of what state law says. As the saying goes, "El trabajo dignifica y la pereza mortifica" (Work dignifies, laziness humiliates). This is why the best translation of the verb *rebuscar* is "to shift," rather than "to hustle." Paying attention to the terms people use and the ideas and practices embedded in those terms is important, and "shifting" describes *rebusque* better than "hustling," because the English term implies an immorality absent from the shift. To hustle, unlike *rebuscar*, connotes an attempt to get ahead by any means. "To hustle" implies there's someone to hustle: the hustler hustles the hustled. "To hustle" is a transitive verb that takes a direct object, while a *rebuscador* does not require a *rebuscado*. *Rebusque* is hard and it is honest work.

Meta, fit and at eighteen in full possession of the self-confidence that comes with youth, a job, and the promise of a steady wage, began to haul jugs of diesel fuel on an afternoon in December 2011. Each jug was made of battered dark blue, orange, or white plastic. A plastic shopping bag had been threaded into the caps to create a seal and keep water out. Each jug held five gallons of liquid and reached up to his knee. A full jug is heavy, but not too difficult to carry. As I helped Meta with the fuel jugs, my shoulders locked from the weight. We had taken off our shirts because of the heat, and we carried one jug in each hand from the pile where Felipe, the muleteer, had dumped them near a plastic shelter about a hundred yards away, over a path made of wooden planks on mud too unstable for the four mules. Felipe had brought the fuel up the quarter-mile gravel road that an excavator had carved into the jungle from the river. As the mules could not make the whole trip because of the mud, Meta and I hauled the twelve jugs two at a time the last few hundred feet. As we worked, what had been a sunny day changed and the clouds broke into rain.

Some workers had followed mine camps across the Pacific region for decades, but it was Meta's first season. Meta was the assistant. His were the odd jobs: lubricating the excavators, carrying food, watching the motor that pumped water to the classifier, and hauling fuel. Meta was not his real name but a nickname that came from a department in eastern Colombia close to Venezuela and from the Spanish word for having a goal or objective. A strange yet not-so-strange nickname. Strange because Meta was from Medellín, not eastern Colombia; not so strange because Meta *was* ambitious. He too had taken the twelve-hour bus ride over the mountains to become just one more young man seeking a fortune, just as young men had done for decades. The work was easy enough, and he could go slow while carrying food, grab a nap in the shade, make calls on a cellphone from a particular spot in the jungle, chat with the woman who did the cooking, or flirt with the washerwoman twice his age. Still, as the assistant, he had little respect from the other workers.

All of the workers on the mine site were men, but there were two women who worked in the village. The two women had taken over a house owned by Esteban's niece, Laura, who lived in the town down the river. The first woman, older with wavy hair and a no-nonsense disposition, worked as the cook. She used the front room of the concrete-block house for food storage and the back room for the kitchen, where she kept massive pots of rice boiling alongside a pressure cooker with beans and salt beef, pork with lentils, salted fish, *yuca*, or plantains. She served sardines from a can and made coleslaw. Breakfast was arepas with fried eggs. She made jugs of *panela*-sweetened lemonade. The cook sold bottles of soda, razors, soap, detergent, and bags of junk food to the mine workers on credit. Beside the kitchen, benches and tables under a tarpaulin roof gave the workers, when not at the mine or sleeping, a place to eat, to chat, and to complain. A second woman did the laundry for the men. She too was late middle aged. We never talked.

Meta rented a wooden hut in the village from Don Alfonso, who had built it for storage. The hut was not much more than wooden box on stilts, just big enough for a bed and a bit of privacy. Meta had a girlfriend, one of the girls who had come home to the village from high school in the city. This was one of the many liaisons between *paisa* miners and Black girls up and down the river. At the time, I wondered if it would end in a small family, or when Meta left for another mine, leaving the girl with perhaps an unwanted child or a sexually transmitted disease. Of course, the relationship *could* work out, I thought. After all, Carlos and Eva had met under the same circumstances. Five years later, on my visit in 2017, the couple was still together.

Meta spent much of his time hauling fuel, which was the lifeblood of the mine. Everything ran on diesel: Geraldo and José said they spent millions of pesos (thousands of dollars) a day to fuel their excavators, truck engine water pumps, boat motors, and generator in the village. Before Meta could fill the machines with diesel, he had to clean the fuel, which had become dirty with leaves and water. Meta unscrewed the cap of each jug, threw aside the plastic bags that had been threaded under the cap to keep out spray from the river, took the jug inside the shelter, and poured the contents through a white sheet covering one of two metal drums. The sheet trapped the leaves and gunk, and the drums cleaned the diesel: the water sank to the bottom of the first drum, while the diesel floated to the top and then flowed through an angled pipe halfway down from the top of the drum into the second drum. Meta refilled the now-empty jugs with the fuel from the second drum.

How had the water gotten into the jugs in the first place? I asked Geraldo, who was watching us work, about that. Geraldo laughed, and explained that the diesel fuel had to be washed, because the truck drivers who brought the fuel to the town down the river had siphoned some away and replaced it with water. The state regulates diesel, gasoline, and kerosene, because fuel, cement, and coca leaves are the components of coca paste, the raw ingredient for cocaine. Workers make the paste by chopping up coca leaves and then mixing in cement and fuel. The chemicals draw the active ingredient of cocaine out of the leaves. One kilogram of cocaine requires between 280 and 325 liters of fuel, and economists estimate this chemical process accounts for perhaps 1.5 percent of gasoline consumption and 2 percent of cement production in Colombia.[13] This might explain the construction boom in Medellín, and the unfinished building projects scattered through the Chocó. Cement and fuel flow in, cocaine flows out.[14] Despite their illegality, miners could get permission to transport large quantities of fuel into the Chocó, and armed groups taxed the shipments and diverted fuel to their drug production.

Meta had left the city to find work, like so many young men. Sometimes the work they found was legal, sometimes it was not. Meta, like Juan David and Carlos, had come to make money. Meta hoped for a bonanza at the mine. On his time off, he wore nice clothes and carried around a small speaker that played music from a USB flash drive. Perhaps he sent money home to his mother, or maybe he was hoping for the chance to try a different job at the mine with more prestige and better pay. By leaving the city to try and find work as a miner, Meta had hoped to find more than what he might have in the city. The work was hard, but it was respectable a way to make a living. Did Meta have an alternative? A gang in Medellín, or picking coca to the south? Maybe he would try that another season. These were all illegal yet paradoxically honest jobs precisely because they were hard work.

When Meta had cleaned the fuel, he filled the jugs, carried them to the excavators, and refueled the machines. There was a steady rhythm to the work at the mine. Each day, there was fuel to haul and clean, food to deliver, and machinery to lubricate. The work was self-directed in a way, and Meta was often in high spirits, because he had recently brought a cheap smartphone with a touchscreen. When the mine work fell through, he would try something else.

A MULETEER'S PRECARIOUSNESS

Rebusque may be rural and urban, but it is not just the domain of a poor, downtrodden, and disposable urban periphery. Many discussions of *rebusque* describe it as an urban phenomenon—the street vendors and the performers on public transit in Bogotá and Medellín—but many *rebusque* workers are shifting from one rural sector to another to make a living: picking coffee for a season, then turning to the coca crop, then moving to work in road construction for a bit before finding a job at a mine.[15]

Felipe, the handsome and light-skinned muleteer with a confident gait, helped the foreman Andrés unload the jugs from the large, metal-hulled boat on the beach down by the river in the scorching noonday sun before it rained on that same Thursday in December when Meta and I hauled the jugs of diesel fuel. Felipe, sporting a trimmed dark beard and a large *vueltiao* hat, placed the jugs in neat rows on the gravelly sandy beach. He had quick smiles and ready jokes. The beach was beside a stream that flowed into the river. On one side was the jungle through which it was a ten-minute walk to the village. On the other side was a gravel beach the length of a canoe and a cliff nine feet high carved into the earth by the river. On the beach, a truck engine and water pump sat on metal skids. On top of the cliff sat a small wooden shack that Felipe had built over months.

Felipe had five daughters, who lived with their two mothers near the town of Caucasia in the Lower Cauca two days away by bus. Felipe had grown coca on his farm there for years; he had invested twenty-five million pesos ($14,000) into the venture before the coca economy fell apart. He spat on the ground as he explained what had happened: President Álvaro Uribe Vélez had been elected in 2002, and the police and army began to destroy the coca crop. The boom turned to bust. Felipe had to leave the area to find work. He traveled north to Urabá on the Caribbean first but found nothing. Then he traveled to the Chocó and found a job with José and Geraldo. Felipe wired money to his daughters and their mothers every month.

Felipe had two tasks. The first was to carry the jugs of diesel from the beach to a flat area under a tree, and then tie them three at a time onto his four mules. The animals were lean, with short, gray hair. Felipe said he injected the mules with vitamins so they would stay healthy and fed them cane molasses mixed with grain bought in the city. Each mule had a cloth over its back with a wooden frame on top. Felipe lashed the jugs to the wooden frame with a rope with ease and fluidity: one jug on each side, balanced so they did not fall off, and then a third on top. Felipe loaded the mules, patted their backs, scratched their necks, and whispered in their ears. Felipe was a muleteer, an *arriero*—one of Colombia's oldest professions. Mules have brought supplies across the country for centuries. While mule trains no longer crisscrossed the country after tractor-trailer *tractormulas* replaced them, in the hot lowlands mules still bring gasoline to jungle camps of miners and coca paste producers. Felipe loaded the four mules with twelve jugs of diesel (about a fifth of the total), slapped the first mule on the rump and whistled. He and the mules started up the track into the jungle. There were three trails to the mine: the track from the river where the excavators had first entered, the logging trail everyone used from the village, and the short track that an excavator had cut from the mine to the river to Felipe's shack. The mules hauled the fuel from the river to the mine along one of the tracks made by the caterpillar treads. Felipe must have made the trip dozens of times a day to haul the fuel from the river to the mine. His days were load, hike, unload, and repeat.

Felipe's second task was to watch the motor pump on the beach. It was an engine from a tractor-trailer. The motor had been removed from the truck and attached to metal skids. The motor ran twenty-four hours a day to power a pump. The pump moved river water through aluminum pipes that followed a track into the jungle and up to a large reservoir that had been dug near the mine. Felipe's other job, and the reason he lived where he did, was to watch the river water level in case of a flood. When the water levels rose, Felipe would signal by pulling on a long string that snaked through the jungle and had a bell tied to the end. Juan David would bring the excavator down through the mud to lift the motor from the skids using a heavy chain. To watch the motor, Felipe had built his *ranchito* (a small shack) by the river. The building began as a bed: Felipe had slept under a bug net over a bed made of two planks the width of man a few feet off the ground and supported by four posts. Over a few months, Felipe built walls and a roof over his bed: he nailed planks to posts to make a wall, and he made the roof with more planks placed over an A-frame with palm fronds and a plastic sheet against the rain. It was a shack in the jungle almost exactly like the homesteads the older men in the village had built for themselves and their families when they were younger.

Felipe had come with his mules to the Chocó, and like the others, he was a *paisa* migrant to the Chocó looking for work. He had become a mobile *rebusque* worker trying to get away from state violence that was pushing coca growers off their land. *Rebusque* was a rural activity for him. Felipe had not come from the city to a rural mining region but from one peripheral coca and mining region to another. Behind his *ranchito*, he raised a dozen chickens and grew plantains, which he planned to sell to Geraldo and José to make a little money on the side. He had not been paid for his work by José and Geraldo either.

After José washed for gold with a spoon on that afternoon in July 2011, Felipe washed the contents of the fourth sluice box for himself. He took apart the metal sluice, took out the red plastic sack, and shook the sediment into a plastic tub, all the while being careful to not lose any gravel. He shook each sack three times, so that all of the metals and sediments fell into a plastic bowl. He held up the sack for me to photograph.

"Mi rebusque," Felipe laughed.

The order of the sluices mattered: each would give a smaller amount of gold than the previous. Felipe was almost giddy, joking as drops of silver mercury fell into the water and onto the mud and gravel. The heavy metal distracted no one, and everyone focused on their sluice and the gold that would complement their wage. Washing the dregs of what came out of the mine was what Felipe called his *rebusque*. The sluice was his opportunity to make millions of pesos in a moment. It was the wash that kept everyone at the mine. The first sluice was for the co-owners, the second for Andrés as foreman, the third for the workers at the mine, and the fourth for Felipe. The gold would augment their salary, and the possibility of a bonanza was always there. Felipe hoped to strike it rich. He never did when I knew him.

A FOREMAN'S MORALITY

Rebusque is a licit illegality. Consider drug trade and mine work. Both are illegal, yet either can have a certain morality. *Rebusque* is moral when there are few legal avenues for employment. *Rebusque* becomes not only how people make a living but a way of life and a way to get ahead. In a country with few ways to do so for the otherwise unemployed, Colombia's illegal and informal economies give someone with few options a way try to make something. In a world without work, illegal work can become moral work, and the illegal, therefore, becomes licit. *Rebusque*, seen from above, is described as informal and illegal, but not so for the *rebusque* worker who tacks back and forth between the formal and the informal in a moral illicit economy. *Rebusque* is the licit and moral way that people make or find their own work. Like all illegal activity, of course, this is in the eye of the beholder. The successful informal and illegal worker in cocaine becomes an organized criminal in the eyes of the state, yet not necessarily so in the eyes of the people who live in and around those activities. For the people who earn a living through *rebusque*, their livelihood has its own morality.

Early in the morning of the Thursday before Felipe loaded the mules with the tanks of diesel and before Meta and I had hauled the fuel, Andrés maneuvered a flat-bottomed, metal-hulled boat to the town downriver from the village and filled the five dozen jugs with diesel fuel. As a rule, Andrés left for town most days with empty jugs and returned to the village with full ones, but he also decided on the work schedule, disciplined the workers, paid them when there was money, and ordered the wash every few days. Andrés often made the trip to the nearest town during daylight hours, but sometimes he went during the rainstorms, when no other boats were on the water. He might stop to leave packages at the edge of the forest for the guerrillas who lived somewhere in the forest—they had their own form of *rebusque*: the extortion of miners. Andrés filled jugs of diesel in town, and the tanker trucks brought diesel to the river every few days. There is a commodity chain of diesel fuel, just as there is with gold, and getting fuel to the mine involved intermediaries all the way back. As tankers brought fuel over the mountains to Istmina or Quibdó from Pereira or Medellín, paramilitaries and the guerrillas and others took their cut.

The contents of the second sluice box belonged to Andrés. He had the prerogative to decide when to do the wash, and while José and Geraldo had the most valuable sluice box in the classifier, Andrés had the second-most valuable. Other than the sluice box of the co-owners, this second box had the highest earning potential. That first sluice box was where the money came from to pay for the gasoline, to pay the guerrillas, to pay the police, and to pay Esteban's family as co-owners. Andrés took the second. He had worked for decades in the Lower Cauca, which has a history of mining as old as the Chocó's. Indeed, the foreman, the owners, and the workers had all brought their work camps, labor relations, practices, and techniques with mercury and excavators from the Lower Cauca to the Chocó. Each worker had come for a share of the wash, with the hope of a big one just around the corner. When the mine went well, Andrés did well. When the mine went badly, he did badly. Andrés rarely smiled.

FAST MONEY, ABSENT METAL, AND A MINING COOPERATIVE

The *retrero* workers had come from the Lower Cauca to mine, to send money home, and to find work. It is no surprise that the different *retreros* had different goals: José and Geraldo had moved to mine, Carlos had wanted to open a garage to repair dirt bikes, Juan David had hoped to get his own excavator, Meta had come to "make it," Felipe had moved from one rural extractive industry to another, and Andrés had come to keep the mine working and make some money. These brief narratives of a few days' mine work, of course, simplify the labor and hopes of complex individuals in a mining boom that had thousands of participants. My point is that each engaged in a form of *rebusque* beyond a permanent job, even as some hoped to find something more permanent. Each excavator miner came to get a share of the fast money but never really got what they had hoped for. What of the other excavator miners and the other *retreros* beyond the particularities of José and Geraldo and the men I knew who worked for them on Esteban's family land?

Don Pablo, taciturn with his employees but talkative with me, perhaps because he saw me as a potential supporter, wove his battered red Toyota Land Cruiser along the potholed road for the drive between Quibdó and our destination, Istmina, on an early April morning in 2011. Don Pablo helped organize one of the small-scale miners' cooperatives. While Geraldo and José and their workers had nothing to do with them, the cooperatives claimed to represent all the *retreros* in the Chocó. Our trip to Istmina that morning was to attend a meeting of one of the cooperatives. These *retreros* bristled when journalists, politicians, or I used the term "illegal" to describe their mines. They preferred the term "informal," implying that steps should be taken to regularize their operations. Most *retrero* mines working the alluvial gravels employed techniques similar to those used by the workers on Geraldo and José's mine. The operations required large investments in capital and machines and a steady supply of mercury and fuel, and yet could be quite marginal. There were more excavator miners in the San Juan than in the Atrato region, and the landscape around Istmina had been flattened over decades of small-scale mining.

Istmina had narrow, winding streets and the cadence of both Spanish and Portuguese, the latter from the Brazilian *garimpeiros* who found their way to the Chocó to mine gold. Miners sold at the cash-for-gold *compraventas* scattered throughout the town, but there were other sources of money in the area. The San Juan River cuts through Istmina on its way to the Pacific, in a region where coca is grown, cocaine is moved, gold is dug, and money is laundered. Istmina is a rough frontier town where *cocaleros* and *narcos* and *paracos* and *retreros* come to rest, to eat a thick steak, to drink cold beer, to visit small bars with stairs leading to rooms above, to find company, to sleep in proper beds with air conditioning, and to eat a good breakfast.

Don Pablo invited me for breakfast at a restaurant called El Paisa. The town of Istmina has a mixed population, the majority Black but with many *paisas* from Antioquia who had recently arrived or who had descended from earlier waves of migration to the Chocó. El Paisa served a breakfast of light broth with beef chunks, arepas, and milky sweet coffee in a small white cup with the Colombian flag. On the wall, by the door to the toilet, hung a poster of a massive, three-story dredge, one of the machines that had dug into the landscape of the Lower Cauca and the Nechí River. The image had the names of all those who had worked on that dredge in small writing on the bottom and the logo of Mineros S.A.

Mineros S.A. is the largest legal gold producer in Colombia and was privatized in 2001. But its state-owned predecessor operated from the 1970s to 2001 on the Nechí and Lower Cauca Rivers. Mineros S.A. was the product of the nationalization of the most important dredging operation in Colombia in the twentieth century. Its sister company, the Chocó Pacífico Mining Company, no longer existed. Chocó Pacífico had operated in the town of Andagoya, a twenty-minute dirt-bike-taxi ride from the restaurant in Istmina. By 2011, all that remained of the company's facilities were the detritus of a former mining town, the skeletal frames of buildings, and the pipes that connected the welding equipment to the fuel tanks. Colombian journalist turned novelist Gabriel García Márquez described a visit to the town in the 1950s, with its wooden bungalows and screened-in windows for the workers, tennis courts for the bosses, and pressed linens for the white American and Caribbean management; blue-eyed, dark-skinned children lived in the small-town of Andagoyita across the river.[16] The once-bustling mining enclave became a sleepy town on the edge of the jungle after the Chocó Pacífico Mining Company went bankrupt and the *paisas* came to mine with their excavators.

After breakfast, Don Pablo took me to attend a meeting of the cooperative in a school classroom. Photocopies of the internal regulations of a Black community council covered the walls of the entrance to the school: how much to pay communities to mine, how to reforest, what the working conditions ought to be, and so forth. The dozen men and the few women who came to the meeting were almost all *paisas*. At the morning meeting, they talked about what their industry needed: a government policy for informal mining, a way to legalize their status, protection from the guerrillas who kidnapped them, protection from the soldiers who burned their machinery, investment in national mining rather than in multinational mining, programs to train miners, and funds for exploration, mapping, environmental studies, and technical reports. The attendees spoke about the future of their industry, about a belligerent government in Bogotá more interested in foreign capital than in supporting a national mining industry for Colombians, and the threat to their mines from multinational mining corporations based in Toronto.

A convoy of white Toyota SUVs with black-tinted windows took me and a half dozen of the men and women from the meeting to an empty open-air restaurant. We ordered thick steak and cold beer.

"Why is a Canadian interested in mining in the Chocó?" a man—who with a mustache and curly black hair looked like Pablo Escobar—asked me. He did not let me respond but went on, "I am glad you are here. I am sick of people portraying small-scale miners as terrible. We are hardworking people, and we are victims. The guerrillas kidnap us, and make our families pay ransom."

The man complained about the bad reputation of the excavator owners. These men and their mining industry across the Colombian Pacific and the Lower Cauca were in the crosshairs of the state. The *paisas* spoke about their problems, and about the Canadians pushing excavators from the land.

"The Canadians are coming," another man said. "The Canadians are pushing us out of our mines. It is like that movie about Africa and conflict diamonds, *Blood Diamond*. Canadian gold is blood gold. They come here and make all the money."

It was Canadians, the men believed, who had rewritten the national mining legislation that had made small-scale mining illegal,[17] who were coming to take their land, and who were forcing the mining cooperatives to try to legitimize their own status through internal regulations cowritten with Black community councils and posted on the wall. The strategy was inspired by social movements.

In April 2011, there was a march of small-scale miners in Quibdó. Hundreds, perhaps thousands, of *retrero* mine workers and the owners and the associations of *barequeros*—the community members who gleaned a little from *retrero* operations—were all bussed in from across the Atrato and the San Juan to fill the streets of Quibdó. They had come to march in support of small-scale miners. Many of the protestors wore T-shirts with the names of the mines they worked on printed on the front and back. The workers held printed placards or banners and marched through the city. Loudspeakers on the back of trucks magnified the chants of the men and women carrying megaphones. At the end of the march, attendees ate food from white plastic containers in a large assembly on the main steps in downtown Quibdó above the Atrato River. The marchers listened to people on loudspeakers who proclaimed that the small-scale miners wanted to be legal, who said they did not want to be repressed by the state. One speaker called in on a phone, a senator for the main left-leaning party, the Polo Democrático Alternativo, and spoke about his support of Colombian mines for Colombian miners. The year before, I had seen the same senator in Ottawa, Canada, speaking out against a free-trade agreement in similar terms. After that march in April 2011, there were more marches. In 2012, the cooperatives of miners blockaded roads in the Chocó and the Lower Cauca, and they occupied the airport in Quibdó for a few hours.[18] The attempt was to shed the label of illegal and get a state policy in support of their mining industry. The protests failed.

"Nobody can afford to leave," a middle-aged miner said to me as we stood behind the classifier at José and Geraldo's mine just before Christmas 2011. The man's comment might have applied to the owners, but he meant the workers—Juan David, Meta, Felipe, and the others. Everyone hoped to make the two-day bus ride home to visit family in time for December 31 and the New Year celebrations, but nobody had been paid for months. The man explained that in the Lower Cauca, where he used to work, things were different. There the mines would often have ten or more excavators, but here there were just a few old ones. There the machines were always in good repair, but here the machines broke down often. There the excavators had enough fuel, but here getting fuel was a challenge. There the workers had work seven days a week, but here the workers never worked a week without a breakdown. There the workers were paid every two weeks, but here the workers were never paid. What frustrated him was that neither José nor the other miners found anything either, but at least in the Lower Cauca the owners paid everyone on time.

"It was better there where I used to work," the man said.

His complaints left me with a question. How could mine owners in the Lower Cauca pay their workers when they did not produce much, and yet for José and Geraldo the same situation was an unmitigated disaster?

THE HOPE TO GET AHEAD

Not much later, on one of the last times I saw Geraldo, we sat a few hundred feet away from his excavator on a Sunday afternoon and talked. Or rather, he talked and I listened. He spoke about the excavators from Japan and the weapons the soldiers had from Israel. He talked about the money he had to pay to the paramilitaries, the guerrillas, the mayor, the police, and the community council. He talked about cocaine profits. And, he complained, with both hands gesticulating, that Colombians did not make most of their money from drugs any longer.

"The Americans," Geraldo said (and here I am quoting verbatim from notes), "like Donald Trump and George Bush, they are the real narco kings. Bush admitted to doing cocaine, didn't he? They should make cocaine legal—it would make more sense."

If José, Geraldo, Meta, Felipe, Carlos, and all the rest had come to the river as their *rebusque* to try to get ahead at a small-scale mine to which

José washes for gold and mercury in the sluice at the bottom of the classifier.

Esteban and his family had invited them in for much the same reason, the story is one of hundreds of others from mines on many other rivers. For the workers and for Esteban and his family, the excavators were a way to move into the cash economy, as actually producing gold was central to their attempt to accumulate cash and get ahead. Ultimately the mine had far less than everyone had hoped, and it was a disaster. The mine was a failure. The perspective of small-scale miners like José and Geraldo and the landowners on whose land they operated is important to counter overly simplistic narratives of destructive illegal economies. Neither victim nor victimized, everyone was engaged in *rebusque* activities on a mining frontier on which small-scale miners and some rural landowners had embraced each other in an attempt to get ahead. Thus, gold can be understood as not that different from cocaine, as both are part of an illegal but moral *rebusque* economy in which small-scale mining offers a way to accumulate cash. Despite all the optimism that was so clear, the efforts of Esteban and his family and José and Geraldo resulted in failure.

While finding metal proved difficult, what joined them was their hope of accumulating gold quickly, even as the land itself ultimately proved to be far poorer than the tunnel had led Esteban and his family to believe. Their shared hope raises an important feature of the rural economy of mining: local systems of land ownership matter, as do the wider regional economies in which they are embedded. People engage in small-scale mining for various reasons, even when the final benefits can be quite marginal.

Reconsidering small-scale mining from the perspectives of the practitioners shows it to be an industry that, because it uses mercury, can have a devastating impact on the environment but that also exists within a system of local regulations and rules, where miners like Esteban and outsiders like José negotiate the terms of an entry, which everyone more or less agrees on. If the land had been as productive as everyone had hoped, José and Geraldo would not have declared de facto bankruptcy by leaving their machinery rusting in the jungle as they fled the area. If the government was serious about shutting down what it casts as an illegal and criminal industry, a more productive course would be to engage with small-scale miners to create a workable framework for mining and alternatives for the men and women who find in mine work their *rebusque*. For many of the people I met mining, the mines were among their best remaining opportunities. Much writing about small-scale mining focuses on their illegality and criminality, but it is as important to consider how Juan David and Meta and Felipe and Carlos and the others found a living through hard work. What united people engaged in various kinds of *rebusque* alongside those who do subsistence activities was a reliance on producing gold—production that is not always necessary in the gold industry.

PART III

Transformation

Money Laundering and Speculation

CHAPTER FIVE

Simulated Extraction and Gold-Based Money Laundering

MERCEDES and I hiked toward Pie de Pato—the sleepy capital of the municipality of Upper Baudó—on a damp afternoon in 2011. I felt dizzy from the almost two-mile hike over the Baudó Mountains, the thickly forested low mountain range that runs parallel to the Pacific in the northwest of the department. We passed soldiers sleeping in hammocks who waved us on, never looking up, despite a half century of war. After the soldiers, the trail crested between two watersheds. Water drained down the eastern flanks of the mountains into the various rivers heading north to the Caribbean, while the western slopes drained into the Baudó River and southwest to the Pacific. As our trail began its descent, we saw the town open out below, with houses built on stilts to withstand floods, a medical center, a mayor's office, schools, a church, a rectory for the priest, and a dozen shops and canteens and lottery ticket kiosks.

From that interoceanic spot between the two watersheds, far from Pedro and Esteban's village and the mine of José and Geraldo, we saw no excavators, no dredges, and none of the signs of the out-of-control gold rush that had brought me to do fieldwork a year earlier. Later, when I was back in Canada near the end of 2012, I read implausible municipal gold production figures, and being aware of the lack of heavy machinery and workers in Upper Baudó (which had been so common in the areas of the department I knew well), I was forced to reconsider my assumption about the production of value. There was none of the scramble of a mining boom: no machines, gravel, holes, or overflowing bars. Instead, people gardened, cut timber, and did many things other than mine.[1] After I finished fieldwork, I read that the municipalities on the Baudó River had produced, on paper at least, 11,797 kilograms of gold, although they had no mines. Not all that gleams comes

Gold and platinum left behind in the bottom of a *batea*

from under the ground, it seemed. One explanation was that of gold-based money laundering, as the metal itself might have come not from the gravels of the Baudó River but from the gold *compraventas* of Panama.

When confronted with the impossible production figures on the Baudó River, I realized that discussions of mining have not always adequately attended to the ways some forms of extraction are embedded in what anthropologists have called the extralegal global underground economy.[2] Producing gold is part of a dual household economy of rural Black residents, and accumulating cash via a small-scale mine is a way for rural Black residents and outsider miners to survive in the cash economy through *rebusque*. A gold rush, however, can also take the form not of production or accumulation of physical metal but of the transformation of value. On the Baudó River, gold-based money laundering neither produces nor accumulates cash but instead transforms drug cash from an illegal to a legal sphere. Realizing the possibility of money laundering prodded me to rethink the mining as embedded in complex global networks that transform (rather than produce or accumulate) value. Here, the mining generates profit through extralegal "simulacra of extraction," where value is transformed under the guise of resource production. On the Baudó River, money from cocaine—the region's other high-value export commodity—is transformed into cleaned cash through faked mines. Examples of gold-based money laundering at different scales of mining and disparate geographic locales underline the complexities of the global networks that facilitate the transformations of value through this process and connect beyond a river in the jungles of the Chocó to the global economies of gold and cocaine.

My methods for learning about how drug traffickers launder cocaine profits through fake mines come not from under the ground but from other places, including reading newspaper and other reports spanning three decades. By squinting sideways at such reports, it becomes clear how precious metals and drugs are connected not simply because they are high-value export commodities extracted from the jungles of the Pacific,[3] but because the former can help launder money from the latter.

DECENTERING PRODUCTION

The absence of mining on that visit to the Baudó in northwest Colombia was confounding. Where were the miners? On my initial visits to the Chocó the year before, I had read an article in the local newspaper noting that, according to the national mining statistics, the Chocó had become the largest gold producer in Colombia. The tone was strangely proud—the Chocó was first in something for once.[4] By my November 2011 visit to the Baudó River, I had spent the better part of a year working with Afro-Colombian miners who pan for gold using hand tools and manual techniques. When I began to read the statistics on gold production, I came to realize the limits of ethnographic fieldwork based on participant observation and learning how to mine, as I had practiced it. The shadows of the global economy of cocaine proved difficult to access just from fieldwork with gold miners on a river in the Chocó.

A reading of gold statistics published online by the Colombian state suggests that the Chocó was the third largest producer behind the departments of Antioquia and Córdoba in 2004.[5] Between 2004 and 2007, the Chocó recorded steady output. In 2008, it saw a rapid rise in production, so much so that by 2009 the department claimed almost half of Colombia's total gold yield. The production might have been worth $1 billion that year, if my estimate using the average world prices is correct. While the official numbers show where miners registered their output, they prove little about where the metal itself came from, because producers like Pedro and Esteban and Geraldo could sell to buyers in nearby towns, and buyers could register gold in places other than the point of origin. Reasons to change location might include one municipal center being closer than another, as was the case for Pedro; a miner being able to recoup his royalty payments more easily in one place than another, as was the case for Geraldo; or because moving and faking registrations are both ways to launder money and transform value.

All of this movement is common knowledge, and yet it is difficult to talk about. These are public secrets—"that which is known but, for one reason or another, cannot be spoken."[6] Public secrets abound in how gold transforms drug profits when narcotraffickers launder their profits using Colombian gold, which may not even have been mined. I suspect the gold production statistics in the Baudó are best explained by traffickers legalizing profits from their illicit exports. Gold is ideal for illicit transactions because of its fungibility, transportability, substitutability, and liquidity. Indeed, individuals, corporations, and states have long used gold to smuggle, speculate, evade taxes, move capital, amass wealth, commit fraud, finance black-market deals, secure illicit investments, sidestep monetary controls, pay for narcotics, and launder money.[7] A gold bar the size of a package of letter-sized printer paper would weigh 29.6 kilograms and be worth over a million dollars, and yet be relatively easy to move and sell.

In 2012, fresh from fieldwork and unsure how to start writing, I spent weeks poring over the gold statistics published on Colombian government websites.[8] I mapped, animated, and charted gold production from 2004 to 2012 (see figures 1 and 2). As I watched computer-generated animated maps that changed over time, I began to see a shifting constellation of momentary flashes of gold production on paper that helped me understand how the process by which *narcos*—the term for the various laborers, brokers, producers, smugglers, and other intermediaries who move and sell cocaine—convert some of their illicit dollars into pesos. In the year after I finished fieldwork, I saw the map pulsate brightest in the traditional mining region of the Lower Cauca in the department of Antioquia, yet it was the sudden, brief flashes of gold in places with no physical metal to mine that were most illuminating. It was production recorded in municipalities that do not appear on geological surveys as having deposits, and that had little prior or expected future production, that for a few brief months shone bright. The statistics of gold in strange places suggests that miners might sell their output on the market after registering the metal with a local government and paying a small tax of 4 percent.

Yet the production figures were dubious for three reasons: First, in some places, the statistics were too low. For example, thirty dredges worked the Quito River in 2009,[9] yet production remained stable from 2004 to 2012. Meanwhile, while seventy-five excavators mined the banks of the Andágueda

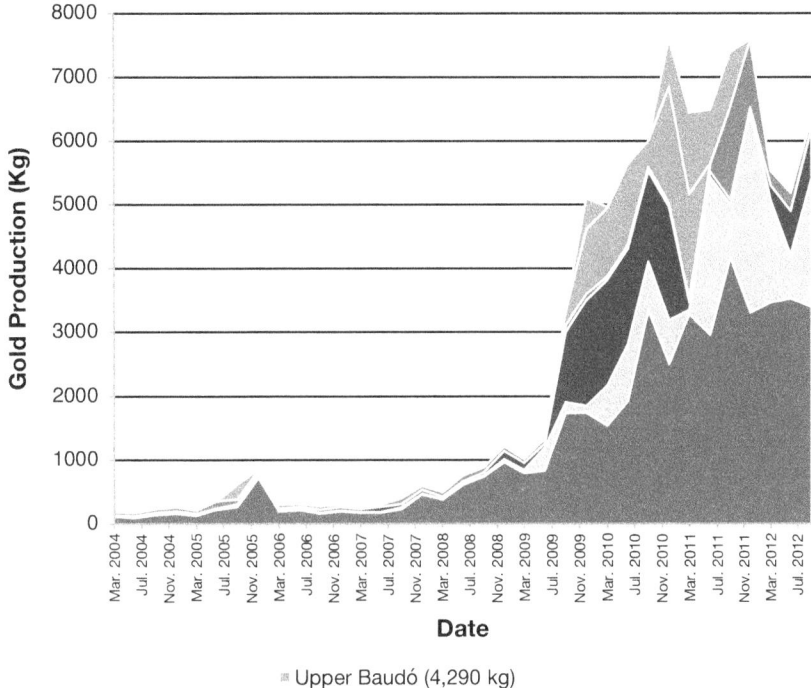

FIGURE 1. Gold production by date and municipality

- Upper Baudó (4,290 kg)
- Middle Baudó (7,786 kg)
- Condoto (5,259 kg)
- Istmina (12,140 kg)
- Nóvita (14,780 kg)
- Other Municipalities (44,814 kg)

River, official output increased only slightly. Second, statistics in some municipalities were too high. In Istmina, Nóvita, and Condoto, gold yields increased an implausible 2,000 percent in a three-month period, from July through September 2008. Third, statistics in some areas were impossible. For example, Upper Baudó registered as the third largest producer in all of Colombia in 2011, despite having no signs of mining and no history of gold.

Of the three municipalities on the Baudó, only two, Upper and Middle Baudó, registered any metal. Middle Baudó reported 279 kilograms between 2004 and 2009, all in the three-month period before September 2005. The two municipalities recorded 11,797 kilograms between January 2009 and December 2011—worth, according to my estimate, $500 million.[10] Yet from January to September of 2012, Upper and Middle Baudó together registered

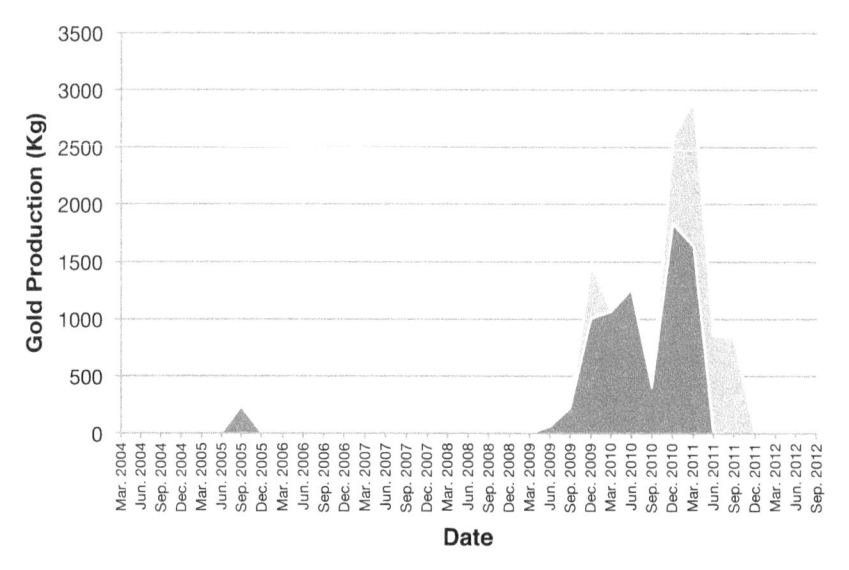

FIGURE 2. Gold production by date in the Middle Baudó and Upper Baudó

about a kilogram of production. The numbers coincided not with the presence of mining but instead with the three-year term of municipal politicians. It was when, in the year after my fieldwork, I read a report written by the state agency that monitors public finances that I realized that not all that glitters comes from under the ground.[11] While Medellín-based refineries were taking advantage of lax controls to register illegal gold with twelve companies, the companies, none of which were in the mining sector, each claimed gold from the Baudó. The companies paid taxes into municipal bank accounts. A judge in Quibdó then transferred those royalties to third-party accounts, apparently to pay for fake debts. Thirteen billion pesos (over $7,000,000) were moved into municipal accounts as royalty payments, and then into third-party accounts to pay civil debts. When the newly elected politicians took office in January 2012, registrations plunged to zero (see figure 2).

What had struck me is that while the excavators and dredges have reshaped the Atrato and the San Juan Rivers for decades, the Baudó itself flowed undisturbed when I visited in 2011. One explanation of how a river that had no mines could on paper be such a large producer is that miners from other places were simply registering their production somewhere else in order to recoup their royalty payments. Second, it could simply be a paper scheme to legalize illegal gold in a town far from Medellín. A third explanation is that the Baudó has produced coca for decades, and that traffickers have long used fishing boats, light aircraft, and small submersibles to smuggle blocks of cocaine from the nearby Pacific Coast northward to Central America and then to Mexican and US markets.[12]

A friend who had worked on the coast explained the trade to me. My friend described walking on a beach and stumbling on what she thought was an old concrete runway where the jungle met the sand. Since the 1980s, narcotraffickers have flown drugs north in light aircraft. The jungle landing strip might have been detritus of that earlier period, or of a more recent one, as traffickers still fly cocaine north. Traffickers also float cocaine out from the remote rivers and forests of the Pacific region in boats and submersibles. Larger shipments head north from the port of Buenaventura. Indeed, newspapers report that the powerful Mexican Sinaloa Cartel has representatives in the city to help orchestrate shipments.[13] If the Pacific Coast is a place to send drugs north, the San Juan River that cuts through Istmina to the ocean is the last leg of a route from the coca fields in the interior on the other side of the Andes. The San Juan traverses the municipalities of Istmina, Condoto, and Nóvita—precisely the ones with the incredible increases in gold registrations. I thought, when studying the figures and staring at those pulsating maps, that it was plausible that the implausible production in Upper and Middle Baudó was tied into trafficking routes. Could cocaine help explain those production figures?

The operation might be simple enough: launder cocaine cash into "clean" money through gold by buying the metal with "dirty" cash and then by selling the metal as if it came from a real mine. Although the miners I knew, like José and Geraldo, faced financial disaster when they had difficulty finding gold, I heard stories of other mining operations that faced no such difficulty. Might these stories have been tied to money laundering? Gold in the Baudó might not have been coming just from the region's mines. Could the informal mining have been implicated not simply in accumulation through production, legal or otherwise, but in a complicated process where value is generated by traffickers of cocaine who then clean their profits through fake gold mines? If so, the public secret of mining is the movement of illegal commodities and capital that sometimes has little to do with shifting stones or digging tunnels or panning gravel, and more to do with cocaine's global connections. Statistics and media reports make clear that cocaine casts a shadow over gold. Across maps that made no sense, I began to see the footprints of money laundering.

COMPLICATING ACCUMULATION

"My father only taught me how to gamble," the mechanic replied to my banal question "Did you learn to fix engines from your father?" The barrel-chested older man had come for the afternoon to repair a truck motor at José and Geraldo's mine on Esteban's family land. He pumped in lubricant with a grease gun, ran his fingers over tubes, lingered on a hunk of metal, filed it down, replaced a spark plug, and turned the ignition. The engine rumbled to life and ran a pump that forced water into a mining classifier, the same one Carlos had operated, which was the two-story contraption that with water from aluminum pipes separated sand and gravel and mud and stones from gold. When the truck motor had broken, the water had stopped. Without the water, the mine had been stalled for days. With the motor now repaired, the mechanic and I spoke above rumble of the engine. "Is gold mining like gambling?" I asked. The mechanic replied with a tale that points to the underground economy as a way to understand everyday transactions as the transformation of value. The story was an everyday account of money laundering through the lottery by people who took advantage of the poverty and naïveté of the mechanic's possibly fictional protagonist, Mario. Indeed, apparently legal activities in trade, finance, and securities become techniques that allow people to launder cocaine profits through quotidian capitalist transactions. In fact, I later realized that newspapers and other scholarly sources support this reading of everyday economic transactions as a process of transformation embedded in the global underground economy, just as the mechanic's story suggested this happened with a lottery ticket. As paraphrased from notes I took afterward, the mechanic's story was as follows:

"Mario was from a mining town in the Lower Cauca River in Antioquia. He worked his whole life as a miner, but he must have been an idiot because he knew nothing about the city. He became a wealthy idiot when he won a lottery worth hundreds of millions. Mario went to claim his prize at the lottery headquarters in Medellín.

"On his way to the office, two men stopped him on the street. 'Where are you going?' one man asked. 'I am going to claim the lottery,' Mario replied. 'What will you do with all the money?' the other man added. 'I don't know,' Mario answered. The first man said, 'The lottery corporation will rip you off. The lottery puts a little every month into your bank account. It will take years to get your winnings. The government will steal from your bank account as well. They take something every time you use the account. Let us buy the ticket. Upfront. In cash.' The other man said, 'You will not have to pay taxes. You can do what you want with it. Buy a house or a car. You won't have to wait.'

"Mario thought for a moment and decided to sell his ticket. The two men paid Mario hundreds of millions of pesos, and Mario went home to the mountains. In his home, he built a house and bought a car. A year later, the police came. 'Where did you find so much money? How could you afford a car? How could you build a house? Have you paid your taxes?' the police demanded to know. Mario explained he had won the lottery, and that he had bought the car and built the house with his winnings. 'Do you have a receipt? A note from the bank? A copy of the ticket?' Mario did not have any such evidence. He could not prove that he had even entered the lottery.

"The police arrested Mario on suspicion of trafficking, and they put him in jail. What happened to the men who bought the ticket? They went to the lottery headquarters and claimed Mario's winning ticket as their own. The lottery company paid the men straight into their accounts every month. The men even paid the tax to the government. Where did the two get the cash to buy Mario's ticket?"

One reading of this story—or at least my rendition—is as an apocryphal tale of a bitter end for someone who found easy wealth, a cautionary tale akin to the stories of cursed wealth that other people told me about incredibly successful miners who found easy money and yet ended up in poverty. However, the story had a significant twist. The two who bought the ticket went free, and Mario went to jail. The twist suggests a reading where the mechanic's story was not just a cautionary tale about gambling, easy money, or gullible people but instead about how the lottery can be used to launder cocaine profits.[14] The insight gained by taking seriously the mechanic's story is that the similarity between miners like Esteban or José and Geraldo and lottery ticket buyers is not just that these activities provide hope but that both mining and lotteries are ways to legalize profits from cocaine sales.

Money laundering and the drug economy are interconnected with the legal economy. Rather than focusing on the large, organized, and mostly fictional cartel systems that appear in newspaper articles and government reports, the entanglements are more mundane. In describing how to launder using gold, I squint at two sources. Stories from men like the mechanic raise questions, but so do the gray literature and newspaper accounts on the diverse techniques Colombian traffickers have used to launder their profits. Consider the following three examples.

In the first, traffickers pioneered the "Black Market Peso Exchange," a trade-based scheme that worked in the following way: Narcos first smuggled illegal drugs into the US, which they then sold for US dollars. Next, traffickers sold the dollars to a peso broker, who moved the money into bank accounts in the US. The peso broker then contacted a Colombian importer in need of dollars to use to buy goods. The importer purchased goods in the US, had them shipped to Colombia and sold them for Colombian pesos. The items might have been hard drives, electronic appliances, televisions, high fashion, and so forth. The importer then returned the pesos to the broker. The broker transferred the pesos to cartel-controlled accounts. In this way, traffickers converted their profits from US dollars into Colombian pesos under the guise of legitimate trade and often paid far better exchange rates for the money exchange than were available from official sources.[15]

In the second, Colombian and Mexican traffickers cleaned millions of dollars utilizing North American and European financial institutions. One case involved the Wachovia Bank, which settled with US authorities in 2011 by admitting to moving $110 million from drug sales into its accounts and to failing to track $376 billion transferred from small Mexican currency exchange houses over a ten-year period. Here, the launderers were using cash, wire transfers, and traveler's checks to move profits from currency exchange houses through Wachovia. Another case involved HSBC, which settled with the US government in 2012. HSBC admitted to a $1.9 billion scheme between 2000 and 2010. The bank received cash worth $881 million from two Mexican cartels and accepted $15 billion over-the-counter bulk payments in Mexico, Russia, and other countries.[16] Narcos, according to the head of the United Nations Office on Drugs and Crime (UNODC), were moving so much cash into the banking system that they softened the blow to the global economy from the 2008 financial crisis: "In many instances, the money from drugs was the only liquid investment capital. In the latter half of 2008, illiquidity was the banking system's main problem, and hence liquid capital became an important factor."[17]

In the third, thousands of clients of the stock brokerage firm InterBolsa stood to lose between $200 and $500 million in Colombia's largest stock market scandal. In early 2013, Simón Gaviria, the head of Colombia's Liberal Party, flagged drug money laundering as the culprit. Gaviria told Congress that the brokerage had financial difficulties because it had been cleaning drug profits through securities markets. Gaviria claimed that Daniel "El Loco" Barrera (who controlled the drug trade from Colombia's eastern regions to Venezuela until his arrest in 2012) and Joaquín "El Chapo" Guzmán (who at the time headed the Sinaloa Cartel and controlled a large part of the Mexican narcotics trade) used the brokerage to transfer cash through the Colombian firm. Officials arrested the stockbroker in November 2012 on instructions from the US Drug Enforcement Agency, and the brokerage defaulted on a loan and declared bankruptcy eleven days later. Gaviria told Colombia's Congress that the Chicago prosecutor's office had records of stockbrokers receiving cash in a luxury hotel in the north of Bogotá and that brokerage employees were using false business records to gain permission from the government to deposit dollars into brokerage firms in Colombia and, in the process, cleaning illicit drug profits.[18]

These three examples of trade-, finance-, and securities-based money laundering rely on what might be called a simulacrum: a representation of an economic transaction that gives the semblance of profit, yet on closer inspection the value (or profits) actually comes from another transaction—the sale of cocaine. While such stories of global connection are not always directly tied to Colombia, and even less to the Chocó, these wider phenomena illuminate the lives of miners. Each scheme—whether based on trade, securities, or finance—is a simulacrum that relies on a representation of something that does not exist.[19] Each is a mimicry of a money-making activity that is a step in a complex process that transforms cocaine profits from one sphere of exchange to another yet does not itself generate value, because the profit has already been generated by the illegal drug trade. The mimicry transforms value, and the simulacra occur, because while the activities might take place, the apparent profits are themselves derived from something else. A loss-making trade has the purpose not of producing but of transforming money, a financial transaction makes the banking system a mechanism not of *storing* but of *hiding* wealth, and a stock market trade has the goal not of investment but of transformation. Each simulacrum was not capitalist per se but a parasitic sleight of hand to move from one sphere of exchange—the illegal economy—into another sphere of exchange—the legal one. The simulacrum of profit making was an activity that aimed to move, hide, store, and transform, yet not generate value.

Bringing together the gold rush with this extralegal world of cleaning drug profits explains why mining, gold smuggling, and narcotics trafficking were all inextricably bound together. But this also begins to point at the limits of my ethnographic fieldwork as I practiced it, which was based primarily on participant observation. While this drew on the richness of direct insight informed by long-term experience, sometimes indirect knowledge requires approaches other than just ethnographic participant observation.

UNDERSTANDING TRANSFORMATION

In the Chocó, miners sell their gold to buying-and-selling shops in nearby towns, which themselves sell to refineries in Medellín, which process the metal to sell on foreign markets. What was the second-largest refinery in Colombia, Medellín-based Goldex, became embroiled in a money laundering scandal in 2015. The police arrested its CEO on January 2, 2015, and the Fiscalía General (Attorney General's Office) alleged that Goldex was at the center of a $970 million laundering scheme. Investigators accused the refinery of laundering gold from illegal small-scale mining operations by mixing it with metal from legal ones.[20] Simulacra of extraction using various forms of money laundering help make sense of frauds, swindles, and deceptions that do not produce or accumulate value but transform it using sometimes apparently legal projects. Reading newspapers spanning three decades shows how similar processes of laundering money through gold have taken place at different scales, for many years.

Salvatore Mancuso, an extradited high-ranking member of the United Self-Defense Forces of Colombia, described one technique to a federal court in Washington, DC, in 2010. Mancuso claimed that the paramilitaries bought gold in Panama using drug cash, smuggled it to Colombia, melted it into bullion, reported the bullion as coming from mines in the department of Córdoba, registered the production with a handful of municipal mayors, sold the metal on legal markets, pocketed their newly laundered profits, and recouped 70 percent of the royalties they had paid to the municipal mayors using fictitious work contracts. At the time, Córdoba, the department where José and Geraldo had originally come from and a key cocaine smuggling route north to the Caribbean and a bastion of paramilitary power for decades, was the country's second-highest gold producer. This changed in 2007 when production fell 99.8 percent in three months.[21]

Newspaper accounts of such laundering abound. In 2011, *El Dinero* ran an article on gold-based laundering, noting that Colombia exported more metal than its miners produced. In 2011, authorities found gold disguised as darkcopper pipes in Alicante, Spain, destined for Colombian narcotraffickers. In 2006, investigators arrested fifty-four people from Haiti, Spain, Colombia, and Guatemala for smuggling gold into Colombia, while an air passenger tried to disguise the metal as sheets of luggage inserts. In 2003, smugglers tried to move metal from New York by recasting bullion as cheap enamel hardware, wallet inserts, belt buckles, wrenches, and screws. In 2000, authorities seized fifty kilograms of "Panamanian" gold in the municipalities of Caucasia and Segovia in Antioquia, while 150 "gold mules" also carried metal worth $150 million from Panama and Mexico into Colombia. In 1999, a woman attempted to smuggle two solid-gold tractor-trailer hitches.[22] Each account could outline a technique to launder money by smuggling gold into Colombia and then passing it off as coming from the small-scale mining sector.

In 1999, similar stories were widely reported. "If the focus remains merely on hard cash and not precious metals, the world's drug barons may yet live to see a new Golden Age," argued investigative journalist David E. Kaplan.[23] Colombian cartels were buying a ton of metal a month from shops across the country. In another memorable arrangement, Swiss refineries sold gold to Italian goldsmiths, who turned the metal into jewelry, which they then exported to the Colón Free Trade Zone in Panama. The port imported twenty-five to thirty tons of Italian gold worth $300 million in 1998. Smugglers then moved the metal into Colombia, where small-scale miners registered it as coming from their mines and sold it back to international buyers. The enterprise produced apparently legitimate sales between four countries.

The case of "La Mina" was the earliest and biggest example of the same basic process. The scheme helped the Medellín Cartel launder their profits between 1985 and 1989. Pablo Escobar, the cartel's flamboyant capo, orchestrated the shipment and sale of Andean cocaine to the US, which created a problem: how to get the profits back to Colombia? The cartel used many techniques; one was to approach an Argentinean man who owned a refinery. The Argentinean proceeded to set up "La Mina" by opening a buy-and-sell shop in Montevideo, Uruguay, and a jewelry business in Los Angeles. The Uruguayan shop first bought gold from Amazonian producers (in the 1980s the Brazilian Amazon was experiencing its own bonanza of small-scale gold mining). Workers in Montevideo cast the metal into bullion, which they exported to the jewelry shop in Los Angeles. Soon the workers in Montevideo began to ship gold-plated lead ingots to California. The plating allowed the lead ingots to pass for pure gold at customs in California, which provided the Los Angeles shop with official paperwork for the imports. Then workers in Los Angeles separated the plating from the lead and sent the lead back to Uruguay; why they sent it back is unclear from the news reports. Meanwhile, narcos were buying scrap gold from jewelers across Los Angeles with cash from cocaine sales. Workers at the store melted the scrap into ingots, and then, with the paperwork from the imports of the disguised lead bars, justified the sale of the now-solid gold ingots to New York buyers. The New York buyers wired their payments to Uruguayan bank accounts. The Argentinean took his commission and sent the rest to accounts controlled by the Medellín Cartel.

Things went well until the narcos ran out of scrap to buy. To solve this problem of scarcity, the Argentinean recruited two New York-based jewelers. The two agreed to ship scrap gold to Los Angeles and accept cash from drug sales in New York. They mixed in narcotics payments with their activities. Soon, the two jewelers in New York faced a shortage of their own, and as the Argentinean was having trouble selling what he was buying, the whole group changed techniques. The New York and Los Angeles companies started to send shipments directly to a refinery in Fort Lauderdale, Florida, which melted the metal down and sold it to another brokerage house in New York. The refinery deposited payments into New York accounts. At first, this new technique relied on physical shipments of gold from New York and Los Angeles to Florida. Later, as this too proved unwieldy, fake shipments of cash disguised as gold were the solution. The jeweler in Los Angeles and the two in New York began to send cash in boxes labeled gold to the Florida refinery, which accepted the cash because it was in financial difficulties. The scheme fell apart on multiple fronts after a few years. A bank official in New York grew suspicious of weekly multimillion-dollar cash deposits from the New York wholesale business, an employee saw wads of cash through a hole in a box labeled "gold," and an antinarcotics agent conducting a sting met a drug broker in Atlanta who mentioned "La Mina." The US authorities arrested 128 people in the three cities in 1989. By the time law enforcement agencies had stumbled onto "La Mina," it had laundered $1.2 billion and made Uruguay the largest source of gold imports to the US, despite the fact that the country had no mines.[24]

For better or worse and with more and less success, the miners I knew, like José and Geraldo, were looking for gold. Thus, while newspaper accounts over a thirty-year period suggest that gold in Colombia does not only come from under the ground, not all production is tied to laundering. The men like José who washed for gold in their metal contraptions by collecting mercury with spoons was evidence the mining sector was alive, even if its practitioners may not be very well. Nevertheless, some gold may be connected to money laundering. Economist Thomas Naylor wrote that "whatever the vagaries of gold's role in legitimate international transactions, its function as an anonymous, portable and highly liquid instrument for covert transactions and hidden savings remains, like the metal itself, untarnished by time or institutional change."[25] Indeed, the phenomenon is widespread, with reports of such smuggling across the Americas.[26] After all, as Juan Pablo Rodríguez, the president of a Colombian mining industry group, noted, "At any point in the business chain [of gold], you can launder money."[27]

GOLD AND THE TRANSFORMATION OF VALUE

While it remains impossible to know which—if any—of the narratives explored above are still true, in the sense that they are current strategies of gold-based money laundering, each is at least plausible, and this plausibility raises unanswerable questions. If the political economy of cocaine works in part through gold, then might the public secret of gold in the Chocó, in Colombia, and in the Americas more broadly, be that the *rebusque* economy of gold and the movement of illegal commodities like cocaine are all deeply intertwined in ways that have little to do with shifting gravel, digging tunnels, or panning and more to do with the machinations of the global underground economy? Decentering production and accumulation shows how gold intersects with the cocaine economy. If Colombian traffickers use everyday capitalist exchanges to legalize their illegal profits, then addressing the transformation of value through money laundering at various scales could confound assumptions about profit in the extractive sector. Rethinking mining suggests that some mines are neither means of production nor accumulation but are instead simulacra of extraction that rely on resource fantasies in out-of-the-way places to transform illicit monies into licit ones.

It is by questioning taken-for-granted narratives of production and accumulation that the interconnections between the legal and extralegal economies become clear, as the latter can masquerade as the former through simulacra of extraction. While some of these examples are distant from the lives of Leidy, Martina, Pedro, Don Alfonso, Esteban and all the rest, walking around Quibdó one starts to see similar simulacra of production in other

Antonio pans at the bottom of a pit.

contexts, where economic activities that seem to be taking place are fronts for something else: the restaurants without patrons, the buildings uncompleted, the casinos open all day and night with few gamblers, and the dozens and dozens of gold buying-and-selling shops everywhere, empty and perhaps unused except for a handful. What to think of stories of moneylenders who will make *gota-a-gota* loans in US dollars (provided they are repaid in Colombian pesos)? What to think of motor-taxis everywhere purchased on high-interest loans—who lent the money? What to think of the public works projects that so often became unfinished white elephants? Even a friend once asked me to participate in a Ponzi scheme that made little sense, except perhaps, as a way to launder money. Each suggests absences in the forms of production of value or attempts to accumulate cash that could serve to transform value. This is where the money laundering could happen. Stories too good to be true become logical and even sensible if they are quotidian ways to launder money. Getting at these phenomena is an urgent but often underexamined topic for those interested in gold mining. The drug trade creates a peculiar economy in which mines produce nothing.

Of course, truly understanding the impacts of a shadow economy that cannot easily be studied proved difficult for me. Fieldwork based on participant observation did not provide me the empirical data on how money laundering works, but it did suggest some questions to ask. While the boardrooms of corporations, the halls of government, and the safe houses of organized crime were inaccessible to me from my fieldwork knee-deep in mud, the long shadows cast by illicit transnational processes were accessible by reading widely. Indeed, a similar technique can be used to make sense of large-scale, open-pit megamines, even before the mines themselves are built. This too is another kind of value transformation.

CHAPTER SIX

Speculative Projects and Multinational Mines

THE workshop, about the arrival of a multinational mining company from Canada, started a day late because getting everyone to the town upriver took much longer than we anticipated. Our boat left Quibdó and traveled up the Atrato River. It paused at one town and then followed the Andágueda River, stopping at half a dozen villages along the way to pick up passengers. The weather had been dry for weeks, and the river was so low that, at points, the passengers had to disembark from the boat so that the craft would float higher in the water over the sandbars and gravel piles that emerged as the river got lower. It was only late in the afternoon that our metal-hulled boat came ashore onto the gravel beach below the town that was our destination. Our group included leaders from Black communities along the river, a handful of people who worked in Quibdó for a Black organization, a lawyer named María Antonia from a nongovernmental organization (NGO) in Bogotá, and myself.

The trail from the river to the town passed kids playing soccer on the left and camouflaged, gun-toting teenage soldiers guarding a sandbag barricade on the right. The barricade protected a concrete bunker painted white and green in the colors of the national police. The fortifications were against guerrilla attacks. Both the Revolutionary Armed Forces of Colombia (FARC) and National Liberation Army (ELN) guerrilla groups operated in the forests between the Quibdó–Medellín and the Tadó–Pereira roads—the same roads that Don Alfonso and I had traveled. The FARC and the ELN had, for example, taken control of the town, injured nine civilians, killed eight policemen, and kidnapped twenty-nine soldiers on December 18, 2005.[1] Most towns on the Andágueda River had a fortified presence of the state in the form of a police bunker with green sandbags and perhaps soldiers. Most smaller villages had little obvious presence of the state beyond a

A planter high in the air, protection against insects and animals

schoolteacher who came during the week. It was only when there was combat between soldiers or police and guerrillas in a village that the government, international agencies, and nongovernmental agencies would descend to hold a workshop. Workshops of more or less similar form were also held by NGOs, government agencies, and Black communities for other reasons. Our workshop was not about the war; instead it was about two mining companies, one from Canada and the other from South Africa, that were coming to the area to open a gold and copper mine—or so everyone thought.

At each of the half dozen workshops I had attended, people gathered together in circles on plastic chairs and ran small group activities; undertook social mapping exercises to sketch their homes, rivers, mines, gardens, and hunting grounds; or held facilitated conversations to discuss topics of forced displacement, illegal mining, and territorial control. At many workshops, an inordinate amount of time was spent on attendance forms and paperwork and record keeping. Workshops themselves were not cheap to run. Each required transport for attendees, food from the city, and honoraria for participants. The record keeping was thus not inconsequential, as funders demanded the paperwork. The workshops often took place during the hottest parts of the day, even though some attendees whom I knew preferred early morning workshops, which would give them a chance go to work in their gardens or mines, or late evening workshops, after they had spent the day working. The daylong workshops fit best the schedule of the visitors who came to run them.

In 2011 and 2012, I attended various workshops to prepare people for what everyone, so it seemed, worried would be an imminent prior consultation process about the multinational mining project in the forest-covered hills north of the town, between the headwaters of the Andágueda and the Atrato Rivers. Or, at least, it was about the potentiality of such an open-pit gold and copper mine.

For the communities in the upper reaches of the Andágueda and Atrato, the idea of a large-scale open-pit mine in the headwaters of the river began to matter significantly in 2008, so much so that by the early 2010s, NGOs were sending María Antonia and others to hold workshops. Although that mine still does not exist as of the writing of this chapter in 2019—and may yet never exist—it has already done something. Although no gold has been produced, what appears as the endless stock market speculation of a Canadian mining industry can be understood as a transformation of value. The modus operandi of the junior mining industry is to prospect for open-pit mines and, based on the exploratory work, raise funds from investors. It is not the same transformation as drug money laundering, but money can be made and lost and moved through mines that are never even built.

Understanding the mobile capital of Canadian junior mining companies illustrates the centrality of speculation in the mining industry, which is a process that transforms rather than produces or accumulates value. Such mines are, often, ultimately failures, conjured only on paper. Yet they can allow profit to appear in extractive industries that have little to do with production or accumulation, and much more to do with the transformation of stories of out-of-the-way jungle deposits into investments on Canadian stock markets. Such mining projects can have impacts long before any operations take place. Despite the absence of actual mining, these multinational projects have real consequences for people living in the areas where they propose to operate, consequences that cannot be understood without also understanding the local histories of a place. That mine that has never been built and that may never be built had already by 2012 done many things: it had inspired workshops, it had created rumors, and it had exacerbated interethnic conflicts over land and mines and territory intimately connected with decades of armed conflict.

WORKSHOPPING SMALL- AND LARGE-SCALE MINES

The town was built on a promontory at the highest easily navigable point on the Andágueda River. A school overlooked the tree-filled central plaza beside the pale-yellow church where the meeting would be held. As the sun stretched into the horizon on the Friday night before the workshop, María Antonia and I walked along the trail upriver from the town toward the last Black community before the Indigenous communities of the Upper Andágueda. As we walked, we talked about the small-scale excavator mining in the Chocó, about the mining project of the Canadian and South African companies in the forests north of the town, about the Spanish colonial mines of Dabaibe in those same hills, and about the three decades of conflict between the two Indigenous Embera Katío communities who lived in the forests between the two roads Don Alfonso and I had traversed and where a dispute over gold had raged for decades. Would the multinationals really move forward with their plans for an open-pit megamine that would, we worried, displace everyone, Black and Indigenous alike? As we walked, we met three teenage soldiers coming the other way. One soldier carried two rusting guns along with his own rifle. The other soldiers escorted two younger boys with terrified faces. Had the guns belonged to the boys? Had the boys been hunting in the forest? What would the teenage soldiers accuse the boy hunters of having done? Were the kids in trouble? María Antonia and I kept walking. What could we do on a trail, at dusk, as the sun gave way to darkness in the midst of the jungle? We fell silent, subdued, turned around, and walked back to the town.

The next morning, María Antonia stood at the front of a circle of pews in the church, talking to the two dozen representatives from the various Black communities on the Andágueda River. It was they who we had picked up by boat the day before. Most of the representatives were older men or women, but a handful were younger. A couple of European NGOs with offices in Quibdó had provided funding. The Black activists, the various NGOs, and the Catholic dioceses of Quibdó were all worried about the potential large-scale mine of the Canadian and South African companies with title in the region. María Antonia was a lawyer with a Bogotá-based NGO—the same NGO that many years later was part of the Constitutional Court challenge that granted the Atrato River legal rights as a person. She ran the workshop in two parts: The morning was about the *retreros* on the Andágueda River. The afternoon was about preparing for prior consultation about the multinational mining project.

María Antonia asked about the impacts of the *retreros* halfway through the morning workshop, and men and women attending yelled out their answers, which María Antonia wrote with marker on newsprint at the front of the room.

"The *retreros* bring problems. Navigating the river is harder. They bring environmental destruction," one man said.

There had been dozens of excavators in the area in 2009. Indeed, a pair of illegal excavators had just started digging on the bend in the river opposite the police barracks at the entrance to the town. The complaints about the *retreros* grew.

"The government owns this problem. We do not have any machines. We do not have anything good. The government should take the blame. The ecological damage the machines do is bad. There are almost no fish coming up the river any more. The water has become undrinkable. The machines leave the water contaminated with oil."

"Sometimes there are conflicts between the community, the landowners, and the excavators. Sometimes an owner of the land might not want an excavator, but the landowner cannot stop the miners. The miners come anyway."

"Our children go hungry. There have been more than six years of excavators, but they have left us nothing. They came to the villages and to town. But we now have better conditions to fight against the mining."

Not everyone complained about the *retreros*, of course. Like Esteban and others, many saw the excavators as a good thing.

"Sometimes the excavators do good. They open roads through the jungle when they bring in the excavators from the highway, and this brings benefits."

"The excavators bring jobs: some people come back to their land from the city, and the excavators let people pan for gold, which gives people money."

Paradoxically, it seemed to me, some of those very leaders, the ones who articulated the most forceful critique of the *retreros*, came from families who had brought in excavators onto their land. There was also a cacophony of voices expressing divergent opinions about the *retreros*: environmental destruction versus jobs; cash versus fish; and rivers unnavigable in the dry season versus dirt tracks through the jungle to the road from Tadó to Pereira. There was no one opinion; instead the workshop brought out the divergent perspectives of these men and women from various communities.

After lunch of rice, fried cheese, and bottled juice, María Antonia turned the conversation to the multinational mining companies that held title to the forests north of the town. She elicited similar contradictory responses from the room in the afternoon, as she had in the morning. Some people saw threats from the Canadians, where other people saw opportunities from the multinationals. Everyone agreed, however, that multinational mining companies must consider the views of the communities who lived on the land and by the rivers that would be impacted.

In the afternoon, María Antonia asked, "Who has to be at a meeting for prior consultation?" She answered her own question with a long list: the Ministry of the Interior, the Ministry of Energy, the Ministry of the Environment, the Ombudsman's Office, the Office of the Attorney General, a collection of national and international NGOs, and of course the *entire* community. People nodded both in agreement and from the lunch and the stifling afternoon heat.

María Antonia continued her workshop with a more pedagogical purpose, no longer to elicit comments but to explain multinational mining to the assembled leaders as she and her colleagues in Bogotá understood it. She spoke about large-scale mining; about mining legislation as it evolved since 2001; about a 2010 National Development Plan that called for Colombia to become a mining country, with mining as a locomotive to pull the economy forward; about a recently signed free trade agreement with Canada; about the dozens of Canadian junior mining companies with projects all over Colombia; about the threats posed by large-scale mining; about prior and informed consent; and about the constitutional framework in Colombia, which gives international treaties constitutional status. This last point was important, because the Colombian constitution gave Indigenous and Black communities a right to prior consultation under Article 15 of the International Labor Organization's Indigenous and Tribal Peoples Convention 169 (1989). Black and Indigenous communities, María Antonia said, could use Article 15 to claim a constitutional right of prior consultation around mining projects that would impact them. Prior consultation, she argued, offered a legal tool for communities to protect their collective territories from a mining project. She emphasized that while the protection gave people neither the right to prior consent nor the right to veto a mining project on their territory, it did give them the right to be consulted. María Antonia's goal on that hot and humid afternoon under the tin roof of the church was to get people thinking about processes of prior consultation. How should a prior consultation process be directed—by the Black communities being consulted, or by the employees of the mining corporations doing the consultation? One worry was that a mining company might try to circumvent a wider consultation process by simply flying a handful of leaders to Bogotá and undertaking a paper consultation process without actually involving the whole community. María Antonia's workshop was, it seemed to me, an attempt to forestall such a possibility.

In a conversation I had after the workshop with an older gentleman, it became clear that people had diverse perspectives on large-scale mining as well. The late-middle-aged man who had not attended the meeting asked me what had been discussed. After my explanation, he replied with little interest:

"Great. A mine will bring jobs. We need work."

On the one hand, the workshop showed people's concerns about the effects of a large-scale mine on the territory, the environment, and the food supply. On the other hand, there was hope for benefits from the proposed mine, including a chance for jobs, and a chance to improve their lives. The mining project in the jungles north of the Andágueda River elicited both the hope and the fear so common to many resource projects, wherein the possibility of good jobs was weighed against potentially damaging changes. As with similar mining projects around the world, activists were opposed to multinational corporations. Yet, critic and supporter alike, everyone seemed to take for granted how the corporate backers of a mine would actually make their money. Workshops like the one María Antonia held actually reinforced a shared assumption that the extraction of the mineral deposits was imminent, and that the foreign corporations in question aimed to make their money from these minerals under the ground. This might be less clearly the case than is often assumed, as many mining ventures have less to do with producing minerals and more to do with financial speculation.

The proposed mine in the headwaters of the Atrato and Andágueda Rivers, in a mountain called Dojurá, was supposed to become another part of the gold rush. Yet ten years have passed, and the mine may never be built. However, it may have facilitated value being transformed from one economy to another. To understand artisanal and small-scale mining that does exist, it is important to consider the impacts of large-scale mining that does not exist. The workshop and the fears of the attendees stemmed from an assumption that the mine was relatively imminent and that by producing gold and copper and accumulating profit, the mining companies would make money, and that local people would be able to get their cut—in a way just like Esteban and the Black community leaders with *retreros* on their land had. This is not always the case, however. Just as some mines serve to transform value by laundering cocaine money, speculation seems central to the Dojurá project. The story of a mine in the jungle suggests a transformation of value from investors to corporate insiders, without necessarily building a productive gold mine.

SPECTACLE AND SPECULATION

About three years before that Saturday workshop up the river in the last navigable town, Ximena, the Black woman described in chapter 3 who dove for gold with a stone on her back when she was younger, watched soldiers disembark from a helicopter onto a garden on the Andágueda River across from her home village on August 15, 2008. Later, she remembered those soldiers as *muchachos*. Boys.

She wondered what they wanted. She was worried, because along with the soldiers, the helicopters had disgorged a handful of geologists. Ximena suspected that the unexpected visitors were after gold. In the months and years following the visit, it became clear that various companies claimed legal title to the subsoil mineral rights in the area north of her village. Although the Canadian and South African mining companies that control mining concessions in the area have made little to no progress in opening a mine eight years after the helicopter visit, the Canadian company described on its website its titles to deposits of gold and copper. The project existed only as words on a website and corporate reports, not as facts on the ground. This gap between words and actions is normal for the Canadian mining industry.

The Canadian mining sector is, in a sense, an industry of spectacle. Anthropologist Anna L. Tsing undertook a postmortem of one such mining project.[2] Bre-X was a Canadian mining company that became infamous in the 1990s when insiders committed a massive fraud in the jungles of Indonesia. The so-called junior mining company claimed to have found one of the world's biggest gold deposits in an area of Borneo where no such deposit actually existed. Tsing described the scandal as an example of an economy of appearances, as a theatrical economic performance that raised funds from investors rather than from selling gold mined from under the ground. Company documents, online forums, and media reports all showed how Bre-X positioned itself as a successful mining company on the brink of exploiting the most promising gold deposit in the world. The company's stock price soared, which made instant millionaires of early investors. Then the price crashed, erasing these paper fortunes. The crash followed the apparent death of the company's geologist, who jumped—or was pushed—from a helicopter. At the same time, auditors began to raise questions about the validity of the core samples.

In short, Tsing shows how Bre-X conjured a project in the jungles of Borneo that fed into the fantasies of North American investors of a resource frontier that, like simulacra of extraction, never need produce anything. Spectacle underpinned speculation. The trick was to promote a project around a legal claim to a distant and remote, out-of-the-way place, then sell that story to investors in Canadian stock markets. Physical mineral production was irrelevant. The mine was never opened, and yet money was transferred from investors to corporate insiders. As the latter spun compelling stories, they turned investor cash into their own rising stock values and salaries, a neat transformation of value. Might this strategy be in use by the Canadian mining company in Colombia that had Ximena, María Antonia, and everyone else so worried? Nevertheless, while no actual mineral extraction need ever take place, such a speculative mining project can still have real consequences for Black and Indigenous communities.

The multinational project for a gold and copper mine in the forests between the roads from the Chocó over the Andes highlights a tension between a gold mine's corporate promoters and its activist opponents. The project near the two communities was one in which no actual mining had happened, and yet lots has happened because of the idea that a mine was coming. Black activists like Ximena worried over multinational mining corporations. Mine promoters raised funds on Toronto stock markets. Black community organizations held workshops on prior and informed consent. Armed groups engaged in violence to gain control of mineral deposits.

One way to understand the delays in the project was through contested property regimes. First, the Colombian Ministry of Mines gave title to foreign corporations for the subsurface mineral rights in the area. Second, the Colombian government's Institute for Rural Development (INCODER) granted collective title to legally constituted Black communities. Third, rural members of the Black communities recognized their own customary kin-based rights to family gardens and artisanal gold mines, in the same way that Esteban and his family did with their tunnel. Together, these created overlapping property regimes operating at different scales on the same physical land. Could the resulting uncertainties over ownership actually facilitate stock market speculation? Opposition from communities, legal challenges, and even armed conflict all sowed enough doubt to excuse long delays in a project moving forward, and indeed justify the lack of progress in the minds of investors. Could such legitimate delays be a central—or at least common—feature of speculation by multinational corporations? If a junior mining company need not exploit any minerals because of delays caused by tension between Black property rights to the land, Black claims to collective territory, and corporate control of subsurface mineral rights, then the project could become merely theatre to facilitate speculation. Nevertheless, even stalled projects have diverse consequences.

PERCEIVED THREATS, LIVED CONSEQUENCES

"Why are you still here?" a soldier asked a neighbor of Ximena's in 2008. "Haven't you displaced yet? You should just displace. Go to another town or find a job with the mining company. It pays well."

Details of the soldier's visit are unknowable. Were these the exact words the soldier spoke, or were Ximena's 2011 recollections colored by intervening events? The reports from an NGO in Quibdó published in the month and year afterward agree, however. Soldiers accompanied a team of geologists, and the unexpected and uninvited visitors made camp.[3]

"It was a day like any other," Ximena continued. "We were at a funeral of a neighbor who had died. We looked to the other side of the river, opposite the town, and we saw some boys who wore the uniform of the military. Along with the boys, there were a lot of *señores*. Did the army have plans to camp there?"

By "there" Ximena meant the garden plot of a neighbor across the river from her home. The three streets of her village step up a hill at a river bend. While Ximena herself had spent many years as a domestic worker in Pereira, when I met her, she was looking after her grandchildren in her home. Her neighbors hunted, logged, gathered medicinal herbs, mined gold using hand tools, and cleared plots for forest gardens on the edges of the river.

"We thought the helicopters strange," Ximena said. "They flew overhead three times that day. We don't have those machines here. Later, we got together; we had a meeting. We asked ourselves, what were those people doing there? They are flying helicopters; they have made a place to land a helicopter. What do they want? Why did they come?"

The helicopters had landed on a plot of land that belonged to a neighbor of Ximena. Wind from the rotor blades flattened some crops. The *muchachos* destroyed the rest. They cut down trees and palms and *yuca* plants, they pulled up laurel and other herbs, and they flattened two-month-old corn. The soldiers cleared space for a heliport with chainsaws, stripped tree trunks of branches to make tent poles, left plastic waste strewn about, and prohibited people from coming near the camp to travel to their gardens or gather food.

"There was a moment when a solider said, 'Why don't you clear out,'" Ximena told me, before continuing. "I said, 'Clear us out if you can. If you have that right, that autonomy, then take us if you think we should not be here. But you come here, and we are from here. We are Colombians. How sad, truthfully, that this stuff still happens in the twenty-first century.'"

Would the soldiers forcibly displace people? Ximena worried they would, because as much as half the population had already left because of the violence and the terror of the armed conflict or to find work.

"I can't explain it to myself," Ximena said. "Why did the army have to come? Might it be to intimidate us? So that we would stay quiet because we are afraid?"

Ximena was not exactly sure what the geologists wanted or who they worked for, but she had her ideas.

"What did it matter?" Ximena said when asked about the company's name. "If it was not one company, perhaps it was the other company. The same company, though. They just changed their name. When in one place they get kicked out, they go to another place and change their name. That's how it is."

The army came to protect the geologists; the geologists worked for an exploration company; the exploration company worked for one of the multinational companies that controlled mining titles in the area. A NGO in Quibdó reported that the company was called one thing; some people said it was a subsidiary of a different company, which was connected to a South African mining giant. In 2011, the South African company AngloGold Ashanti controlled most of the mining titles across Colombia, according to the Colombian Mining Register.[4] In the hills around Ximena's village, AngloGold Ashanti had title to thousands of hectares. Other companies, including Anglo American, a mining company based in the United States; Continental Gold, listed on the Toronto Stock Exchange; and dozens of Colombian companies and individuals, owned or had filed paperwork to own forty titles to over 50,000 hectares in the Upper Andágueda and Upper Atrato. I heard rumors the companies were after oil, natural gas, and various minerals, including gold, copper, zinc, uranium, and coltan. In a corporate filing, Continental Gold reported an aerial survey of its claim as indicative of a copper and gold deposit.[5]

In the Chocó, the term "multinational" is used in ways that do not always coincide with large-scale, foreign-owned, legal mining corporations. I often heard Brazilian small-scale mining operations, which used dredges and excavators to mine gold with mercury, labeled *las multinacionales*. Newspapers reported that owners of *retreros* came from the US, Korea, and even China—the last having bought dredges and excavators with fake permission, paid thousands of dollars to start a mine, and then fled after receiving death threats. All these were described as *multinacionales* because of the nationality of their owners, even as they operated just like any of the hundreds of other small-scale, illegal, Colombian-owned operations. The Canadian, South African, and Colombian corporations that had international funding, legal backing, official mining titles, expert geologists, and money to spend on exploration expenses, helicopters, head offices, and websites were a different genre of multinational. While the small-scale illegal operations owned by foreigners actually mined gold, these foreign corporations sold investors stock on their claims of legal title to subsoil minerals.

Continental Gold controls some of the titles north of Ximena's village. The Canadian company has a polymorphous legal structure[6] and described its project in the hills north of the village as a 45,380-hectare, forty-square-kilometer zone of three registered concessions, six concessions awaiting registration, and five concessions in the process of being registered, all located near an area that had been surveyed in the 1960s with the potential for gold and copper deposits—near where miners have worked for four hundred years. The chairman of Continental Gold and AngloGold Ashanti signed a joint-venture agreement for eleven concessions on October 4, 2006, called the Dojurá project, in which AngloGold Ashanti promised to pay $200,000 to Continental Gold to explore on Continental Gold's titled land. AngloGold Ashanti conducted an aerial geophysical survey, which reported the potential gold and copper deposits. In 2012, the security situation in the area had worsened, Continental Gold reported, so no further exploration had taken place.[7] As I read the reports published by NGOs and Continental Gold, I asked myself a lot of questions: Where exactly is the project? What did the mining titles with the Colombian Ministry of Mines and Energy referenced in the agreement between Continental Gold and AngloGold Ashanti include? Which of the dozens of companies and individuals with claims were involved? How serious had the soldiers been when they had asked Ximena, "Why are you still here?"

Ximena worried the geologists were prospecting for minerals.

"They explained they had come by mistake. They claimed they came looking for an Indigenous community. We said to them, 'We're sorry, but everything that you see from here to wherever you can see is Black territory. There are no Indigenous communities.' The engineer said that they had come to explore. They said, 'I want you to understand, we did not come to work, we came to see what was going on. We came to take samples.' They did not say they were looking for the hills of Dojurá."

An airplane leaving Quibdó for Bogotá rises over the foothills of the Andes and follows the Andágueda River. Looking out the window in 2012, I once mused that the hills of Dojurá must be visible somewhere in the forest. They are the highlands north of Ximena's village. But finding where exactly the hills were on the ground was tricky. Where were the titles in relation to the hunting grounds of the people who lived in the village and the dozens of other Black and Indigenous communities in the area? Were the titles to the land owned by Black or Indigenous communities? On the official online maps from the national mining register, it was difficult to locate Dojurá. In 2012, the website of the Colombian Mining Register was slow, confusing, and unwieldy. The maps had few features and no details: a crisp grid of a mining title mapped onto an empty white square. The complex interactions of the rivers and forests and communities and people become the digital white space of a mining title.

Dojurá—the name that Continental Gold used on its website and in its corporate filings—comes from the Embera Katío language of the Indigenous communities that live upriver from Ximena's home. The Atrato River is fed by the Andágueda, Capá, and Tumbertumbedo Rivers, which in turn are fed by springs that drain the hills of Dojurá. The hills, if I had been able to see them from the airplane window, would be almost equidistant between the two roads that snake their way through the jungle from Quibdó and Tadó to the cities of Medellín and Pereira in the more populous Coffee Axis just to the other side of the Andes Mountains. The hills of Dojurá, not too far from where Don Alfonso and I had breakfast on the road to Medellín, were an in-between space. Black communities lived on the middle and lower reaches of those four rivers; Indigenous Embera Katío communities lived in the upper reaches. The mining claims, people worried, were centered on this interethnic zone between the Black and Indigenous communities.

Ximena worried about the geologists' visit, their lack of information, and the fact no one had even bothered to ask permission before they started exploration with dozens of soldiers. Why had the geologists not known that Black people lived on the river? she asked.

"When a company like that comes, it is our destruction. We will be left with nothing. Because they are not interested that we people progress. Better we drown. The hills of Dojurá are important for us, not just for this municipality, but also the neighboring one. It is like our reserve. The reserve of the Blacks. As a person, as a human being, I think that before mining companies try to enter, they must tell the communities whether they [the mining companies] want to or not. Because it is our reserve for the future. If they come, they have to come and dialogue with the communities. What is it that they want? What if they want to do something? They cannot come arbitrarily. We deserve respect."

By "we" Ximena meant the Black community for which she had been an activist for decades. As a young woman, Ximena had traveled a lot. She went to the city of Pereira, the capital of the department of Risaralda, to work as a domestic worker. When Ximena came back to her town for periods in the 1980s to the 2000s, she participated in a nascent Black social movement, which had mobilized to make claims for collective ownership of territory under Colombia's 1991 constitution. For a period, Ximena had worked as a lay missionary with the local Catholic diocese of Quibdó. She lived at home but walked on trails to the different communities up and down the river to run classes, hold theater workshops, and do other "consciousness-raising"—her words—events to promote "the process." She became one of the leaders of the Black community in her village.

"Do we have some necessity of being here?" Ximena said. "We do not have to be here. Our ancestors were forced to come here; they forced us to come. Therefore, everything here belongs to us. It belongs to us because we should not even be on these lands. But they brought us here. They brought us here to serve them, to have us as slaves, to subjugate us, to force us to do the things that we did not want to do. Now, they claim nobody lives here? After they spread us about like wasps? No. Impossible. They have to take into account that these communities and people exist. We are not as stupid as we were before. How are they going to tell us that nobody lives here? If no one is here, then who are you talking to at this moment?"

Who did Ximena mean by "they"? The Spanish who had enslaved her ancestors from Africa to mine for gold? The mining company that did not know Black communities lived in the area? Or the national government, which, at the time of my interview in the 2011, still had not recognized the rural Black residents who lived in the area? For Ximena, the mining project seemed a decisive reason to explain why the national government had not recognized the Black communities on her river. One branch of the Colombian state had granted mining titles to multinational corporations, and so another branch delayed recognizing the presence of the Black communities that actually lived on the land. Ximena thought this the likely explanation.

"Will they"—here I assume the mining company—"put themselves against the community? We are an organized community. Nobody can come here without telling us. We have our autonomy. The engineers came and said that they had come by mistake. But they wanted to talk to us anyway. We said they had to go to Quibdó and talk to the council. Why? Because it's the council who represents us."

This council was the *mesa directiva*, the highest administrative body of the Consejo Comunitario Mayor de la Organización Popular Campesino del

Alto Atrato (the Greater Community Council of the Popular Peasant Organization of the Upper Atrato), or in its acronym the Cocomopoca. At the time of the interview with Ximena in March 2011, the Cocomopoca was still six months from receiving a collective title it had been seeking for almost twelve years.

"They do not recognize our rights," Ximena complained. "They do not recognize that we were brought here, our ancestors, as slaves. Why don't they recognize that those persons did not return to where they were brought from, that they had to stay somewhere? Then, because they had to stay somewhere, they stayed here. Why don't they converse with the communities?"

THE FIGHT FOR COLLECTIVE TITLE

The Cocomopoca, which represents forty-three Black communities in the watershed of the Upper Atrato River, received a collective title to 72,000 hectares of forests, gardens, and villages in the municipalities of the Upper Atrato, Andágueda, Capá, and Tumbertumbedo Rivers from the Colombian government on September 17, 2011. The ceremony took place in an assembly hall, hours downriver from Ximena's home and a convenient half-hour drive from Quibdó. It was attended by clergy, politicians, journalists, activists from Quibdó, representatives from regional and national NGOs, and many dozens of delegates from the forty-three towns and villages in the territory. Ximena, a handful of representatives from her town, and dozens of others sat near the back of the hall. The event was the culmination of the twelve-year land claims process. All the leaders had wanted it to be a celebration of victory in a process that had taken more than a decade and that had often seemed unlikely to be fulfilled, yet the mood was somber because of a large mine accident a few days before, wherein seven people had died. A family had gone to work on a small-scale mine in the predawn hours during a rainstorm, and there was a cave-in. There was no talk of canceling the ceremony, however, because more than a decade had passed since the process had begun in 1999. The Cocomopoca's land claims process had taken a decade longer than many similar claims in the Pacific.

The Black communities that lived on the four rivers—the Atrato, Andágueda, Capá, and Tumbertumbedo—formed the Cocomopoca with the support of the Catholic diocese of Quibdó in 1994. By 1999, the Cocomopoca asked the Colombian government for a collective title to an area of 140,000 hectares in the watershed of the Upper Atrato. The government delayed giving the title despite countless meetings and extensive documentation provided by Cocomopoca activists. Over the years, local, national, and international NGOs had come together with the Cocomopoca to lobby state agencies through meetings, workshops, assemblies, delegations, and mapping exercises. As that first decade turned into the second, Ximena attributed the delay to the state's failure to recognize an essential fact: people lived on the land.

The process to claim their collective property rights to territory was remarkable compared to hundreds of others in the Colombian Pacific region because it took so long. The Colombian state had already awarded title across the region to dozens of Black communities, which formed in response to the loggers, miners, traffickers, and armed actors who arrived the 1980s and 1990s to disrupt rural livelihoods and who pushed Black residents from their homes. The Black activists developed a discourse that tied culture, history, social life, and livelihood to particular places. These community organizations demanded and, by and large, quickly won (except for the Cocomopoca) territorial control in the form of collective title.[8]

Across the Colombian Pacific region, legal recognition coincided with the violent displacement of civilian populations and a disarticulation of the rural economy caused by a low-intensity war, large-scale monoculture oil palm plantations, cattle ranching, drug production, gold mining, and out-migration. The legal recognition of collective property rights for Black communities stemmed not from a legal recognition of preexisting forms of collective ownership within Black communities by the Colombian state but from the political demands of Black organizations themselves. While Pedro and Don Alfonso and Esteban recognized inherited customary rights to lots based on whose ancestors had cleared the land, they all had a collective understanding of shared-use areas in the forest, which with the official collective titles the Colombian state had recognized as Black owned. This legal recognition came from Article 55 of the 1991 constitution, and Law 70 from 1993, which implemented the article. Law 70 protected ethnic and cultural rights by recognizing "Black communities" as ethnic groups, and by creating legal frameworks for their protection; granted collective landownership by creating mechanisms for Black communities to claim ownership to the rural river regions where they lived; and promoted socioeconomic development by creating state-funded education, development, credit, and technical support programs and granting land use rights for subsistence logging, fishing, hunting, gardening, and mining. The constitutional framework created what it enshrined. Black communities formed to claim collective territories under the legal structure of community councils.[9]

The fight for legal recognition of collective territories was no panacea for problems in rural areas. Legal recognition of the Black communities projected a grid of collective property rights onto the forests and rivers of the Pacific, accompanied by the processes of mapping, surveying, and dividing land titles. Since Black and Indigenous communities often share the same rivers, when the state came mapping, different communities began to contest the same locations. By creating Black communities, enshrining them with legal status, and giving them collective land rights to the surface, the government made the region more governable through formal incorporation into a property regime, which, however, fueled interethnic tensions. Worse, despite legal ownership of the surface rights and a long history of exploiting gold by rural Black residents, the community councils had no legal collective title to subsoil mineral rights.

Ximena worried that one of the reasons for the delay in the Cocomopoca receiving the collective was the mining claims by multinational corporations to the same territory claimed by the Cocomopoca.[10] Other reasons might have been changing priorities as national governments came and went, or conflicts with municipal elites over where the line between rural and urban areas would be drawn. One outcome of racialized and contested property claims to the surface and subsurface was the legal conflict over mineral rights in light of the armed conflict.

DISPLACEMENT, MINING, AND ARMED CONFLICT

A land restitution judge in Quibdó issued a five-year suspension of forty mining titles and ten applications for title to 54 percent of the Embera Katío territory upriver from the Cocomopoca's collective territory on January 30, 2013.[11] The judge cited Embera Katío communities displaced by mining over thirty years and the worry that the mining projects of the multinational corporations would exacerbate preexisting conflicts. The mining titles, which covered 80 percent of Embera Katío territory, were controlled by a handful of individuals and corporations based in Medellín, the US, South Africa, and Canada. The judge suspended the mining title because the communities in the area had been displaced by violence related to mining for decades.

Both the Upper Atrato and the Upper Andágueda might be described as historical shatter zones (areas that people escaped *to* in order to get away from the Spanish colonial and slave economy)[12] and contemporary zones of displacement (areas *from* which thousands of people fled to get away from rural violence). In the first instance, the Indigenous communities living in the upper reaches of the Atrato and Andágueda Rivers had run away, not only from the Spanish and later Republican powers but also from the formerly enslaved but freed or escaped Black men and women who also settled in the upper reaches of the Atrato River and the lower reaches of the Andágueda. If the Black communities fled a slave mining economy by going up the rivers to the least cultivable lands in the hot and humid lowlands of the Pacific region, the Indigenous peoples went further upriver to settle the headwater of both rivers. These racialized histories of settlement in the Chocó still shape human settlement patterns in the 2000s. In the lower reaches of the rivers and the urban areas, Black people make up most of the population, with *paisa* settlers from Antioquia controlling commerce in lumber and gold and trade goods, while in the upper reaches of the Atrato and Andágueda Rivers, the communities are Indigenous.[13] Over the Andes Mountains, there are *paisa* communities in the coffee valleys of Antioquia and Risaralda, the ones Don Alfonso and I passed through on our way to Medellín.

In the second instance, much of the contemporary displacement is tied to how the region is perceived as a dangerous place. Jesús Botero Restrepo, an Antioquian novelist, wrote the novel *El Andágueda* about the *paisa* colonization of the Upper Andágueda in 1946.[14] Botero wrote about the traders and the miners who supplied and worked the mines in a jungle inhabited by *indios*. In the novel, a young *paisa* migrant comes of age when he crosses from the Coffee Axis in southwestern Antioquia into the jungles of the Upper Andágueda to mine and later marry an Indigenous woman. This account was a representation of the mid-twentieth-century mining on the Andágueda—Botero briefly mentioned the *"negros"* living on the river yet dwelt primarily on the lives of the *paisas* and the *indios*. His was a literary representation of what he saw as a positive expansion and incorporation of the Andágueda into the zones of influence of southwestern Antioquia—a novel of *paisa* colonialism. The connections run deep between the Chocó and the western slopes of the western arm of the Andes on one side, and Antioquia on the other side. Smugglers used the Andágueda River to move between the Caribbean and Antioquia and avoid paying taxes to the Spanish crown in the colonial period.[15] Today, cocaine is moved. The Spanish crown itself closed the Atrato River to traffic for a hundred years in the seventeenth century to prevent *contrabandistas*, who moved goods from the Caribbean Bay of Urabá up the Atrato River, and from there up the Andágueda over the Andes into southern Antioquia.[16] Missionaries came at the beginning of the twentieth century and built a Catholic school in Aguasal, where they evangelized Indigenous communities, destroyed traditional practice and culture, and raised cattle. It was then that miners arrived after gold.

Guillermo Montoya and Ricardo Escobar, two *paisas* from Los Andes, a town on the Antioquia side of the western range of the Colombian Andes, took control of a gold mine in the Upper Andágueda in 1927, which they and then their families controlled for much of the twentieth century. They developed close-knit relations in the area with kinship ties and support from the Indigenous communities. The two *paisa* partners owned the productive mine until one of them died in 1974, whereupon the remaining partner and the heirs of the other fought to control it. For a while, both families agreed to mine in peace. However, they drifted apart just as a second gold mine was discovered by Aníbal Murillo, an Indigenous man from one of the two Embera Katío communities. Conflicts over control of this new mine divided the Indigenous communities into two groups. Hundreds died and thousands were displaced to nearby towns, to Quibdó, to those shacks along the highways between Quibdó and Medellín and between Tadó and Pereira that Don Alfonso and I passed heading to Medellin, or to beg homeless on the streets of Bogotá, Medellín, or Pereira. These conflicts worsened in 1987 when the grandson of one of the original partners and an Indigenous group attacked and forced 150 hired workers to leave because the family had denied access to the new mine and attackers took control of it, the cyanide plant, fourteen mules, and fifty-seven cows. That evening, the group smuggled gold along remote mountain trails over the Andes and into Antioquia to purchase guns. The police moved in to retake the mine.[17]

    The conflicts intensified as armed groups arrived to fight for control the mine over the next thirty years. The guerrillas came first, then the soldiers, and then the paramilitaries. On the left, these were the Nineteenth of April Movement (M-19), the National Liberation Army (ELN), the Popular Liberation Army (EPL), and the Revolutionary Armed Forces of Colombia (FARC). On the right, various paramilitary groups, Colombian soldiers, and police fought to control the Upper Andágueda and the Upper Atrato. A peace agreement in the area lasted a little while in the early 1990s, before the FARC and ELN arrived to use the area as a transit route, a retreat, a supply zone, and a place to hide from the Colombian army. In 2012, armed confrontations between soldiers and guerrillas were common and led to greater displacement.[18] Colombian army helicopters bombed Indigenous communities in the Upper Andágueda an hour before the sun rose on July 18, 2012. Nobody died, yet fifteen hundred Embera Katío people fled to Aguasal. On April 18, 2015, almost three years later, government soldiers and ELN guerrillas fought each other in nearby villages.[19]

    It was this history of violence that the land restitution judge in Quibdó cited in his decision to suspend the titles of the Canadian and South African companies mining in the same area that the *paisas* had worked for years. While the multinational mine has never exploited the area and may never be able to because of the decision by the judge in Quibdó, mining in the hills of Dojurá, the western range of the Colombian Andes, and the headwaters of the Atrato and Andágueda Rivers already has a long, violent history.

THE FIGHT FOR THE FUTURE

An antimining organization in Barcelona produces an online map of hundreds of multinational mining projects in Latin America.[20] The maps list the project of Continental Gold and AngloGold Ashanti in the hills of Dojurá as "being in progress." It was the visit of the helicopters in 2008 that brought multinationals into the imagination of Ximena and the Black activists of the Cocomopoca and their national and international allies. It was these fears that led the Cocomopoca to hold workshops about multinationals, mining, and prior and informed consent. Ximena was worried, and not without reason. Three decades of war in the Upper Andágueda had already displaced thousands of Indigenous people. Were the helicopters the harbingers of a giant mine that would do the same to the Black communities? It is impossible for me to know to what extent the project in the Upper Andágueda operates in the economy of appearances that Anna Tsing described.[21] Might selling shares based on the potential profits from a mine in the Upper Andágueda be more lucrative than building a mine itself? Probably not, but it is too soon to know. Still, the conflict over a proposed large-scale mine in the twenty-first century is not just one of digging minerals from under the ground but also one of fears of the future. The project has prehistory embedded in local interethnic conflicts over gold, in divergent property regimes, and in conflicting claims to surface and subsoil mineral rights. The delays in the Dojurá project must be understood as a continuation of rural contestations over property and the history of a conflict in a particular place.

By 2019, a decade after the visit of the helicopter and seven years after that workshop, the project in the hills of Dojurá had still made little progress,[22] partly because the land restitution judge in Quibdó had suspended the mining titles in 2013, and partly because of the legal successes of María Antonia and the lawyers in Bogotá. Indeed, while Continental Gold advertised on its website other projects in other regions of Colombia, in 2016 it barely mentioned the Dojurá project in its corporate filings. A 2015 report by British NGO Agencias Británicas e Irlandesas Trabajando en Colombia (ABColombia) about mining in Black collective territories quoted a representative of Continental Gold as saying it planned to soon begin a process of prior consultation with the Indigenous and Black communities in the Upper Andágueda.[23] Ximena's worries about a future large-scale mine that would bring violence might yet come true. Even if the multinational corporations never fully arrive, however, Ximena's neighbors already perceive the foreign corporation as a threat and already see prior consultation as much a means to prevent and delay a mining project as a place from which to negotiate. The mines of Dojurá had already had a significant impact—as shown by highlighting the particular local histories of multiethnic conflicts between Black, Indigenous, and *paisa* communities that had displaced so many people.

Ultimately, the Dojurá project in this chapter relied on a paper conjuring, where stories were told in ways that have little to do with production or accumulation, and much more to do with the transformation of value. Tales of a mine in the out-of-the-way jungles of the Chocó become stories to be used for corporate reports on Canadian stock markets embedded in a system of spectacle and speculation.

Going to a workshop with Ximena and hearing about a mining company that may never quite arrive gives insight into the uncertainties, fears, and hopes that a mining project engenders for a community. It also suggests how important a good story is in serving a mining company for a decade, despite little apparent progress on the ground. This is a process of speculation that is also a transformation of value, which in a way is not so different from the gold-based money laundering that has gone on in Colombia for decades. To fully consider a gold rush requires turning to processes that are neither about the production nor accumulation of value but instead are about the transformation of value, be it through money laundering or stock market speculation. Such activities do not produce a profit from under the ground and they are not get-rich-quick schemes, but instead they are processes to transform value. These processes of value transformation have real consequences, not least the drug conflicts in Colombia facilitated by money laundering, but also the fears encapsulated by that workshop in the town. It was not gold as a material commodity produced by miners trying to make a little cash that matters for money laundering or stock market speculation, but instead it is stories of gold that provided the lubricant for transformations of value. These processes were sometimes contested, as with Ximena and her concerns over the mining company, but were also embedded in particular local economies of narcotrafficking and mining. To understand gold, one has to consider not merely the particularities but also the ways that local events—be they workshops or rivers with no mines—are manifestations

Elisabet cooks rice cakes to sell as her *rebusque*.

of broader and harder-to-pin-down processes. Money laundering and speculation neither produced nor accumulated gold; they instead transformed value. Both required stories that relied on distance and the imagined remoteness of the Chocó. In neither case, though, was producing gold necessary.

Gold enables such stories in the jungles of the Pacific, with great consequence for rural people like Pedro and Don Alfonso and Ximena who rely on subsistence production and *rebusque*. It is clear that for some, producing minerals from under the ground is far less important than weaving complex stories of remote mines and fueling what are simulacra of extraction. Mines have a significant impact in their early phases, long before production. The mobile capital of the Canadian junior mining sector becomes central to this financialization, through speculation, which has real consequences for people living on a river. Mines that produce little metal become part of broader processes, transforming rather than producing or accumulating value. This connection sheds light on the shadows cast by broader economic processes that exist to transform value rather than produce gold. Understanding these networks of contemporary capital is required to make sense of a twenty-first-century gold rush. Drug money laundering and stock market speculation are both about the transformation of value. In the former, the metals and drugs are not merely export commodities destined for foreign markets that come from the jungles of Colombia but also intertwined in global legal and extralegal markets, as gold helps launder cocaine. In the latter, the idea of a mine helps to facilitate speculation, as transformations of value through the projects of junior mining companies in Canada become a way to transform investors' cash into insider profits. Both rely on compelling stories that enable processes to transform value.

Conclusion

Life after a Gold Rush

THE first time I saw the river run clear was on the first morning of 2012. The water reflected the shore with a rare clarity. Gone were the coffee-with-milk shades from water heavy with mine tailings. I sat in Pedro's green-and-yellow boat, tired from the festivities the night before, and watched four boys, the children of Pedro and Martina's niece, play on the rocks beside the dock. The river embraced the boys as they cartwheeled in, floated to a beach, splashed to shore, and clambered back up the rocks to relaunch themselves with shouts of glee. The river ran clear for the first time in many years because the *retreros* had stopped work and gone home for the New Year's celebration. I was leaving too, and I already felt nostalgic. I would spend the next four months in Quibdó writing, and although I visited the village often—even going mining and hunting pacas with a camera for those few memorable days—I was already beginning to think not as mineworker or fieldworker but as a writer. By May 2012, I would head back to Canada to teach a summer course.

The last time I saw the river run clear was for thirteen days in May 2017. Water the color of the sky glistened on little girls cavorting on an air mattress as they played in the river in the afternoon sun. The river ran clear because the *retreros* had gone, this time for good.

"Where is all the mining?" I asked friends.

"The gold has left," they replied.

In a way, gold was something alive, almost a mineral, nonhuman animate, something that could move on its own volition. This counterintuitive idea was grounded in a certain agency that Black artisanal miners attributed to the gold on their family mines. The gold wasn't just gone; *it had left*.

Marchers carry the green, gold, and blue tricolor flag of the Chocó during an indefinite, peaceful general strike against state abandonment.

During the boom times between 2008 and 2014, the gold had not yet gone. Polluted river water left clothes gritty, made one's skin itch, and was undrinkable. Excavator gold-mining operations—like the one owned by José and Geraldo—spewed mine runoff into increasingly turbid waters. Collectively, the excavators reshaped rivers, filled them with sediment and gravel, acidified water, and poisoned fish with mercury. Studies say parts of Colombia have the highest levels of mercury contamination in the world.[1] The Quito River, not so far from the departmental capital Quibdó, had been dredged for over a decade by multistory machines that had twisted the river's course so much so that the municipal capital of Paimadó has been threatened with erosion. The Atrato River had been filled with so much runoff, I heard once, that the water level was rising and floods were becoming common.

Things were different on the river that flowed by Pedro's village in 2017. I saw little sign of mining. Dozens of excavators had operated along the river and carved into the landscape that Antonio and I had surveyed when we crested that rise in 2011. All of them were gone by May 2017. With the gold having left and the small-scale miners long gone, the contrast in the river water was stark. Still, questions remained. Could that crystalline water even support life, or had acid runoff from former mine sites contaminated the river? How resilient were the fish, really? What would the mercury contamination mean? What problems had decades of mining left behind? What were the impacts of the leftover pools of standing water that dotted the landscape? While there is a need for more research to answer these questions, on that 2017 visit I could not but help feel a little giddy. Little girls lounged on the river on their air mattresses, and people said that the water no longer made them itch and that the fish were returning.

Anthropologists spend years doing fieldwork, taking notes, recording videos, asking questions, and doing our best to observe and record and describe and interpret. Sometimes, it is easy to forget the passage of time. The boys I remembered so well swimming on New Year's Day in 2012 were young men by 2017. The young mothers like Leidy I remembered had themselves become grandmothers. The boom times I lived and worked in, off and on, from 2010 to 2012 had ended by 2017, at least on the river that flowed by Pedro and Esteban's village. What happens after a gold rush?

AQUATIC AGENCY

When the Atrato River became a legal person in November 2016, it was through a landmark decision by the Constitutional Court of Colombia, which defined the river as a subject and a legal holder of rights. The river had a different genre of a subjecthood than what my friends had meant when they said the gold had left. In the court's decision, the Atrato River became a form of rights-holding nature within a Western legal ontology. It was not, however, a recognition of local sociocultural understandings of the river per se—rivers mattered but people did not see rivers as animate in the same way that gold is. Instead, the Atrato became a subject in a legal response to mining that has devastated life in the river's basin over the last thirty years. The court found that the state had failed to protect the Atrato from mining, and in its decision, it ordered new schemes of protection through better state policies framed around the legal personhood of the river.

One challenge faced by the Constitutional Court decision is that of implementing all such schemes. The department remains one of the most peripheral and marginalized zones in a country once called a lawless land.[2] There is plenty of law in Colombia, to be sure. Rural Black activists like Ximena quoted progressive laws and constitutional precedents to make claims for their rights. Yet all of these laws sometimes exist more in the imagination than in practice. In many areas, the laws of the jungle predominate, as armed groups on the left and right implement their own forms of rough justice, while human rights activists and Indigenous and Black activists, who are themselves increasingly threatened and victimized, continue to make claims to the Colombian government for protection through the 1991 constitution and international human rights decisions. On the ground, the transformation of a conflict and a state of incompetence make implementing these laws a challenge.

Another challenge faced by the court is that the decision grants rights to nature, and yet rural people by and large find their own forms of agency, not from the law or legal protections but through shifting livelihood strategies of *rebusque*, which often articulate with export-oriented commodity production. When mining ended on the river, not only did this have little to do with state laws and policies but it also meant that there were fewer possibilities for *rebusque*. If *rebusque* was the strategy by which the poorest and most marginalized in Colombia find a degree of agency, then the actions of Esteban and Pedro and Don Alfonso and the others must be understood not as the product of a state failure to prevent a gold rush but as the consequence of how people respond to the real and imagined possibilities that a gold rush presents. Esteban's family's decision to bring in the *retreros* (and Pedro's decision not to) had much in common with the decisions of so many *paisa* men and women pouring into the Chocó on their own *rebusque* after fast cash. These decisions demonstrate local forms of agency within difficult structures of poverty that marginalize and render invisible the lives of people living on a precarious periphery. Their decisions were, in some ways, little different than the work of Elisabet, who came with Antonio and me to visit the *retrero* mine and sell *agua panela*. Elisabet was in a difficult position: she lived on a river long ignored by the state, in the midst of an armed conflict, and in the midst of many structures of race, class, and gender stacked against her. She had no stable employment, few prospects of finding one, and few sources of income, and yet she took a boat to Pedro's village to sell lemonade, boiled rice cakes cooked in banana leaves, sugar cookies, *yuca* cakes, and fried donuts.

While the environmental results of the gold rush were devastating, as the court decision and a growing literature have made clear, the human story is more complex. Gold enabled various forms of *rebusque*. It was *rebusque* on a mine that allowed Elisabet to find her way. For both Pedro and Don Alfonso, the same techniques of artisanal production allowed for their dual household economy—an inward-oriented subsistence and an outward-oriented cash production—that made gardening, fishing, hunting, and out-migration complementary to mining, logging, or itinerant labor. For each, artisanal mining was part of a package of diverse activities and at the center of an autonomous dual household economy. For them, their mining with wooden pans was a successful stratagem to make some cash, which would let them stay on their river. Mines also provided the hope that cash would be made. The story is much more complex than just primitive accumulation, as Esteban and José and Geraldo all show. The Constitutional Court decision misses the ways that, for some people, producing gold was the core of the good life, and for others a way to accumulate cash and get ahead. It also missed how the wider gold rush is embedded in the transformation of value, because gold provided a way to launder cocaine cash and a story to fuel speculation by multinational corporations.

The boom in mining did not just occur because the state failed to prevent it, and the gold mining that still exists in other regions of the Chocó is unlikely to end because of the state either. Decades of the prohibition of cocaine suggest as much. The negative impacts of the gold rush may even have been exacerbated by a state that has criminalized small-scale miners while supporting international mining projects, instead of creating robust public policy to formalize artisanal and small-scale miners. If the livelihoods of artisanal and small-scale miners, *paisa* and Black, are in tension with the court decision, balancing both will be a challenge. Supporting and strengthening local agency for people like Pedro and Esteban matters, as do their rights to clean water and good health. And yet, visiting the village in May 2017 suggested to me that the most pressing issue on the river may no longer be the *retreros*, just as in 2012 it was already no longer the multinationals. By the time activists and NGOs and the state became focused on one existential threat, the threat had already begun to pass. On my return visit to the river, the gold seemed to be gone, some activists were talking of the rights of a river and a peace process with the FARC, while others were mobilizing a civic strike against the ongoing inability of multiple levels of government to deliver on important services. Yet the people I knew best were most worried about mosquitos.

AFTER THE GOLD RUSH

When fast cash turned Esteban and his family into rent-seekers of mechanized mining operations or wage-laborers on the same mines, when the guerrillas levied their war taxes, and when the economy was booming even as the mine runoff rendered the river into a coffee-colored, turgid soup, I asked Esteban's son Marco, "What comes after gold?"

"Cocaine," he replied.

With the benefit of hindsight, he was wrong. Sun-loving shrubs, fast-growing trees, pineapple, silence, more artisanal mining deeper into the forest, a transformation of the armed conflict, a general strike against state abandonment, and mosquitos carrying malaria would be better answers.

During the boom times, on the edge of the river, gravel piles overshadowed water-filled holes in the ground, and everything seemed to be a landscape of rock and clay and sediment left by gold miners, over which Antonio and I looked out and interpreted so differently. After the gold rush, grass and bushes and shrubs terraformed the minescape left by excavators. By 2017, what had been gravel became grasses. What had been grasses became secondary-growth forest.

This is best imagined from the side of the road. Driving from Istmina to Nóvita along the San Juan River in 2010, the remnants of a mobile mining frontier carved into the landscape were obvious. Beside the dirt track, huge swaths of gravel and stone had replaced the jungle for kilometers. Yet to the north, new-growth forest had already filled in. On Pedro's river, the mines were never so expansive, and a handful of years after the *retreros* had left, the trees were already returning. The gravel flats downriver from the village had become grassland, with *paco* trees shooting up. The areas that I had remembered being open were light forest. Where outsider-owned excavators and dredges had denuded the forest down to the bedrock by washing away rich alluvial gravels, leaving behind a postindustrial scene, the rain forest was again reclaiming gravel and leftover holes in the ground. While some said the forests were useless, others planted crops.

After the gold rush, a silence I had not experienced before descended. It felt good. It was the absence of music in the town down the river and in the two bars in the village. The bars stood empty; nobody had money to celebrate. *Vallenato* music did not play. Nobody danced the night away. The girls did not have boyfriends who were miners. During the gold rush, single miners, men from other regions of Colombia, especially Medellín and the Lower Cauca, drank beer or aguardiente or whiskey and played dominos and danced to *vallenato* and seemed destined to leave behind young mothers with broken hearts, or worse. With the bars and the blaring music and the dance parties most nights, a general feeling of tension was palpable. By 2017, the bars had closed, the music was silent, and a feeling of silence had come to the river.

After the gold rush, Esteban and his family returned to gardening. During the gold rush, he and his family had focused their energy on mining, giving up their forest lots to the *retreros* who promised cash without labor, washing the land below the forest over a mercury-filled sluice and leaving behind a buttery amalgam of heavy and precious metals. Four years later, with the *retreros* gone, Esteban and his family returned to the subsistence production that Pedro had never stopped doing. They opened new lots to plant sugarcane along the river, plantains a little inland, cacao trees higher still, and pineapple stands. Everywhere, pineapple stands. It's hard to describe how many people had planted pineapples. Prices in town had consequently crashed to almost nothing.

After the gold rush, the conflict was transformed. With the *retreros* gone, some said the *elenos*—the National Liberation Army (ELN) guerrillas—had left the river. The area was tranquil. Contrast that to a few years earlier, when the owners of the excavators paid a percentage of their profits not just to the families who owned the land but also to the municipal government, to the soldiers, to the police, to the *paracos* (the paramilitaries), and to the guerrillas. One friend called the guerrillas "rats eating in the bush." Over the last decade, newspapers often reported that mining had become the largest money-making scheme for armed groups in Colombia. Mining was becoming an important economic activity, and like all others (small stores, buses, and coca production), armed groups were charging protection monies.

After the gold rush, there was supposed to be peace. In 2016 the FARC signed a definitive peace agreement with the Colombian government, ending a fifty-year conflict, and in May 2017, the same weeks I was visiting, the FARC guerrillas began handing over their weapons to the state and fully demobilizing. It was unsettling, then, to hear all my contacts in Quibdó telling me that something had arrived, but it was not peace. While the FARC had demobilized, the ELN and right-wing Gaitanista paramilitaries were expanding into areas the FARC formerly controlled.

Peace has proved elusive, at least into 2019. Perversely, beyond the river I know best, the conflict was worse in 2017 than it had been in 2010. The peace process failed to end the violence in the Chocó, as the seeds of a new conflict can be found in the earlier one. Still, particular geographies matter, and where I did fieldwork, the guerrillas had moved on. The FARC never had much presence previously.

This peace was not reflected in the rest of the Chocó. Newspaper accounts described the ELN as stepping up its campaign and as having kidnapped eight young miners in early May 2017 in Nóvita, the day I arrived in Quibdó, where, due to the homicide rate, people told me it was no longer the city I knew. The paramilitaries had returned to the towns and municipal centers near where I did fieldwork, and newspapers described how they and the ELN were fighting for control of the new mining frontiers and the areas that had been controlled by the FARC. According to news reports in 2018 and 2019, at best one can say the implementation of the peace process between the FARC, which has now become a political party, and the government has been difficult. Not just in the Chocó but especially in Antioquia, the Cauca, and the Valley of Cauca, social movement leaders and organizers have become the target of violence and selective assassinations. While the Colombian Constitutional Court decision in November 2016 granted the Atrato River, the department's largest, rights as a subject of law, the failure of the state to implement its own peace accord and to protect the lives of social movements leaders suggests many challenges. As I write these words in January 2019, twenty-one men and women were killed by a car bomb at a police station in the south of Bogotá, the worst such massacre in a decade. The ELN claimed responsibility.

After the gold rush came a general strike. In May 2017, in Quibdó and across the Colombian Pacific region, a *paro cívico* (general strike) was called. Stores were closed, government offices shut down, the downtown was boarded up, the transport system stopped, the restaurants and street vendors were gone, and small and large businesses did not open. The central plaza became the headquarters of the strike. People spent the afternoon listening to protest music from the 1970s. The morning and evening were filled with long marches throughout the city with thousands more people, including musicians and mimes all dressed in black and others covered in full body paint in the regional colors of gold and green. People held banners, and a group carried a twenty-foot flag of the Chocó. The ostensible purpose of the strike was ten demands that the national government had agreed to the previous year, during a similar strike. They were basic: road repairs, hospital repairs, medical provisions, and a recognition of a political decision regarding the boundaries of the Chocó and Antioquia, among others. The language was of being forgotten by the state, of being disrespected, and of the state being unable to keep its promises. The strike took place simultaneously across the whole Pacific region, and at the core of the protest was that the central, regional, and local governments were unable or unwilling to keep their promises.

After the gold rush came the mosquitos and their malaria, which people called *paludismo*.[3] During that visit in 2017, and when I called in 2018 and 2019, I heard people complain not of the dirty river or the mercury or the mining but of *paludismo*. The first three months of 2015 and 2016, the Ombudsman's Office of Colombia registered almost 20,000 cases of *paludismo*; in 2017, thirty adults and children died from the disease. When I talked to Pedro and Mauricio, they told about those holes in the jungle that have become breeding grounds for malaria. While the trees had come back, the river ran clear, artisanal miners continued their work, an armed conflict had transformed, and a general strike had raged, what had people most worried were the mosquitos that bit as the day turned to night.

WAITING FOR THE NEXT BOOM

On one river, between 2008 and 2013, miners and their small-scale mechanized mines were everywhere. The evidence of their negative impact was abundant: while it was a booming frontier town on the edge of the jungle and the bars were full, the rivers were dirty, people said the fish had stopped running, the forests were gone, and the guerrillas were extorting the miners. It was all of this in other areas as well, which led the Constitutional Court decision to grant the Atrato River rights. In a way, the challenge of implementing the court decision is the same faced by the peace process: state capacity and desire.

After the gold rush, there was little small-scale mining; while the bars were empty, the river flowed clear, the fish had returned, the forests were growing back, the guerrillas had left for other places, and people had returned to their gardens, even as a wave of *paludismo* carried by mosquitos breeding in holes in the ground had worsened. While I'm no expert on forest succession, freshwater ecology, acidification, mercury contamination, or sedimentation, the story for the rivers, forests, gardens, and people when the gold disappeared was unexpectedly positive, and to some extent negative. Perhaps the notorious inability of the Colombian state to implement its own policies may perversely be a good thing, assuming the gold, having its own agency, as people explained, continues to go of its own volition. Strategies are needed not just to remediate a river but also eradicate *paludismo*.

Although the boom in mining where I did fieldwork has ended, the bust has brought some people back to their dual household economy of subsistence peasant production. Despite the peace process with the FARC, the Chocó was anything but postconflict in 2019, and armed groups have moved to extort other miners and other drug traffickers. While the gold had left the river and some things were improving—except for the malaria—in Quibdó I spoke with activists who warned me that the mining frontier had merely moved north along the Atrato River and south along the San Juan River.

Rural black communities in the Colombian Pacific region have long articulated their livelihoods to boom-and-bust extractive economies—rubber tapping, tagua gathering, lumber booms, and on-again-off-again gold mining—anthropologist Daniel Varela Corredor argues that rural Black peasants in Andagoya shifted from an extractive, export-oriented gold production when the boom times of a US-owned mining company ended in the early 1980s.[4] After the company left, people returned to a rural peasant economy embedded in subsistence production and familial territory. People often had their feet in two economies, a household economy for domestic subsistence production and a market-oriented economy. Varela Corredor,

The Atrato River from the air

building on anthropologist of the Colombian Pacific region Norman Whitten,[5] suggests that people participated in an export-oriented gold boom, and when the bust came, they returned to their forests and subsistence.

When I first did fieldwork, some people were heavily articulated with mining. When I returned, they had shifted back to gardening and hunting and fishing. When I returned in 2017, I also heard stories of development projects funded by the national government, international agencies, and internationally funded NGOs. Everyone, it seemed to me, had planted pineapple or cacao because they could get a loan from the Agrarian Bank of Colombia. I heard rumors of similar projects coming for a reconstruction promised by the end of the conflict with the FARC. Might what comes after the gold be a bonanza of development projects, postconflict reconstruction, and funding to restore a river? Some will be able to articulate themselves to this new bonanza, at least until the NGOs, the UN, and the government pack up, as that new boom turns to bust.

In 2017, I spoke with Pedro's son Antonio on the phone. He lived in Quibdó.
"How are things?" I ventured.
"Good," he replied.
We talked about the children we've both had. His two-year-old daughter was learning to speak. My three-year-old son was speaking a little more.
"Did the *retreros* ever come back?" I asked.
"No, long gone. They left nothing."
"Pedro?"
"Working at his mine. He works hard. He has a sore back."
Over the New Year, I had heard from Esteban's son Marco. The young had left, but the old had stayed behind. Esteban was in the village mining again, but now somewhere else deeper into the forest. Don Alfonso was "vacationing" in Medellín, as he had resumed his travels despite his protestations to me. Don Gabriel and Guapi and Martina's mother and too many others had died in the months and years since I had left. The *retreros* were gone, and they had left nothing. Yet Pedro still had his mine, which gave him a certain freedom. I imagined Pedro and Martina eating their fingerling bananas for breakfast, with Martina wearing her gold filigree earrings. The last time I spoke to Pedro, in 2019, he was recovering from a bout of *paludismo*.

NOTES

FOREWORD

1 See, for example, Taussig, *Devil and Commodity Fetishism*; and Nash, *We Eat the Mines*.
2 See, for example, Bain, *Ores and Industry in South America*; and Kneas, "Necessary Illusions."

PREFACE

1 Pronounced "Lady."
2 Sánchez Juliao, "El Flecha." (This book's epigraph, in English translation, is from Farnsworth-Alvear, Palacios, and Gómez López, *Colombia Reader*, 499–500.)
3 Oxford English Dictionary Online, "Shift."
4 Gudeman and Rivera, *Conversations in Colombia*.
5 This method was inspired by various authors who adopted apprenticeship, enskilment, or embodiment approaches to fieldwork by working in a factory, going to the gym, apprenticing in *vodou*, learning to hand drum, working in the North Atlantic fishery, or learning to box. In each case, these researchers relied on embodied practice and not just participant observation to gain a long-term enskilment, which provided them a base from which to develop their analysis. See Cooper, "Apprenticeship as Field Method"; Crossley, "Circuit Trainer's Habitus"; Landry, "Moving to Learn"; Lindsay "Hand Drumming"; Pálsson, "Enskilment at Sea"; and Wacquant, "Carnal Connections."
6 Lahiri-Dutt, in *Between the Plough and the Pick*, offers an excellent collection of chapters by experts on artisanal and small-scale mining around the world, including work on Colombia by Alexandra Urán and Marjo de Theije and Ton Salman. Indeed, the field of critical studies on artisanal and small-scale mining is burgeoning, with excellent work emerging on the gold rush around the world, from South America and

Africa to South Asia and Southeast Asia. In this book, I have not attempted to synthesize this growing and important literature, some of which is emerging as I revise these pages.

7   Dollar amounts are given in US$. These estimates are from Ed Prior, "How Much Gold Is There in the World?" BBC News, April 1, 2013.
8   Sebastian Chrispin, "How Is the Price of Gold Set?" BBC News, May 23, 2014.
9   On this point made by Galeano, in *Open Veins*, see the introduction.
10 On the history of colonial mining in Colombia, see West, *Colonial Placer Mining*. On the Chocó, see Orián, *El Chocó*.
11 Escalante, *La minería del hambre*.
12 The literature on the anthropology of mining, on small-scale and artisanal mining, and on large-scale resource projects has both been growing rapidly and is too vast to summarize here. The classical contributions in anthropology are synthesized in two review articles, first in the 1980s by Godoy, "Mining," and later in a follow-up by Ballard and Banks, "Resource Wars." The literature on small-scale and artisanal mining continues to evolve rapidly. A good place to start is the work by Brian Brazeal on emeralds in Colombia and the global gemstone trade, Andrew Walsh on sapphires in northern Madagascar, Kuntala Lahiri-Dutt on South Asia, and Marjo de Theije on Suriname and the Amazon. The pages of *The Extractive Industries and Society*, edited by Gavin Hilson, are an invaluable resource. On large-scale corporations and their critics, the work of Stuart Kirsch, Fabiana Li, Alex Golub, and others is fundamental. This book makes no attempt at a systematic treatment of these three literatures, for a couple of reasons, some defensible, others less so. First, the book develops a narrative and analysis from eighteen months of practice-based participant observation fieldwork on a particular river in the Chocó, between 2010 and 2012. Giving space to this fieldwork and writing this as a short book required that I limit discussions of the wider debates. Second, some of this excellent literature has been emerging at the same time as this book, meaning that the timely completion of the latter required less engagement with the former than I would have liked.
13 See Gaghan, *Gold*.
14 Lahiri-Dutt, in "Extractive Peasants," discusses the ongoing movement of peasants from agricultural fieldwork to informal mine work.
15 Following Dove, *Banana Tree at the Gate*, dual household economy refers both to inward-oriented subsistence production as a source of livelihood and export-oriented commodity production as a source of cash. The concept is discussed further in the introduction.

ACKNOWLEDGMENTS

1   Tubb, "Muddy Decisions," and "Everyday Social Economy."

INTRODUCTION

1. The term "department" refers to a *departamento*; Colombia is divided into 32 departments, each a subnational division with regional autonomy roughly equivalent to a province in Canada or a state in the US.
2. Arturo Escobar, in *Territories of Difference* (41–42), unpacks the politics of the terms for the Colombian Pacific.
3. Germán Poveda and Oscar J. Mesa, in "On the Existence of Lloró," cite annual average precipitation in one municipality as between 8,000 and 13,000 millimeters.
4. Ulrich Oslender, in *The Geographies of Social Movements*, has described the riverine Black communities living further to the south as an aquatic culture.
5. This and the next paragraph draw heavily on the court decision, Corte Constitucional, *Sentencia T-622/16*, 43, 47, 58, 71, 78–80, 94, 135.
6. Colombians make a distinction between *malaria* and *paludismo*—*paludismo* being a milder case of *malaria*. However, the terms refer to the same mosquito-borne disease that kills hundreds of thousands of people a year. On *paludismo* and malaria globally, see WHO, "Paludismo." On *paludismo* in the Chocó, see "El fuerte auge de la malaria en Colombia," *El Tiempo*, August 27, 2016.
7. Corte Constitucional, *Sentencia T-622/16*, 47.
8. On cocaine exports, see UNODC, "Coca Crops in Colombia at all-time high." A good place to start on the conflict in Colombia is a special issue of the *Canadian Journal of Latin American and Caribbean Studies* edited by LeGrand, Van Isschot, and Riaño-Alcalá, "Land, Justice, and Memory."
9. On the growing literature on artisanal and small-scale mining, a good place to start is Lahiri-Dutt, *Between the Plough and the Pick*, for example, de Theije and Salman, "Conflicts in marginal locations." On the situation in the Amazon, see Cremers, de Theije, and Kolen, *Small-Scale Gold Mining*.
10. On primitive accumulation, see Marx, *Capital*, vol. 1, part VIII.
11. Marx, *Capital*, vol. 1, 875.
12. Marx, *Capital*, vol. 1, 918.
13. Marx, *Capital*, vol. 1, 918.
14. Veiga, "Artisanal Mining"; Hinton, Veiga, and Veiga, "Clean Artisanal Gold Mining."
15. Innis, *Cod Fisheries* and *Fur Trade in Canada*.
16. On this early history, see Williams, *Between Resistance and Adaptation*.
17. On slavery in the Chocó, see Sharp, "Profitability of Slavery" and *Slavery on the Spanish Frontier*.
18. On the Chocó Pacífico Mining Company and Andagoya, see Varela Corredor, "Los saberes del monte."

19 On campaigns for formalization, see Urán, "La legalización de la minería."
20 For more on this figure, see chapter 5 and SIMCO, "Producción de oro."
21 On the staples theory, see Watkins, "Staple Theory of Economic Growth" and "Staple Theory Revisited."
22 On this neo-extractivism literature, see Farthing and Fabricant, "Open Veins Revisited."
23 Galeano, *Open Veins*, 2.
24 On Potosí today, see Francescone, "Tracing Indium Production."
25 Restrepo, *Estudio sobre las minas de oro*.
26 On the history of maroon communities in what is today Ecuador, see Lane, *Quito 1599*.
27 This reverses the dynamic that Scott, in *The Art of Not Being Governed*, describes for highland Southeast Asia. In Colombia, the hot lowlands are the less governed places.
28 Asher, in *Black and Green* (58), discusses why the Chocó is Colombia's worst performer for most indicators of human development.
29 Wolf, *Europe and the People* and Braudel, *Mediterranean*.
30 Sidney Mintz, in *Sweetness and Power*, made following the commodity de rigueur. A rich genre of commodity analysis resulted, for example, on silver, guano, cochineal, rubber, gold, and cocaine; see Topik, Marichal, and Zephyr, *From Silver to Cocaine*.
31 García Márquez, *Crónicas y reportajes*, 187–207.
32 On this history, see Roldán, "Violencia, colonización y la geografía."
33 Bryant, in *Rivers of Gold, Lives of Bondage*, suggests this smuggling route.
34 Leal, "La Compañía Minera Chocó Pacífico."
35 Leal, "Disputas por tagua y minas."
36 Gudynas, "El nuevo extractivismo progresista."
37 Alayza and Gudynas. *Transiciones y alternativas*; Gudynas, "Más allá del nuevo extractivismo."
38 The resource curse is the argument that the resource extraction leads to negative outcomes. Indeed, many resource-rich countries in the Global South face intractable conflicts of resource wars, complex political emergencies, conflict traps, resource securitization, petro-violence, petro-populism, and blood diamonds. McNeish and Logan, in *Flammable Societies* (10), call for careful and empirical consideration, rather than assuming that resource extraction is inherently good or bad. The question is not of negative or positive social and economic outcomes but of which and how.
39 On the dual household economy, see Dove, *Banana Tree at the Gate*.
40 Tsing, *Mushroom at the End of the World*.
41 Millar, *Reclaiming the Discarded*.
42 On mining in the Colombian Pacific, see Friedemann, *Minería, descendencia y orfebrería artisanal*; West, "Folk Mining in Colombia"; and Taussig, *My Cocaine Museum*.

43 Leal, *Landscapes of Freedom*.
44 *Paisa* means something different depending on place. Broadly, the term refers to someone from the western coffee region, in particular the department of Antioquia. In the Chocó, where the population is mostly Black or Indigenous, *paisa* refers to any white or mestizo person from somewhere else. Settlers and miners from Antioquia, European priests, Mercedes from Bogotá, and even I, a white Canadian male anthropologist, were all *paisas*.
45 Tania Murray Li, *Land's End*.
46 Standing, in *The Precariat*, coined this new name for the class of those precariously employed.
47 Ferguson, *Give a Man a Fish*.
48 Beck, *Brave New World of Work*.
49 Marx, *Eighteenth Brumaire*, 1.
50 Holmes, in *Fresh Fruit, Broken Bodies*, describes a different kind of physical labor, with his ethnography of the bodily brutality of picking strawberries faced by Oaxacan farmworkers in Washington State.
51 On financialization, see Gunnoe, "Political Economy of Institutional Landownership;" Haiven, *Cultures of Financialization*; and Sippel, Larder, and Lawrence, "Grounding the Financialization of Farmland."
52 Peyton, *Unbuilt Environments*.
53 Scott, *Seeing Like a State*.
54 Ferguson, *Anti-politics Machine*.
55 Tania Murray Li, "Beyond 'the State' and Failed Schemes."
56 Marx, *Capital*, vol. 3, 525–42.
57 Polanyi, *Great Transformation*.
58 Friedman and Friedman, "Globalization as a Discourse."
59 Campbell, *Conjuring Property*.
60 Brito and Barreto, "Did Land Regularization Advance in the Amazon?"
61 Kneas, "Subsoil Abundance and Surface Absence."
62 Tania Murray Li, "What is Land?"
63 I read articles and newsletter accounts promoting dozens of Canadian junior mining corporations in Colombia from 2010 to 2012. For an overview, see Mining Watch and CENSAT-Agua Viva, *Land and Conflict*. By 2018, all but a handful had pulled out.
64 On commodity circulation, see McKay, "Agrarian Extractivism in Bolivia"; and Francescone, "Tracing Indium Production."
65 Hart, "Informal Income Opportunities."
66 Oxfam, *Economy for the 1%*.
67 UNODC, *World Drug Report 2017 V*; Gootenberg, *Cocaine* and *Andean Cocaine*; and Kernaghan, *Coca's Gone*.
68 Grosse, *Drugs and Money*, 3–12.
69 Bohannon, "Impact of Money."

70 Ferguson, "Cultural Topography of Wealth."
71 Weiner, *Inalienable Possessions*.
72 Ferry, *Minerals, Collecting, and Value*.
73 Fabiana Li, *Unearthing Conflict*.
74 High, *Fear and Fortune*.
75 Muehlmann, *When I Wear My Alligator Boots*.
76 Guyer, *Marginal Gains*, 46. Elizabeth Ferry and Peter Gose suggested this connection to me.
77 Kirsch, *Mining Capitalism*; Fabiana Li, *Unearthing Conflict*; Golub, *Leviathans*; and Rajak, *In Good Company*.
78 On the gold rushes in the Amazon in the 1980s, see Bunker, *Underdeveloping the Amazon*; Cleary, *Anatomy of the Amazon Gold Rush*; and Gray, *And after the Gold Rush*.

CHAPTER ONE: GOLD AND THE HOUSEHOLD ECONOMY

1 The dual household economy draws on Dove, *Banana Tree at the Gate* and refers to the way households combine subsistence production as a source of livelihood and commodity production as a source of cash.
2 I didn't record the names of the fish that people caught, but the Atrato River is home to a plethora of aquatic fish species. In a 2018 study of fish consumption in Quibdó, the most common species consumed were three freshwater fish: *bocachico* (*Prochilodus magdalenae*), *cachama* (*Colossoma macropomum* sp.), and *dentón* (*Leporinus myscorum*), according to van Vliet et al., "Wild Animals," 10.
3 I use an exchange rate of 1,800 Colombian pesos to 1 US dollar throughout this book, which was appropriate in 2010 to 2012. The value of the US dollar to the Colombian peso rose markedly after 2014.

CHAPTER TWO: GOLD AND THE CASH ECONOMY

1 Oslender, in "Banality of Displacement," assesses displacement statistics in Colombia.
2 Escobar, in "Displacement, Development, and Modernity," outlines how the arrival of the war caused displacement.
3 Andrew Willis, "Gold Beats Cocaine as Colombia Rebel Money Maker: Police," *Bloomberg*, June 21, 2013.
4 Simon Romero, "In Colombia, New Gold Rush Fuels Old Conflict," *New York Times*, March 3, 2011.
5 "Accidente en la vía Medellín-Quibdó destapó el mal estado de la malla vial nacional," *El Tiempo*, February 7, 2009.
6 Appelbaum, in *Muddied Waters*, and Roldán, in *Blood and Fire*, discuss *paisa* identity in Colombia.

7   Asher, in *Black and Green* (32–35, 200), discusses race in the Chocó and critiques these common estimates of demographic data as unreliable.
8   Safford and Palacios, *Colombia*.
9   Wade, *Blackness and Race Mixture*.
10 See "Odin Sanchez Freed: Colombia's ELN Rebels Release Key Hostage," *BBC News*, February 2, 2017; "Hijo de líder afro, nueva víctima en la convulsionada región del Atrato chocoano," Verdad Abierta, October 30, 2016; Comisión Intereclesial de Justicia y Paz, "Amenaza indiscriminada."
11 Appelbaum, *Muddied Waters*.

CHAPTER THREE: FAMILY MINES AND SMALL-SCALE MINING

1   Tania Murray Li, in *Land's End*, makes a similar point for the Indigenous frontier of central Sulawesi, Indonesia, where highland people planted a cacao cash crop, which enclosed their once-collective land and ultimately brought disastrous results.
2   The discussion of black communities continues in chapter 5. See also Asher, *Black and Green*; Escobar, *Territories of Difference*; Ng'weno, *Turf Wars*; Oslender, Camacho, and Restrepo, *De montes, ríos y ciudades*; and Oslender, *Geographies of Social Movements*.
3   On kinship and lot ownership, see Oslender, *Geographies of Social Movements*, 116–19; and Friedemann and Arocha Rodríguez, *Herederos del jaguar*, 205.
4   The September 2011 price was not the highest price ever, which, in inflation-adjusted terms, occurred in January 1980. See US Geological Survey, "Gold Statistics and Information."
5   Leal, in "Black Forests" and "Disputas por tagua y minas," describes gold and tagua as export commodities.
6   Leal and Restrepo, in *Unos bosques sembrados de aserríos*, describe the history of logging in the Colombian Pacific region.
7   Restrepo, in *Estudio sobre las minas* (191), described women diving for gold as *zambullidoras* in 1888.
8   Friedemann, *Minería, descendencia y orfebrería*; West, *Colonial Placer Mining* and "Folk Mining in Colombia."

CHAPTER FOUR: *REBUSQUE* ON THE PRECARIOUS PERIPHERY

1   Farnsworth-Alvear, Palacios, and Gómez López, in *Colombia Reader* (499–500), make this point.

2. On this transformation in Medellín, see Farnsworth-Alvear, *Dulcinea in the Factory*, and Tubb, "Narratives of Citizenship."
3. On the Chocó Pacífico Mining Company and Andagoya, see Escalante, *La minería del hambre*; O'Neill, *From Snowshoes to Wingtips*, 129–42; and Varela Corredor, "Los saberes del monte."
4. Rojas, "Securing the State."
5. Hylton, in "The Cold War That Didn't End" and "Medellín's Makeover," describes this story of modernization in Medellín. See also Civico, "'We Are Illegal.'"
6. Hart, "Informal Income Opportunities."
7. Ferry and Ferry, in *La Batea*, discuss gold in the Lower Cauca more recently.
8. On the informality and illegality of small-scale mining, see Urán, "La legalización de la minería."
9. María Teresa Ronderos, "La fiebre minera se apoderó de Colombia," *Semana*, September 6, 2011; "Chocó, tierra de dragones," *Semana*, March 29, 2013.
10. See CODHES, *La crisis humanitaria*.
11. This is a reference to the Mothers of Soacha scandal in which soldiers took teenagers from the slums of Bogotá to the north of Santander, assassinated the kids, dressed their bodies up as combat kills by the guerrillas, and then claimed extra pay and vacation—a perverse *rebusque*. See del Pilar Castillo V., "¿Qué tan perverso puede llegar a ser un sistema de incentivos?"
12. See Vox, *Diccionario avanzado*, and Real Academia Española, *Diccionario*.
13. Mejía and Rico, *La microeconomía de la producción*.
14. Taussig, in *My Cocaine Museum* (160–61), describes the movement of cement for cocaine to the Putumayo, in southern Colombia.
15. Belén Fonseca, in "It's Not Just about Money," writes about street performers and *rebusque*.
16. García Márquez, *Crónicas y reportajes*, 187–207.
17. On this allegation, see Ramírez Cuellar, "State Terrorism and the Dirty Business."
18. "Mineros del Chocó se toman aeropuerto de Quibdó," *El Espectador*, July 19, 2013.

CHAPTER FIVE: SIMULATED EXTRACTION AND GOLD-BASED MONEY LAUNDERING

1. Meza Ramírez, in *Tradiciones elaboradas y modernizaciones vividas*, describes these ways of life on the Baudó River through his ethnography of an unbuilt highway to the sea.

2   Nordstrom, *Global Outlaws*.
3   This is a point that Taussig, in *My Cocaine Museum*, and Civico, in *Para-State* (119–43), make. Others have as well.
4   Asher, *Black and Green*, 58.
5   SIMCO, "Producción de Oro."
6   Taussig, *Defacement*, 5.
7   Naylor, "Underworld of Gold."
8   SIMCO, "Producción de Oro."
9   Juan José Hoyos, "Dios y el diablo en la tierra del oro," *Semana*, August 25, 2012.
10 My estimate came from multiplying municipal registrations per year with the average world price for the years in question.
11 Contraloría General de la República, *Informe actuación especial*, 163; Contraloría General de la República, *Minería en Colombia*, 178–81; "Posible lavado de activos con regalías ficticias, advierte Contraloría," *El Espectador*, July 15, 2013; "Autoridades investigan posible lavado de activos con dinero de minería y regalías," La W Radio, January 16, 2013; "Más pistas de lavado de activos vía regalia," *El Dinero*, July 23, 2013.
12 Jesús Duva, "'Narcos' colombianos transportan droga en submarinos fabricados por ellos mismos," *El Espectador*, January 27, 2009.
13 Dudley Althaus, "Report: 'Chapo' Guzman Grabs More Market Share in Colombia," InSight Crime, January 10, 2013, www.insightcrime.org/news-analysis/report-chapo-guzman-grabs-more-market-share-in-colombia; "A la cárcel 10 integrantes de combo delincuencial 'Los Chacales,'" *El Espectador*, September 16, 2013.
14 Juan David Laverde Palma, "El crimen que 'La Gata' no pudo burlar," *El Espectador*, January 12, 2013.
15 As one anonymous reviewer pointed out, the black market peso exchange may have emerged in the age of fixed exchange rates, not long gone, in which Colombia was the only country in the Americas where the black market price of the US dollar was worse than the official price, as huge inflows of dollars lead to a tendency to discount the price in the illegal economy to facilitate money laundering. For example, FATF, *Trade-Based Money Laundering*.
16 Ed Vulliamy, "Western Banks 'Reaping Billions from Colombian Cocaine Trade,'" *The Observer*, June 2, 2012.
17 Quoted in Rajeev Syal, "Drug Money Saved Banks in Global Crisis, Claims UN Advisor," *The Observer*, December 12, 2009.
18 "Investigan si el Chapo Guzman lavó dinero a través de Interbolsa," *El Espectador*, April 11, 2013; "InterBolsa y el dinero de los narcos," *Semana*, May 18, 2013.
19 Baudrillard, *Simulation and Simulacra*.

20 Cecilia Jamasmie, "Colombian Gold CEO Involved in $970m Laundering Case Arrested," Mining.com, January 22, 2015.
21 "Con oro lavan dinero y se roban regalías, reveló el ex jefe 'para' Salvatore Mancuso," *El Tiempo*, July 31, 2010.
22 "Carteles lavan dinero con oro comprado en Panamá," *Crítica*, September 2, 2000; "La nueva lavandería," *El Dinero*, June 9, 2011; "Desmantelan banda colombiana de lavado de dinero," *Emol*, August 6, 2000; Germán Jiménez Morales, "El Dorado de las bandas criminales," *El Colombiano*, October 3, 2010; M. C. Sánchez, "Un comercio de Alicante blanqueaba dinero del mayor cártel de la droga suramericano," *La Verdad*, July 27, 2011; Benjamin Weiser and Daisy Hernández, "Drug Money Laundered into Gold, U.S. Says," *New York Times*, June 6, 2003.
23 David E. Kaplan, "The Golden Age of Crime: Why International Drug Traffickers Are Invading the Global Gold Trade," *U.S. News & World Report*, November 21, 1999.
24 On "La Mina," see Naylor, "Underworld of Gold" (205); and Evan Lowell Maxwell, "Gold, Drugs, and Clean Cash: Colombians Sent Tons of Dirty Cocaine Money to the Los Angeles Jewelry District, $1.2 Billion Came Out Spotless," *Los Angeles Times*, February 18, 1990.
25 Naylor, "Underworld of Gold," 192.
26 Wagner, *Organized Crime and Illegally Mined Gold*.
27 Nadja Drost, "Gold Rush," *Money Laundering Bulletin*, March 6, 2012.

CHAPTER SIX: SPECULATIVE PROJECTS AND MULTINATIONAL MINES

1 "Capturado guerrillero que participó en toma a San Marino," *El Mundo*, June 22, 2013.
2 Tsing, "Inside the Economy of Appearances."
3 FISCH, in "El ejército nacional," described the visit a month afterwards. The Ontario Public Service Employees Union published a report, "Black Communities," the following year.
4 CMC (in English, the Colombian Mining Property Register), in "Consulta expediente," shows that AngloGold Ashanti controlled subsoil mineral rights to hundreds of thousands of hectares across Colombia.
5 Continental Gold, "Annual Information Form."
6 S&P Capital IQ, in "Market Access Profile: Continental Gold Ltd.," reported that prior to a 2015 reorganization, which moved the head offices to Canada, Continental Gold Ltd. was based in Bermuda; had Canadian tax resident status; was listed on the Toronto Stock Exchange; had a series of Medellín-based holding companies for its Colombian operations; had been formed in Bermuda in 2010 from the amalgamation of Continental Gold Ltd., which had been incorporated in Bermuda in

2007, and Toronto-based Cronus Resources Ltd., which had been incorporated in British Columbia in 1986 as Crest Resources Ltd. Crest Resources changed its name to Sentinel Resources Ltd. in 1992, then to Ulysses International Resources Ltd. in 1995 when it moved to Bermuda; it then changed its name to Auric Resources Ltd. in 2001, then moved to the Yukon Territory in 2001, then changed its name to Lalo Ventures Ltd. and returned to British Columbia in 2005, where it changed its name to Sunrise Minerals and then to Cronus Resources Ltd. in 2008, followed by a move to Ontario in 2009.

7 Continental Gold, "Annual Information Form."
8 Asher, in *Black and Green*, describes the collective titling process of Black communities in the Chocó.
9 Escobar, in *Territories of Difference* (53), discusses this new territorial order.
10 On the Cocomopoca and these delays, see Martínez Basallo, *Configuraciones locales del estado*.
11 On the decision of the judge who worked for the Land Restitution Office of the Directorate of Ethnic Affairs in Quibdó, see Unidad Administrativa Especial de Gestión de Restitución de Tierras Despojadas, "Medida Cautelar"; and Karen Tatiana Pardo, "La promesa incumplida a los emberas katíos del Alto Andágueda," *El Espectador*, January 3, 2016.
12 Scott, in *The Art of Not Being Governed*, describes the areas people flee to escape state violence. Scott builds on Clastres, who in *Society against the State* was writing of the borderlands of Brazil and Paraguay.
13 Gniset, *Poblamiento, hábitats y pueblos*; Romero, "Procesos de poblamiento."
14 Botero Restrepo, *Andágueda*.
15 Roldán, in "Violencia, colonización y la geografía de la diferencia," writes about the closure of the Atrato and the imagination of space in Colombia.
16 On the *paisa* expansion to Western Antioquia, see Parsons, *Antioqueño Colonization in Western Colombia* and *Antioquia's Corridor to the Sea*.
17 Hoyos, in *El oro y la sangre*, offers an excellent account of gold in the Upper Andágueda. For updates on this history, see José E. Mosquera, "Adoctrinados para la guerra," *El Mundo*, June 26, 2008; José E. Mosquera, "El oro de Dabaibe," *El Mundo*, June 19, 2008; José E. Mosquera, "Guerra entre indios," *El Mundo*, July 3, 2008; José E. Mosquera, "Historia de una guerra tribal por el oro del Chocó," *Las 2 Orillas*, September 22, 2015; José E. Mosquera, "La paz con hambre," *El Mundo*, July 11, 2008; and José E. Mosquera, "La tragedia de los indígenas," *El Mundo*, September 6, 2012. See OREWA, *Minería*, for a perspective from civil society.

18 Observatorio Pacífico y Territorio, "Ejército colombiano"; ONIC, "Graves confrontaciones."
19 Asociación OREWA, "Bombardeo del Ejército"; Autoridades Tradicionales Indígenas, "Comunicado bombardeos."
20 Environmental Justice Atlas, "Dojura, Chocó, Colombia."
21 Tsing, "Inside the Economy of Appearances."
22 CEJS, in *La minería en Chocó*, offers a panorama of mining in the Chocó in 2016.
23 ABColombia, *Fuelling Conflict*.

CONCLUSION

1 Cordy et al., in "Mercury Contamination from Artisanal Gold Mining," suggest that Antioquia has the highest per capita mercury contamination in the world.
2 Taussig, *Law in a Lawless Land*.
3 "El fuerte auge de la malaria en Colombia," *El Tiempo*, August 27, 2016.
4 Varela Corredor, "Los saberes del monte."
5 Whitten, *Black Frontiersmen*.

BIBLIOGRAPHY

ABBREVIATIONS

ABColombia	Agencias Británicas e Irlandesas Trabajando en Colombia
Asociación OREWA	Asociación de Cabildos—Autoridades Tradicionales Indígenas Embera Dóbida, Katío, Chamí y Dule
CEJS	Centro de Estudios para la Justicia Social (Tierra Digna)
CMC	Catastro Minero Colombiano
CODHES	Consultoría para los Derechos Humanos y el Desplazamiento
FATF	Financial Action Task Force
FISCH	Foro Interétnico Solidaridad Chocó
ONIC	Organización Nacional Indígena de Colombia
OPSEU	Ontario Public Service Employees Union
OREWA	Consejo de autoridades indígenas de la asociación de cabildos, Embera Dobida Indígenas Wounaan, Katío, Chamí y Tule del departamento del Chocó
SIMCO	Sistema de Información Minero Colombiano
UNODC	United Nations Office on Drugs and Crime
WHO	World Health Organization

SOURCES

Agencias Británicas e Irlandesas Trabajando en Colombia (ABColombia). *Fuelling Conflict in Colombia: The Impact of Gold Mining.* London: ABColombia, 2016.

Alayza, Alejandra, and Eduardo Gudynas. *Transiciones y alternativas al extractivismo en la región andina: una mirada desde Bolivia, Ecuador, y Perú.* Lima, Peru: Centro Peruano de Estudios Sociales, 2012.

Appelbaum, Nancy P. *Muddied Waters: Race, Region, and Local History in Colombia, 1846–1948*. Durham: Duke University Press, 2003.

Asher, Kiran. *Black and Green: Afro-Colombians, Development, and Nature in the Pacific Lowlands*. Durham: Duke University Press, 2009.

Asociación de Cabildos—Autoridades Tradicionales Indígenas Embera Dóbida, Katío, Chamí y Dule, Departamento del Chocó, Colombia (Asociación OREWA). "Bombardeo del Ejército en el Alto Andágueda-Chocó." 2012. Accessed March 7, 2017. www.colectivodeabogados.org/Bombardeo-del-Ejercito-en-el-Alto.

Autoridades Tradicionales Indígenas, Cabildo Mayor Zona del Alto Andágueda, Cabildo Zona 3. "Comunicado bombardeos en el Alto Andágueda." 2015. Accessed April 20, 2016. http://radiomacondo.fm/2015/04/26/comunicado-bombardeos-en-el-alto-andagueda/#_jmp0_.

Bain, H. Foster. *Ores and Industry in South America*. New York: Harper Brothers, 1934.

Ballard, Chris, and Glenn Banks. "Resource Wars: The Anthropology of Mining." *Annual Review of Anthropology* 32, no. 1 (2003): 287–313.

Baudrillard, Jean. *Simulation and Simulacra*. Translated by Sheila Faria Glaser. Ann Arbor: University of Michigan Press, 1994.

Beck, Ulrich. *The Brave New World of Work*. Cambridge: Polity, 2000.

Belén Fonseca, Ana. "It's Not Just about Money: An Ethnography of Rebusque Performances and Life-Stories on Public Transportation Buses in Downtown Bogota Colombia." MA thesis, Carleton University, 2011.

Bohannon, Paul. "The Impact of Money on an African Subsistence Economy." *Journal of Economic History* 19, no. 4 (1959): 491–503.

Botero Restrepo, Jesús. *Andágueda: Novela*. Medellín: Ediciones Teoría, 1946.

Braudel, Fernand. *The Mediterranean and the Mediterranean World in the Age of Philip II*. 2 vols. New York: Harper and Row, 1972–73.

Brito, Brenda, and Paulo Barreto. "Did Land Regularization Advance in the Amazon? Two Years of the Legal Land Program." 2011. Accessed November 1, 2018. https://imazon.org.br/PDFimazon/Ingles/books/RESEXEC_TerraLegal_v2ING_24nov2011.pdf.

Bryant, Sherwin K. *Rivers of Gold, Lives of Bondage: Governing Through Slavery in Colonial Quito*. Chapel Hill: University of North Carolina Press, 2014.

Bunker, Stephen G. *Underdeveloping the Amazon: Extraction, Unequal Exchange, and the Failure of the Modern State*. Chicago: University of Chicago Press, 1985.

Campbell, Jeremy M. *Conjuring Property: Speculation and Environmental Futures in the Brazilian Amazon*. Seattle: University of Washington Press, 2015.

Catastro Minero Colombiano (CMC). "Consulta expedientes." Database of mining registries; search the department Chocó and municipality Bagadó. Accessed January 1, 2016. www.cmc.gov.co:8080/CmcFrontEnd/consulta/busqueda.cmc.

Centro de Estudios para la Justicia Social (Tierra Digna). *La minería en Chocó, en clave de derechos: Investigación y propuestas para convertir la crisis socio-ambiental en paz y justicia territorial*. Bogotá: CEJS, 2016.

Civico, Aldo. *The Para-State: An Ethnography of Colombia's Death Squads*. Oakland: University of California Press, 2016.

———. "'We Are Illegal, but Not Illegitimate': Modes of Policing in Medellin, Colombia." *PoLAR: Political and Legal Anthropology Review* 35, no. 1 (2012): 77–93.

Clastres, Pierre. *Society against the State: The Leader as Servant and the Humane Uses of Power among the Indians of the Americas*. Translated by Robert Hurley and Abe Stein. New York: Urizen Books, 1977.

Cleary, David. *Anatomy of the Amazon Gold Rush*. London: MacMillian, 1990.

Comisión Intereclesial de Justicia y Paz. "Amenaza indiscriminada a habitantes de ZH Nueva Esperanza en Dios." 2017. Accessed March 1 2019, www.justiciaypazcolombia.com/29366-2/amenaza-indiscriminada-a-habitantes-de-zh-nueva-esperanza-en-dios/.

Consejo de Autoridades Indígenas de la Asociación de Cabildos, Embera Dobida Indígenas Wounaan, Katío, Chamí y Tule del Departamento del Chocó (OREWA), Dirección de Investigación. *Minería: Estratégias del Despojo en los Pueblos Indígenas del Chocó*. Quibdó: OREWA, 2013.

Consultoría para los Derechos Humanos y el Desplazamiento (CODHES). *La crisis humanitaria en Colombia persiste: El Pacífico en disputa: Informe de desplazamiento forzado en 2012*. Bogotá: CODHES, 2013.

Continental Gold. "Annual Information Form for the Year Ended December 31, 2015." 2016. Accessed February 21, 2017. www.sedar.com/GetFile.do?lang=EN&docClass=1&issuerNo=00037284&issuerType=03&projectNo=02463773&docId=3889084.

Contraloría General de la República. *Informe actuación especial. Regalías generadas en el municipio Alto Baudó: Operaciones riesgosas y embargos*. Bogotá: Contraloría General de la República, 2013.

———. *Minería en Colombia: Fundamentos para superar el modelo extractivista*. Bogotá: Contraloría General de la República, 2013.

Cooper, Eugene. "Apprenticeship as Field Method: Lessons from Hong Kong." In *Apprenticeship: From Theory to Method and Back Again*, edited by Michael W. Coy, 137–48. Albany: State University of New York, 1989.

Cordy, Paul, Marcello M. Veiga, Ibrahim Salih, Sari Al-Saadi, Stephanie Console, Oseas Garcia, Luis Alberto Mesa, Patricio C. Velásquez-López, and Monika Roeser. "Mercury Contamination from Artisanal Gold Mining in Antioquia, Colombia: The World's Highest Per Capita Mercury Pollution." *Science of the Total Environment* 410–411 (December 2011): 154–60.

Corte Constitucional de Colombia. *Sentencia T-622/16. Principio de precaución ambiental y su aplicación para proteger el derecho a la salud de las personas: Caso de comunidades étnicas que habitan la cuenca del río Atrato y manifiestan afectaciones a la salud como consecuencia de las actividades mineras ilegales.* Bogotá: Corte Constitucional de Colombia, 2016.

Cremers, Leontien, Marjo de Theije, and Judith Kolen, eds. *Small-Scale Gold Mining in the Amazon: The Cases of Bolivia, Brazil, Colombia, Peru and Suriname.* Cuadernos del CEDLA 26. Amsterdam: Centre for Latin American Studies and Documentation, 2013.

Crossley, Nick. "The Circuit Trainer's Habitus: Reflexive Body Techniques and the Sociality of the Workout." *Body & Society* 10, no. 1 (2004): 37–69.

del Pilar Castillo V., María. "¿Qué tan perverso puede llegar a ser un sistema de incentivos?" *El observador regional* 8 (2008): 1–4.

de Theije, Marjo, and Ton Salman. "Conflicts in marginal locations: Small-scale gold-mining in the Amazon." In *Between the Plough and the Pick: Informal, Artisanal and Small-Scale Mining in the Contemporary World*, edited by Kuntala Lahiri-Dutt, 261–74. Acton, Australia: Australian National University Press, 2018.

Dove, Michael R. *The Banana Tree at the Gate: A History of Marginal Peoples and Global Markets in Borneo.* New Haven: Yale University Press, 2011.

Environmental Justice Atlas. "Dojura, Chocó, Colombia." 2016. Accessed July 10, 2016. https://ejatlas.org/conflict/dojura-choco-colombia.

Escalante, Aquiles. *La minería del hambre: Condoto y la Chocó Pacífico.* Barranquilla: Tipografia Dovel, 1971.

Escobar, Arturo. "Displacement, Development, and Modernity in the Colombian Pacific." *International Social Science Journal* 175 (2003): 157–67.

———. *Territories of Difference: Place, Movements, Life, Redes.* Durham: Duke University Press, 2008.

Farnsworth-Alvear, Ann. *Dulcinea in the Factory: Myths, Morals, Men and Women in Colombia's Industrial Experiment, 1905–1960.* Durham: Duke University Press, 2000.

Farnsworth-Alvear, Ann, Marco Palacios, and Ana María Gómez López, eds. *The Colombia Reader: History, Culture, Politics.* Durham: Duke University Press, 2017.

Farthing, Linda, and Nicole Fabricant. "Open Veins Revisited: Charting the Social, Economic, and Political Contours of the New Extractivism in Latin America." *Latin American Perspectives* 45, no. 5 (issue 222) (2018): 4–17.

Ferguson, James. *The Anti-politics Machine: Development, Depoliticization, and Bureaucratic Power in Lesotho*. Minneapolis: University of Minnesota Press, 1990.

———. "The Cultural Topography of Wealth: Commodity Paths and the Structure of Property in Rural Lesotho." *American Anthropologist* 94, no. 1 (1992): 55–73.

———. *Give a Man a Fish: Reflections on the New Politics of Distribution*. Durham: Duke University Press, 2015.

Ferry, Elizabeth E. *Minerals, Collecting, and Value Across the US-Mexico Border*. Bloomington: Indiana University Press, 2013.

Ferry, Elizabeth E., and Stephen Ferry. *La Batea*. New York: Red Hook Editions, 2017.

Financial Action Task Force (FATF). *Trade-Based Money Laundering*. Paris: FATF Secretariat, 2006.

Foro Interétnico Solidaridad Chocó (FISCH). "El ejército nacional al servicio de compañías mineras en el Chocó, en detrimento de la población afrodescendiente." September 10, 2008. Accessed January 23, 2016. www.sicsal.net/articulos/node/662.

Francescone, Kirsten. "Tracing Indium Production to the Mines of the Cerro Rico de Potosí." *Economic Anthropology* 6, no. 1 (2019): 110–22.

Friedemann, Nina S. de. *Minería, descendencia y orfebrería artesanal, litoral pacífico (Colombia)*. Bogotá: Universidad Nacional, Facultad de Ciencias Humanas, 1974.

Friedemann, Nina S. de, and Jaime Arocha Rodríguez. *Herederos del jaguar y la anaconda*. Bogotá: Carlos Valencia Editores, 1982.

Friedman, Jonathan, and Kajsa Ekholm Friedman. "Globalization as a Discourse of Hegemonic Crisis: A Global Systemic Analysis." *American Ethnologist* 40, no. 2 (2013): 244–57.

Gaghan, Stephen, dir. *Gold*. 2016; Black Bear Pictures, Boies/Schiller Film Group, Hwy61, and Living Films.

Galeano, Eduardo. *Open Veins of Latin America: Five Centuries of the Pillage of a Continent*. New York: Monthly Review Press, 1997.

García Márquez, Gabriel. *Crónicas y reportajes*. Bogotá: Oveja Negra, 1982.

Gniset, Jacques Aprile. *Poblamiento, hábitats y pueblos del Pacífico*. Cali: Centro Editorial, Universidad del Valle, 1993.

Godoy, Ricardo. "Mining: Anthropological Perspectives." *Annual Review of Anthropology* 14, no. 1 (1985): 199–217.

Golub, Alex. *Leviathans at the Gold Mine: Creating Indigenous and Corporate Actors in Papua New Guinea.* Durham: Duke University Press, 2014.

Gootenberg, Paul. *Andean Cocaine: The Making of a Global Drug.* Chapel Hill: University of North Carolina Press, 2008.

———. *Cocaine: Global Histories.* London: Routledge, 2002.

Gray, Andrew. *And After the Gold Rush . . . ? Human Rights and Self-Development Among the Amarakaeri of Southeastern Peru.* Copenhagen: International Work Group for Indigenous Affairs, 1986.

Grosse, Robert E. *Drugs and Money: Laundering Latin America's Cocaine Dollars.* Westport, CT: Greenwood Publishing Group, 2001.

Gudeman, Stephen, and Alberto Rivera. *Conversations in Colombia: The Domestic Economy in Life and Text.* Cambridge: Cambridge University Press, 1990.

Gudynas, Eduardo. "El nuevo extractivismo progresista." *El Observador* 4, no. 8 (2010): 1–16.

———. "Más allá del nuevo extractivismo: transiciones sostenibles y alternativas al desarrollo." In *El desarrollo en cuestión: reflexiones desde América Latina*, edited by Fernanda Wanderley, 380–410. La Paz, Bolivia: Plural Editores, 2011.

Gunnoe, Andrew. "The Political Economy of Institutional Landownership: Neorentier Society and the Financialization of land." *Rural Sociology* 79, no. 4 (2014): 478–504.

Guyer, Jane I. *Marginal Gains: Monetary Transactions in Atlantic Africa.* Chicago: University of Chicago Press, 2004.

Haiven, Max. *Cultures of Financialization: Fictitious Capital in Popular Culture and Everyday Life.* New York: Palgrave Macmillan, 2014.

Hart, Keith. "Informal Income Opportunities and Urban Employment in Ghana." *Journal of Modern African Studies* 11, no. 1 (1973): 61–89.

High, Mette M. *Fear and Fortune: Spirit Worlds and Emerging Economies in the Mongolian Gold Rush.* Ithaca, NY: Cornell University Press, 2017.

Hinton, Jennifer J., Marcello M. Veiga, and A. Tadeu C. Veiga. "Clean Artisanal Gold Mining: A Utopian Approach?" *Journal of Cleaner Production* 11, no. 2 (2003): 99–115.

Holmes, Seth. *Fresh Fruit, Broken Bodies: Migrant Farmworkers in the United States.* Berkeley: University of California Press, 2013.

Hoyos, Juan José. *El oro y la sangre.* Bogotá: Planeta Publishing Corporation, 1994.

Hylton, Forrest. "The Cold War That Didn't End: Paramilitary Modernization in Medellín, Colombia." In *A Century of Revolution: Insurgent and*

Counterinsurgent Violence During Latin America's Long Cold War, edited by Greg Grandin and Gilbert M. Joseph, 338–67. Durham: Duke University Press, 2010.

———. "Medellín's Makeover." *New Left Review* 44 (2007): 70–89.

Innis, Harold, A. *The Cod Fisheries: The History of an International Economy*. New Haven: Yale University Press, 1940.

———. *The Fur Trade in Canada: An Introduction to Canadian Economic History*. New Haven: Yale University Press, 1930.

Kernaghan, Richard. *Coca's Gone: Of Might and Right in the Huallaga Post-Boom*. Stanford: Stanford University Press, 2009.

Kirsch, Stuart. *Mining Capitalism: The Relationship between Corporations and Their Critics*. Oakland: University of California Press, 2014.

Kneas, David. "Necessary Illusions: Fetishism and the Becoming of Subsoil Resources." *Extractive Industries and Society* 4 (2017): 846–51.

———. "Subsoil Abundance and Surface Absence: A Junior Mining Company and Its Performance of Prognosis in Northwestern Ecuador." *Journal of the Royal Anthropological Institute* 22, no. S1 (2016): 67–86.

Lahiri-Dutt, Kuntala, ed. *Between the Plough and the Pick: Informal, Artisanal and Small-Scale Mining in the Contemporary World*. Acton, Australia: Australian National University Press, 2018.

———. "Extractive Peasants: Reframing Informal Artisanal and Small-Scale Mining Debates." *Third World Quarterly* 39, no. 8 (2018): 1561–82.

Landry, Timothy R. "Moving to Learn: Performance and Learning in Haitian Vodou." *Anthropology and Humanism* 33, no. 1-2 (2008): 53–65.

Lane, Kris. *Quito 1599: City and Colony in Transition*. Albuquerque: University of New Mexico Press, 2002.

Leal, Claudia. "Black Forests: The Pacific Lowlands of Colombia, 1850–1930." PhD diss., University of California, Berkeley, 2004.

———. "Disputas por tagua y minas: recursos naturales y propiedad territorial en el Pacífico colombiano, 1870–1930." *Revista colombiana de antropología* 44, no. 2 (2008): 409–38.

———. "La Compañía Minera Chocó Pacífico y el Auge del Platino en Colombia, 1897–1930." *Historia crítica noviembre* 39, no. 1 (2009): 150–64.

———. *Landscapes of Freedom: Building a Postemancipation Society in the Rainforests of Western Colombia*. Tucson: University of Arizona Press, 2018.

Leal, Claudia, and Eduardo Restrepo. *Unos bosques sembrados de aserríos: Historia de la extracción maderera en el Pacífico colombiano*. Medellín: Editorial Universidad de Antioquia, 2003.

LeGrand, Catherine, Luis Van Isschot, and Pilar Riaño-Alcalá. "Land, Justice, and Memory: Challenges for Peace in Colombia." *Canadian Journal of*

Latin American and Caribbean Studies / Revue canadienne des études latino-américaines et caraïbes 42, no. 3 (2017): 259–76.

Li, Fabiana. *Unearthing Conflict: Corporate Mining, Activism, and Expertise in Peru.* Durham: Duke University Press, 2015.

Li, Tania Murray. "Beyond 'the State' and Failed Schemes." *American Anthropologist* 107, no. 3 (2005): 383–94.

———. *Land's End: Capitalist Relations on an Indigenous Frontier.* Durham: Duke University Press, 2014.

———. "What is Land? Assembling a Resource for Global Investment." *Transactions of the Institute of British Geographers* 39, no. 4 (2014): 589–602.

Lindsay, Shawn. "Hand Drumming: An Essay in Practical Knowledge." In *Things as They Are: New Directions in Phenomenological Anthropology,* edited by Michael Jackson, 196–212. Bloomington and Indianapolis: Indiana University Press, 1996.

Martínez Basallo, Sandra Patricia. *Configuraciones locales del estado: Titulación colectiva, economías de enclave y etnicidad en el Pacífico colombiano.* Cali: Universidad del Valle, 2013.

Marx, Karl. *Capital: A Critique of Political Economy.* Vol. 1. London: Penguin, 1990.

———. *Capital: A Critique of Political Economy.* Vol. 3. London: Penguin, 1991.

———. *The Eighteenth Brumaire of Louis Bonaparte.* Moscow: Progress Publishers, 1972.

McKay, Ben M. "Agrarian Extractivism in Bolivia." *World Development* 97 (September 2017): 199–211.

McNeish, John-Andrew, and Owen J. Logan. *Flammable Societies: Studies on the Socio-Economics of Oil and Gas.* London: Pluto Press, 2012.

Mejía, Daniel, and Daniel M. Rico. *La microeconomía de la producción y tráfico de cocaína en Colombia.* Bogotá: Documentos Centro de Estudios sobre Desarrollo Económico (CEDE), Universidad de los Andes, 2010.

Meza Ramírez, Carlos Andrés. *Tradiciones elaboradas y modernizaciones vividas por los pueblos afrochocoanos en la vía al mar.* Bogotá: Instituto Colombiano de Antropología e Historia, 2010.

Millar, Kathleen. *Reclaiming the Discarded: Life and Labor on Rio's Largest Garbage Dump.* Durham: Duke University Press, 2018.

Mining Watch and CENSAT-Agua Viva. *Land and Conflict: Resource Extraction, Human Rights, and Corporate Social Responsibility: Canadian Companies in Colombia.* Ottawa: Inter Pares, 2009.

Mintz, Sidney. *Sweetness and Power: The Place of Sugar in Modern History.* New York: Viking-Penguin, 1985.

Muehlmann, Shaylih. *When I Wear My Alligator Boots: Narco-Culture in the U.S.-Mexico Borderlands*. Berkeley: University of California Press, 2013.

Nash, June. *We Eat the Mines and the Mines Eat Us: Dependency and Exploitation in Bolivian Tin Mines*. New York: Columbia University Press, 1993.

Naylor, Thomas. "The Underworld of Gold." *Crime Law and Social Change* 25, no. 3 (1996): 191–241.

Ng'weno, Bettina. *Turf Wars: Territory and Citizenship in the Contemporary State*. Stanford: Stanford University Press, 2007.

Nordstrom, Carolyn. *Global Outlaws: Crime Money and Power in the Contemporary World*. Berkeley: University of California Press, 2007.

Observatorio Pacífico y Territorio. "Ejército colombiano bombardea viviendas indígenas del Alto Andágueda, Chocó." 2012. Accessed January 13, 2014. https://perma.cc/Y4V2-4VQF.

O'Neill, Patrick. *From Snowshoes to Wingtips: The Life of Patrick O'Neill*. Fairbanks: University of Alaska Foundation, 2007.

Ontario Public Service Employees Union (OPSEU). "Black Communities and the OREWA Indigenous Organization." August 28, 2009. Accessed January 24, 2016. http://opseu-colombia.blogspot.ca/2009/08/black-communities-and-orewa-indigenous.html.

Organización Nacional Indígena de Colombia (ONIC). "Graves confrontaciones armadas en territorios indígenas del Alto Andágueda." 2013. Accessed January 13, 2014. https://perma.cc/TVF3-H26B.

Orián, Jiménez. *El Chocó: Un paraíso del demonio: Nóvita, Citará, y el Baudó: Siglo XVIII*. Medellín: Editorial Universidad de Antioquia, 2004.

Oslender, Ulrich. "The Banality of Displacement: Discourse and Thoughtlessness in the Internal Refugee Crisis in Colombia." *Political Geography* 50 (2016): 10–19.

———. *The Geographies of Social Movements: Afro-Colombian Mobilization and the Aquatic Space*. Durham: Duke University Press, 2016.

Oslender, Ulrich, Juana Camacho, and Eduardo Restrepo. *De montes, ríos y ciudades: Territorios e identidades de la gente negra en Colombia*. Bogotá: Instituto Colombiano de Antropología, 1999.

Oxfam. *An Economy for the 1%* (Oxfam Briefing Paper). Cowley, UK: Oxfam GB, 2016.

Oxford English Dictionary Online. "Shift." 2018. Accessed October 20, 2018. www.oed.com.

Pálsson, Gísli. "Enskilment at Sea." *Man* 29, no. 4 (1994): 901–27.

Parsons, James J. *Antioqueño Colonization in Western Colombia*. Berkeley: University of California Press, 1968.

———. *Antioquia's Corridor to the Sea: An Historical Geography of the Settlement of Urabá*. Berkeley: University of California Press, 1967.

Peyton, Jonathan. *Unbuilt Environments*. Vancouver: University of British Columbia Press, 2017.

Polanyi, Karl. *The Great Transformation: The Political and Economic Origins of Our Time*. Boston: Beacon Press, 2001.

Poveda, Germán, and Oscar J. Mesa. "On the Existence of Lloró (the Rainiest Locality on Earth): Enhanced Ocean-Land-Atmosphere Interaction by a Low-Level Jet." *Geophysical Research Letters* 27, no. 11 (2000): 1675–78.

Rajak, Dinah. *In Good Company: An Anatomy of Corporate Social Responsibility*. Stanford: Stanford University Press, 2011.

Ramírez Cuellar, Fransisco. "State Terrorism and the Dirty Business of Transnational Mining in Colombia." In *Community Rights and Corporate Responsibility: Canadian Mining and Oil Companies in Latin America*, edited by Liisa North, Timothy David Clark, and Viviana Patroni, 181–83. Toronto: Between the Lines Productions, 2006.

Real Academia Española. *Diccionario de la lengua española*. Madrid: Real Academia Española, 2014.

Restrepo, Vicente. *Estudio sobre las minas de oro y plata de Colombia*. Bogotá: Silvestre y Compañía, 1888.

Rojas, Cristina. "Securing the State and Developing Social Insecurities: The Securitisation of Citizenship in Contemporary Colombia." *Third World Quarterly* 30, no. 1 (2009): 227–45.

Roldán, Mary. *Blood and Fire:* La Violencia *in Antioquia, Colombia, 1946–1953*. Durham: Duke University Press, 2002.

———. "Violencia, colonización y la geografía de la diferencia cultural en Colombia." *Análisis Políticos* 35 (1998): 3–22.

Romero, Mario Diego. "Procesos de poblamiento y organización social en la costa pacífica colombiana." *Anuario colombiano de historia social y de la cultura* 18–19 (1991): 9–31.

Safford, Frank, and Marco Palacios. *Colombia: Fragmented Land, Divided Society*. Oxford: Oxford University Press, 2001.

Sánchez Juliao, David. "The Arrow." In *The Colombia Reader: History, Culture, Politics*, edited by Ann Farnsworth-Alvear, Marco Palacios, and Ana María Gómez López, 499–500. Durham: Duke University Press, 2017.

———. "El Flecha." In *Una década: 1973–1983*. Bogotá: Plaza y Janes, 1983.

S&P Capital IQ. "Market Access Profile: Continental Gold Ltd." 2015. Accessed January 21, 2017. http://reports.standardandpoors.com/aidata/maccess/pdf/2385010.pdf.

Scott, James C. *The Art of Not Being Governed: An Anarchist History of Upland Southeast Asia*. New Haven: Yale University Press, 2009.

———. *Seeing Like a State: How Certain Schemes to Improve the Human Condition Have Failed*. New Haven: Yale University Press, 1998.

Sharp, William Frederick. "The Profitability of Slavery in the Colombian Chocó, 1680–1810." *The Hispanic American Historical Review* 55, no. 3 (1975): 468–95.

———. *Slavery on the Spanish Frontier: The Colombian Chocó, 1680–1810*. Norman: University of Oklahoma, 1976.

Sistema de Información Minero Colombiano (SIMCO). "Producción de oro." 2013. Accessed July 1, 2013. www.upme.gov.co/generadorconsultas/Consulta_Series.aspx?idModulo=4&tipoSerie=116&grupo=357&Fechainicial=01/01/2004&Fechafinal=31/03/2013.

Sippel, Sarah Ruth, Nicolette Larder, and Geoffrey Lawrence. "Grounding the Financialization of Farmland: Perspectives on Financial Actors as New Land Owners in Rural Australia." *Agriculture and Human Values* 34, no. 2 (2017): 251–65.

Standing, Guy. *The Precariat: The New Dangerous Class*. New York: Bloomsbury Academic, 2011.

Taussig, Michael T. *Defacement: Public Secrecy and the Labor of the Negative*. Stanford: Stanford University Press, 1999.

———. *The Devil and Commodity Fetishism in South America*. Chapel Hill: University of North Carolina Press, 2010.

———. *Law in a Lawless Land: Diary of a "Limpieza" in Colombia*. New York: New Press, 2003.

———. *My Cocaine Museum*. Chicago: University of Chicago Press, 2004.

Topik, Steven, Carlos Marichal, and Frank Zephyr. *From Silver to Cocaine: Latin American Commodity Chains and the Building of the World Economy, 1500–2000*. Durham: Duke University Press, 2006.

Tsing, Anna Lowenhaupt. "Inside the Economy of Appearances." *Public Culture* 12, no. 1 (2000): 115–44.

———. *The Mushroom at the End of the World: On the Possibility of Life in Capitalist Ruins*. Princeton: Princeton University Press, 2015.

Tubb, Daniel. "The Everyday Social Economy of Afro-Descendants in the Chocó, Colombia." In *The Black Social Economy in the Americas: Exploring Diverse Community-Based Markets*, edited by Caroline Shenaz Hossein, 97–117. New York: Palgrave Macmillan, 2018.

———. "Muddy Decisions: Gold in the Chocó, Colombia." *Extractive Industries and Society* 2, no. 4 (2015): 722–33.

———. "Narratives of Citizenship in Medellín, Colombia." *Citizenship Studies*, 17, no. 5 (2013): 627–40.

Unidad Administrativa Especial de Gestión de Restitución de Tierras Despojadas, Dirección de Asuntos Étnicos. "Medida cautelar Alto Andágueda—rama judicial." 2013. Accessed July 3, 2013. https://pacificocolombia.org/wp-content/uploads/2016/05/0112574001410107090.pdf.

United Nations Office on Drugs and Crime (UNODC). "Coca Crops in Colombia at All-Time High, UNODC Report Finds." 2018. Accessed February 9, 2019. www.unodc.org/unodc/en/frontpage/2018/September/coca-crops-in-colombia-at-all-time-high--unodc-report-finds.html.

———. *World Drug Report 2017 V: The Drug Problem and Organized Crime, Illicit Financial Flows, Corruption and Terrorism*. Vienna: UNODC, 2017.

Urán, Alexandra. "La legalización de la minería a pequeña escala en Colombia." *Letras Verdes: Revista Latinoamericana de Estudios Socioambientales* 14 (2013): 255–83.

US Geological Survey. "Gold Statistics and Information." 2016. Accessed February 1, 2017. https://minerals.usgs.gov/minerals/pubs/commodity/gold/index.html#mcs.

van Vliet, Nathalie, Björn Schulte-Herbrüggen, Liliana Vanegas, Eric Yair-Cuesta, François Sandrin, and Robert Nasi. "Wild animals (fish and wildmeat) contribute to dietary diversity among food insecure urban teenagers: The case of Quibdó, Colombia." *Ethnobiology and Conservation* 7, no. 2 (2018): 1–15.

Varela Corredor, Daniel. "Los saberes del monte: Desindustrialización, crisis y reinvención campesina en Andagoya, Chocó (1974–1991)." Ph.D. diss., Universidad Nacional de Colombia, 2013.

Veiga, Marcello. "Artisanal Mining: Perspectives from the Field." Presentation at the Intergovernmental Forum on Mining, Minerals, Metals and Sustainable Development, October–November 2013. Available at https://www.yumpu.com/en/document/view/24561593/igf-2013-artisanal-mining-perspectives-from-the-fiels-marcello-veiga.

Vox. *Diccionario avanzado de la lengua española*. Barcelona: SPES Editorial, 2003.

Wacquant, Loïc. "Carnal Connections: On Embodiment, Apprenticeship, and Membership." *Qualitative Sociology* 28, no. 4 (2005): 445–74.

Wade, Peter. *Blackness and Race Mixture: The Dynamics of Racial Identity in Colombia*. Baltimore: Johns Hopkins University Press, 1993.

Wagner, Livia. *Organized Crime and Illegally Mined Gold in Latin America*. Geneva: Global Initiative Against Transnational Organized Crime, 2016.

Watkins, Mel. "A Staple Theory of Economic Growth." *Canadian Journal of Economics and Political Science* 29, no. 2 (1963): 141–58.

———. "The Staple Theory Revisited." *Journal of Canadian Studies* 12, no. 5 (1977): 83–94.

Weiner, Annette B. *Inalienable Possessions: The Paradox of Keeping-While-Giving.* Berkeley: University of California Press, 1992.

West, Robert C. *Colonial Placer Mining in Colombia.* Baton Rouge: Louisiana State University Press, 1952.

———. "Folk Mining in Colombia." *Economic Geography* 28, no. 4 (1952): 323–30.

Whitten Jr., Norman E. *Black Frontiersmen: A South American Case.* New York: Schenkman Publishing, 1974.

Williams, Caroline A. *Between Resistance and Adaptation: Indigenous Peoples and the Colonisation of the Chocó, 1510–1753.* Liverpool: Liverpool University Press, 2004.

Wolf, Eric. *Europe and the People without History.* Berkeley: University of California Press, 1982.

World Health Organization (WHO). "Paludismo." 2018. Accessed February 10, 2019. www.who.int/es/news-room/fact-sheets/detail/malaria.

INDEX

Italic page numbers indicate illustrations.

A

accidents, mining, 99–100, 163
accumulation: complicating, 140–43; narrative and assumptions, 25–26, 147; primitive, 10–12, 87. *See also* family mines and small-scale mining; *retreros*
afrocolombianos (Afro-Colombians), 19, 61
afrodescendientes (Afro-descendants), 61
agency: aquatic, 174–77; family mines and, 103; of gold, 172–73; mining and, 80–81; *rebusque* and, 23–24. *See also* freedom or liberation
Agrarian Bank of Colombia, 182
agua panela, 42, 45
Andagoya (town), 13, 16–17, 126, 181
Andagoya, Pascual de, 13
Andágueda River, 149–52, 165, 166
Anglo American (mining company), 159, 160
AngloGold Ashanti, 159, 192n4. *See also* Dojurá mine project, multinational

Appelbaum, Nancy, 72–73
aquatic culture, 6–8
artisanal mining: as cash source, 40, 46–47, 67–68; criminalization of, 9–10; danger and risk, 99–100; defined, 10, 12; description of mine, 43; diving techniques, 97–98, 100; emancipatory potential of gold, 41, 59–63, 82; with excavator-dug reservoirs, 50–51; excavators compared to, 12; intrinsic rewards of, 80–81; *mazamorreo* technique of panning, 55; panning, 46; process, 46, 48–49, 64, *65*; skill and problem-solving, 47–48; tunneling, 85, *86*, 89, 94, 99; water pump technique, 93, 97
Atrato River, *181*; about, 7–8; Cocomopoca and, 162–63; Commission of Guardians of the Atrato, 9; Dojurá mine project and, 151; estimated number of mines along, 110; flooding of, 173–74; history of, 15, 16; mining frontier moved north, 181; personhood and

Atrato River (*continued*)
rights of, 8–10, 88, 174–76, 180; Upper Atrato as shatter zone and displacement zone, 165

B

bandeja paisa, 76
banking systems and money laundering, 142
bareque panning, 95–96
Barrera, Daniel "El Loco," 142
Baudó River, 7–8, 133–35, 138–39, 190n1
Beck, Ulrich, 22
Black Market Peso exchange, 141–42, 191n15
Bolivian silver mines, Potosí, 14–15
boom-and-bust commodity cycles, 97, 121, 181–82
borojó, 45
Botero, Fernando, 74
Botero Restrepo, Jesús, 166
Brazilian Amazon, paper conjuring in, 27
Brazilian *garimpeiros*, 125
Bre-X, 156–57
Buenaventura, 66, 73, 78, 139
bus travel, 68–73

C

cacao, 21–22, 178, 182
campesinos (peasants), as term, 61
Canadian International Development Agency, 53
Canadian mining companies: paper conjuring and, 27–28; "pushing out" *retreros*, 127; speculation, transformation of value, and, 151, 156–57, 169–71. *See also* Dojurá mine project, multinational
canoeing, 51–52
Capá River, 161, 163
cash economy: artisanal mining as cash source, 40, 46–47, 67–68; dual household economy undermined by, 102–3; family mines as entering into, 87, 96–97, 102–3; gold and, 67–68; *retreros* and, 129; wholesale shopping trip to Medellín with Don Alfonso, 66–80
cash transfers, redistributive politics of, 22
Cauca (department), 5, 179
checkpoints, 68–69, 78–79
the Chocó: environment and aquatic culture in, 5–8; gold as defining export of, 13; gold mining statistics for, 135; history of gold in, 15; mining in Lower Cauca compared to, 128; as racialized region, 72–73; racialized settlement histories, 165–66; as source of displaced persons, 73
Chocó Pacífico Mining Company, xxi–xxii, 13, 16–17, 50, 107, 126
civil wars, Colombian, 9–10, 65, 69
Clastres, Pierre, 193n12
cocaine: boom and bust in coca farming, 121; criminalization of, 9; factory closures and boom in, 107; gold compared to, 129; smuggling methods, 139
cocaine money laundering. *See* money laundering; transformation of value
Cocomopoca (Consejo Comunitario Mayor de la Organización Popular Campesino del Alto Atrato), 162–65
Coffee Axis, 71, 72–73
coffee picking, 71–72
collective land title (*título colectivo*), 91–93, 157, 162, 163–65

Colombian Mining Register, 159, 161
Commission of Guardians of the Atrato, 9
commodification of nature, 12–14, 25
commodity trade, 15–17, 97. *See also* cocaine; gold
community councils (*consejos comunitarios*), 92–93, 95
compraventa shops, 96, 109
comunas (slums), Medellín, 74
comunidades negras (Black communities), collective territory of, 91–93
Condoto, 137, *137*, 139
constitution, Colombian, 154, 164, 175
Constitutional Court of Colombia, 8–9, 88, 174–76, 180
Continental Gold, Ltd., 159–61, 168–69, 192n6. *See also* Dojurá mine project, multinational
cooperatives of small-scale miners, 106, 125–27
corn cultivation, 44
criminalization, 9–10
Cronus Resources, Ltd., 193n6
customary property regime, kinship-based, 91–93, 157

D

Dalik communities, Borneo Highlands, Indonesia, 19–20
dangers of mining, 99–100
debt, *gota-a-gota*, 77, 101
dependency, 14–15
de Theije, Marjo, 183n6
development projects, 182
diesel fuel. *See* fuel
dirt-bike-taxi service, 6, 104

displacement, human: the Chocó as source of, 73; Dojurá mine project and, 158–59, 165–68; internally displaced persons, 110–11; primitive accumulation and, 10–11; *rebusque* vs. displacement to city, 82
distrust, 95
diving techniques, 97–98, 100
dogs, hunting with, 39–42, 52–59
Dojurá mine project, multinational (Continental Gold and AngloGold Ashanti): Canadian stock market speculation and transformation of value, 151, 156–57, 169–71; Cocomopoca fight for collective titles, 163–65; community workshop, 149–56; consequences of, 151; displacement, armed conflict, and, 158–59, 165–68; Embera Katío, racialized regional history, and, 161, 165–67; future of, 168–71; geologists with soldiers arriving in helicopters, 158, 160; hills of Dojurá, 160–61; judge's suspension of mining titles and, 165, 167–68; *"las multinacionales,"* 159–60; prior consultation rights, 154–55; property regimes, overlapping and contested, 157–58, 160–63
Dove, Michael, 20
dual economy. *See* household economy, dual

E

economy of appearances, 156, 168
El Andágueda (Botero Restrepo), 166
el invierno (wet months), 7
el verano (dry months), 6

Embera Katío communities, 71, 152, 165–67
environmental consequences of excavator mining, 8, 90, 153
Escobar, Pablo, 107, 145
Escobar, Ricardo, 166–67
excavator mining. *See* family mines and small-scale mining; *retreros*
export trade: boom-and-bust commodities, 97; dual household economy and export-oriented commodity production, 20–21; gold as defining export of the Chocó, 13; Latin American governments and export-oriented resource economies, 18

F

family mines and small-scale mining: after the gold rush, 172–74, 177; *bareque* panning at, 95–96; cash economy, entering into, 87, 96–97, 102–3; classifiers, *105*, 109, 113–14, 140; community council's share of gold, 95; criminalization of, 9–10, 106; defined, 10, 12; distrust and, 95; division of the gold, 94–95; environmental and health consequences of, 8, 90, 153; kinship, property rights, and, 89–93, 94; labor-based vs. lot-based revenue sharing, 93–94; mercury use, 8, 109–10; money laundering and, 146; motor pumps, 122; numbers of mines, estimated, 110; pairs of excavator machines, 116–17; process, 109–10; profitability, marginal, 88, 100–101; reasons for calling in *retreros*, 85–88, 97–98, 101; risk-shifting, 98–99; scale of mining at one location, 90; size of operations, 56; washing, 112–14, *129*. *See also retreros*

FARC (Revolutionary Armed Forces of Colombia), 149, 167, 176, 178–79
"fast money," 104–5
Ferguson, James, 22
fictitious capital, 26–28
fish as food, 53, 188n2 (chap. 1)
formal employment, permanent (*fijo*): with mining companies, 107; *rebusque* and, 28, 108, 112, 123; in textile industry, 107
freedom or liberation: dual household economy and, 21; emancipatory potential of gold, 41, 59–63, 82; *rebusque* and, 23–24. *See also* agency
Friedemann, Nina S. de, 20
fuel: in cocaine production, 120; commodity chain of, 124; hauling, 118, 119–20; state regulation of, 120

G

Galeano, Eduardo, 14–15
García Márquez, Gabriel, 16, 126
gardening. *See* horticulture
Gaviria, Simón, 142–43
general strike (*paro cívico*), *173*, 179–80
Geographic Institute Agustín Codazzi, 70
gold: accessing, 97–99; agency of, 172–73; cash economy and, 40, 46–47, 67–68; cocaine compared to, 129; as defining export of the Chocó, 13; emancipatory potential of, 41, 59–63, 82; as global

commodity, 14; the gold rush, 13–14; history of, in the Chocó, 15; as ideal for illicit transactions, 136; international history of, xx; physical and financial components of, 73; place of origin, changing, 135–36; production statistics, 135–39, *137, 138*; royalty payments, 138–39; selling, 96–97; smuggling of, 144–45. *See also* money laundering
Goldex, 144
gold mining. *See* artisanal mining; family mines and small-scale mining; multinational, large-scale mine projects
Gold Museum, Bogotá, xvii
gold refineries, 143–44
gota-a-gota loans (loan sharks), 77, 101, 112, 148
Gudynas, Eduardo, 18
guerrillas: Andágueda fortifications against, 149–50; Dojurá mine project and, 149–50; extortion by, as *rebusque*, 124; kidnappings by, 127, 149, 179; military presence and, 61; Upper Andágueda mine and, 167; in villages, 60
Guzmán, Joaquín "El Chapo," 142

H

Highland Clearances, Scotland, 10–11
Holmes, Seth, 187n50
horticulture: gardening in dual household economy, 42–45; return to, after gold rush, 178; slash-and-mulch, 15, 40, 44, 91
household economy, dual: after the gold rush, 177–78, 181–82;

diverse strategies, 67, 80–82; emancipatory potential of gold, 41, 59–63, 82; gardening, 42–45, 178; hunting paca, 39–42, 51–59; interconnected livelihood strategies and diversity of activities, 41, 60–61; mining in, 43, 46; on resource frontier, 19–21; unbalanced by excavator mining and cash economy, 100–103. *See also rebusque* ("shifting")
HSBC, 142
hunting, 39–42, 51–59

I

Indigenous communities, Embera Katío. *See* Embera Katío communities
Indigenous communities, neo-extractivist account of, 19
Indonesia, 19–20, 21–22, 156–57, 189n1 (chap. 3)
"informal economy" vs. *"rebusque"*, 108. *See also rebusque*
Institute for Rural Development (INCODER), 157
InterBolsa, 142–43
internally displaced persons, 110–11
International Labor Organization's Indigenous and Tribal Peoples Convention 169 (1989), 154
International Mining Consortium, 17
Istmina, 96, 125–27, 137, *137*, 139

K

Kaplan, David E., 145
kinship-based customary property regime, 91–93, 157

L

Lahiri-Dutt, Kuntala, xxii, 183n6
"La Mina" case, 145–46
land title. *See* property rights and titles
La Paila de Mi Abuela (My Grandmother's Pan) restaurant, Quibdó, 52–53
large-scale mining. *See* Dojurá mine project, multinational; multinational, large-scale mine projects
Law 70 (1993), 164
Lewisohn, Adolph, 17
Li, Tania Murray, 21–22
libres, 15, 61
Logan, Owen J., 186n38
logging, 50
lottery, 140–41
Lower Cauca, 107, 109–11, 124, 128, 178

M

malaria, 8, 177, 180, 185n6. See also *paludismo*
Mancuso, Salvatore, 144
maps, 69–70
marches and protests, 127–28
Marx, Karl, 10–11, 13, 23, 87
mazamorreo technique of panning, 55
McNeish, John-Andrew, 186n38
Medellín: bus from Quibdó to, 68–73; bus via Pereira back to Quibdó, 78–79; *comunas* (slums), 74; rental properties, 60, 74; taxi driving in, 77; textile industry in, 107; wholesale shopping in, 73–78
Medellín Cartel, 107, 145–46
mercury, 8, 109–10, 173
mesa directiva of the Cocomopoca, 162–63
Meza Ramírez, Carlos Andrés, 190n1
military. *See* soldiers, presence of
Mineros S.A., 126
minidredges, 98, 100
mining, artisanal. *See* artisanal mining
mining, large-scale. *See* Dojurá mine project, multinational; multinational, large-scale mine projects
mining, small-scale. *See* family mines and small-scale mining
Ministry of Mines and Energy, 160
money laundering: the Baudó and lack of mines, 133–35; examples and narratives for understanding transformation, 143–46; gold as ideal for illicit transactions, 136; gold production statistics and decentering of production, 135–39, *137*, *138*; gold smugglers, 144–45; *rebusque* and, 147; simulacra of extraction, 134, 143, 147–48; steps in, 29; trade-, finance-, and securities-based laundering and complication of accumulation, 140–43; as transformation of value, 28–29, 134–35, 143, 146–48
Montoya, Guillermo, 166–67
Mothers of Soacha scandal, 190n11
muleteers (*arrieros*), 121
multinational, large-scale mine projects: *"las multinacionales,"* 159–60; opinions about, 153–54, 155; prior consultation rights, 154–55. *See also* Dojurá mine project, multinational
murder of miners by miners, 100
Murillo, Aníbal, 167

N

Nariño, 5, 107
National Development Plan (2010), 154
National Liberation Army (ELN), 69, 149, 167, 178–79
nature, commodification of, 12–14, 25
Naylor, Thomas, 146
negros (Blacks), as term, 61
neo-extractivism critique, xix–xx, 17–19, 30
Nineteenth of April Movement (M-19), 167
Nóvita, 69, *137*, 139, 179

P

paca, lowland (*guagua*), 39–42, 52–54, 56–59
paisas, 21, 72–73, 125–27, 166–67, 187n44
paludismo, 90, 180, 182, 185n6
pancoger ("daily bread"), 46–47
panela, 45
pangueros, 51
panning: *bareque* panning, 95–96; described, 46; *mazamorreo* technique, 55
paper conjuring, 27–28, 30, 151, 169. See also Dojurá mine project, multinational; money laundering; speculation
paramilitaries, 61, 124, 144, 167, 178–79
Pato Consolidated Mining Company, 107
peace accord with FARC, 178–79
peach palm (*chontaduro*), 44
personhood, judicial, 8. See also Atrato River
physical labor and agency, 24, 187n50
pigs, 53

pineapple, 44, 62, 91, 178, 182
plantains, 44, 47, 178
platinum mining, 16
Popular Liberation Army (EPL), 167
Potosí, Bolivia, silver mines, 14–15
primitive accumulation, 10–12, 87
prior consultation rights, 154–55
production: decentering, 135–39; narrative and assumptions, 25–26, 147–48; simulacra of, 134, 143, 147–48. See also artisanal mining
profit-sharing, labor-based vs. lot-based, 93–94
property rights and titles: collective land title (*título colectivo*), 91–93, 157, 162, 163–65; constitutional framework, 164; Dojurá mine project and, 157–58, 159, 160–63, 165, 167–68; kinship-based customary regime, 91–93, 157
protest and marches, 127–28

Q

Quibdó: dirt-bike-taxi service in, 104; gold buying/selling shops in, 96; La Paila de Mi Abuela (My Grandmother's Pan) restaurant, 52–53; march of small-scale miners (April 2011), 127; movement between forest villages and, 60; rental properties in, 81; rising homicide rate in, 179
Quibdó–Medellín Road, 70–73, 149, 167
Quito River, 173

R

racialized regions of Colombia, 72–73
rains, 5–7, 50

rebusque ("shifting"): around the world, 108; coffee picking, 71–72; displacement to city vs., 82; diverse strategies, 67, 80–82; everyday connections between villages and large cities, 68; excavator miners and, 67; extortion by guerrillas as, 124; formal employment vs., 28, 108, 112, 123; gold and cocaine in, 129; gold rush and, 175; as honest work or licit illegality, 117–18, 123; "hustling" vs., 118; illegal commodities intertwined with, 147; "informal economy" vs., 108; mail-order sales, 115; rental properties, 60, 74, 81; *retreros* and, 112, 114–16, 124–25, 129; in rural sector, 120–21; seen from above vs. from below, 108, 123; shopkeeping, small-scale, 66; structure, agency, and, 22–24; taxi driving, 77, 148; as term, xvi, 21, 22; wholesale shopping trip to Medellín with Don Alfonso, 66–80. *See also* cash economy; household economy, dual

refineries, 143–44
regions of Colombia, racialized, 72–73
rental properties, 60, 74, 81
resource curse, 19, 186n38
resource economies, export-oriented, 18
retreros (excavator owners and workers): assistant's job, 117–20; cook's job, 119; cooperatives and activism, 106, 125–28; definition of, 11–12; departure after the gold rush, 172–74; distrust of, 95; driver's job, 115–17; fast-cash hopes and mine failures, 106, 111–12, 117, 128–30; foreman's job, 123–24; goals of, 124–25; as internally displaced persons, 110–11; muleteer's job, 120–23; negotiating with, 89–90; night work, 114; opinions about, 153; payment and profit-sharing arrangements, 94–95; reasons for inviting, 85–88, 97–98, 101; *rebusque* and, 112, 114–16, 124–25, 129; regular wage plus share of gold, 105–6; transnational, 159–60; washer's job, 112–15; women's positions, 119. *See also* family mines and small-scale mining

risk-shifting, 99–100
Rodríguez, Juan Pablo, 146
rubber, 16

S

Salman, Ton, 183n6
Sánchez Juliao, David, xvi
San Juan River: about, 7–8; after the gold rush, 177; coca trafficking and, 139; estimated number of mines along, 110; history of, 15, 16; Istmina and, 125; mining frontier moving south along, 181; Tadó–Pereira Road and, 70
savings (*ahorros*), gold as, 47, 96–97
scale, 18–19
Scott, James C., 193n12
securities markets, money laundering through, 142–43
"shifting." See *rebusque*
shopkeeping, small-scale, 66
silver mining, 14–15
simulacra of extraction, 134, 143, 147–48. *See also* money laundering
Sinaloa Cartel, Mexico, 139, 142

slash-and-mulch horticulture, 15, 40, 44, 91
slave mining works, remains of, 61
small-scale mining. *See* family mines and small-scale mining
smugglers, 139, 144–45, 166
soldiers, presence of: along Andágueda, 149–50; checkpoints, 68–69, 78–79; in villages, 61
speculation: Canadian mining sector and, 156, 157; Dojurá mine project and, 151, 169–71; in Indonesia, 156–57; paper conjuring and, 27–28
stock market scandal, 142–43
subsistence production. *See* household economy, dual
sugarcane, 42, 45, 47, 91, 178

T

Tadó–Pereira Road, 70, 149, 167
tagua seeds ("vegetable ivory"), 97
Taussig, Michael, 190n14
taxi driving, 77, 148
timber boom in tropical hardwoods, 50
trade-based money laundering, 141–42
transformation of value: assumptions of production and accumulation and, 25–26; Canadian mining sector, speculation, and, 156–57; Dojurá mine project and, 151, 169–71; economy of appearances, 156, 168; fictitious capital and, 26–28; informal economy and, 28–30; money laundering and, 28–29, 134–35, 143, 146–48. *See also* money laundering
tropical hardwoods, timber boom in, 50
Tsing, Anna L., 156–57, 168
Tumbertumbedo River, 161, 163
tunneling accidents, 99
tunneling for gold, 85, *86*, 89, 94

U

Urán, Alexandra, 183n6
Uribe Vélez, Álvaro, 121

V

Varela Corredor, Daniel, 181–82

W

Wachovia Bank, 142
Wade, Peter, 72
wage labor in Medellín, 75
wages of *retreros*, 105–6. *See also* *retreros*
water pump mining technique, 93, 97
Whitten, Norman, 182
Wolf, Eric, 16

Y

yuca (manioc or cassava), 44

Z

zambullir diving, 98

CULTURE, PLACE, AND NATURE
Studies in Anthropology and Environment

Shifting Livelihoods: Gold Mining and Subsistence in the Chocó, Colombia, by Daniel Tubb

Disturbed Forests, Fragmented Memories: Jarai and Other Lives in the Cambodian Highlands, by Jonathan Padwe

The Snow Leopard and the Goat: Politics of Conservation in the Western Himalayas, by Shafqat Hussain

Roses from Kenya: Labor, Environment, and the Global Trade in Cut Flowers, by Megan A. Styles

Working with the Ancestors: Mana *and Place in the Marquesas Islands,* by Emily C. Donaldson

Living with Oil and Coal: Resource Politics and Militarization in Northeast India, by Dolly Kikon

Caring for Glaciers: Land, Animals, and Humanity in the Himalayas, by Karine Gagné

Organic Sovereignties: Struggles over Farming in an Age of Free Trade, by Guntra A. Aistara

The Nature of Whiteness: Race, Animals, and Nation in Zimbabwe, by Yuka Suzuki

Forests Are Gold: Trees, People, and Environmental Rule in Vietnam, by Pamela D. McElwee

Conjuring Property: Speculation and Environmental Futures in the Brazilian Amazon, by Jeremy M. Campbell

Andean Waterways: Resource Politics in Highland Peru, by Mattias Borg Rasmussen

Puer Tea: Ancient Caravans and Urban Chic, by Jinghong Zhang

Enclosed: Conservation, Cattle, and Commerce among the Q'eqchi' Maya Lowlanders, by Liza Grandia

Forests of Identity: Society, Ethnicity, and Stereotypes in the Congo River Basin, by Stephanie Rupp

Tahiti Beyond the Postcard: Power, Place, and Everyday Life, by Miriam Kahn

Wild Sardinia: Indigeneity and the Global Dreamtimes of Environmentalism, by Tracey Heatherington

Nature Protests: The End of Ecology in Slovakia, by Edward Snajdr

Forest Guardians, Forest Destroyers: The Politics of Environmental Knowledge in Northern Thailand, by Tim Forsyth and Andrew Walker

Being and Place among the Tlingit, by Thomas F. Thornton

Tropics and the Traveling Gaze: India, Landscape, and Science, 1800–1856, by David Arnold

Ecological Nationalisms: Nature, Livelihood, and Identities in South Asia, edited by Gunnel Cederlöf and K. Sivaramakrishnan

From Enslavement to Environmentalism: Politics on a Southern African Frontier, by David McDermott Hughes

Border Landscapes: The Politics of Akha Land Use in China and Thailand, by Janet C. Sturgeon

Property and Politics in Sabah, Malaysia: Native Struggles over Land Rights, by Amity A. Doolittle

The Earth's Blanket: Traditional Teachings for Sustainable Living, by Nancy Turner

The Kuhls of Kangra: Community-Managed Irrigation in the Western Himalaya, by Mark Baker

CPSIA information can be obtained
at www.ICGtesting.com
Printed in the USA
BVHW080926040720
582857BV00004B/8